Preston Lee's
Beginner ENGLISH 100 Lessons

For Chinese Speakers (简体版)

Preston Lee Books
prestonleebooks@gmail.com

No unauthorized photocopying

All rights reserved. No part of this publication may be reproduced, stored in a retrieval system, or transmitted, in any form or by any means, without the prior permission in writing of Preston Lee Books.

This book is sold subject to the condition that it shall not, by the way of trade or otherwise, be lent, resold, hired out, or otherwise circulated without the publisher's prior consent in any form of binding or cover than that in which it is published and without a similar condition including this condition being imposed on the subsequent purchaser.

Copyright © 2018 Matthew Preston, Kevin Lee
All rights reserved.

ISBN-13:
978-1724433497

ISBN-10:
1724433490

Letter from the authors

Dear learners,

Thank you for choosing *Preston Lee's Beginner English 100 Lessons*.

It took us over two years to write this book. Our goal was to create the best and most complete book ever written for beginner learners of the English language. We chose the most common and everyday topics, so that you can get the most use out of this book.

A lot of care was put into this book.

Over 20 years of English-teaching experience has taught us a lot about the best and most efficient way of learning English correctly.

We believe the correct process of learning English is extremely important.

The lessons in this book were carefully written, so that the learning development of English grammar and words would seem effortless and understandable.

By the time you complete the lessons in *Preston Lee's Beginner English 100 Lessons,* you will be ready to speak English fluently and be a learner of advanced English.

Kevin Lee and Matthew Preston

CONTENTS

Lesson 1: My family 我的家人　　　　　　　Page 12
Lesson 2: My pencil case 我的铅笔盒　　　　Page 16
Lesson 3: In the classroom 在教室里　　　　Page 20
Lesson 4: The weather 天气　　　　　　　　Page 24

| Test 1 | Lesson 1 - 4 | Page 28

Lesson 5: Places 地方　　　　　　　　　　Page 30
Lesson 6: Sports 运动　　　　　　　　　　Page 34
Lesson 7: At the zoo 在动物园　　　　　　Page 38
Lesson 8: Colors 颜色　　　　　　　　　　Page 42

| Test 2 | Lesson 5 - 8 | Page 46

Lesson 9: Activities 活动　　　　　　　　Page 48
Lesson 10: Food & Drinks 食品和饮料　　　Page 52
Lesson 11: At the fruit market 在水果市场　Page 56
Lesson 12: Shapes 形状　　　　　　　　　　Page 60

| Test 3 | Lesson 9 - 12 | Page 64

4

Lesson 13: At the supermarket 在超级市场   Page 66
Lesson 14: At the ice cream shop 在冰淇淋店   Page 70
Lesson 15: In the refrigerator 在冰箱里   Page 74
Lesson 16: Jobs 工作   Page 78

| Test 4 | Lesson 13 - 16 | Page 82

Lesson 17: Names 名字   Page 84
Lesson 18: More places 更多地方   Page 88
Lesson 19: Meats 肉   Page 92
Lesson 20: Vegetables 蔬菜   Page 96

| Test 5 | Lesson 17 - 20 | Page 100

Lesson 21: At school 在学校   Page 102
Lesson 22: School subjects 学校科目   Page 106
Lesson 23: Chores 家事   Page 110
Lesson 24: At the toy store 在玩具店   Page 114

| Test 6 | Lesson 21 - 24 | Page 118

Lesson 25: In the kitchen 在厨房   Page 120
Lesson 26: In the toolbox 在工具箱里   Page 124
Lesson 27: Transportation 运输工具   Page 128
Lesson 28: Clothes 衣服   Page 132

| Test 7 | Lesson 25 - 28 | Page 136

Lesson 29: More clothes 更多衣服	Page 138
Lesson 30: In the living room 在客厅	Page 142
Lesson 31: In the bathroom 在浴室	Page 146
Lesson 32: In the bedroom 在卧室	Page 150

Test 8 — Lesson 29 - 32 — Page 154

Lesson 33: Around the house 在房子周围	Page 156
Lesson 34: Hobbies 嗜好	Page 160
Lesson 35: Countries 国家	Page 164
Lesson 36: Landscapes 自然景观	Page 168

Test 9 — Lesson 33 - 36 — Page 172

Lesson 37: Everyday life 日常生活	Page 174
Lesson 38: Languages 语言	Page 178
Lesson 39: Pets 宠物	Page 182
Lesson 40: Fast food 速食	Page 186

Test 10 — Lesson 37 - 40 — Page 190

Lesson 41: At the cinema 在电影院	Page 192
Lesson 42: Music 音乐	Page 196
Lesson 43: Feelings 感觉	Page 200
Lesson 44: The calendar 日历	Page 204

Test 11 — Lesson 41 - 44 — Page 208

Lesson 45: World foods 世界食品　　　　　　　Page 210
Lesson 46: Desserts 甜品　　　　　　　　　　Page 214
Lesson 47: Homework 家庭作业　　　　　　　Page 218
Lesson 48: At the hospital 在医院　　　　　　Page 222

Test 12　Lesson 45 - 48　　　　　　　　　Page 226

Lesson 49: On the farm 在农场　　　　　　　Page 228
Lesson 50: In the office 在办公室里　　　　　Page 232
Lesson 51: At the airport 在机场　　　　　　Page 236
Lesson 52: Camping 露营　　　　　　　　　Page 240

Test 13　Lesson 49 - 52　　　　　　　　　Page 244

Lesson 53: Birthday party 生日聚会　　　　　Page 246
Lesson 54: At the park 在公园　　　　　　　Page 250
Lesson 55: On the street 在街上　　　　　　Page 254
Lesson 56: Seasons 季节　　　　　　　　　Page 258

Test 14　Lesson 53 - 56　　　　　　　　　Page 262

Lesson 57: Outdoor activities 户外运动　　　　Page 264
Lesson 58: Skills 技能　　　　　　　　　　Page 268
Lesson 59: Capital cities 首都城市　　　　　　Page 272
Lesson 60: Personalities 性格　　　　　　　Page 276

Test 15　Lesson 57 - 60　　　　　　　　　Page 280

Lesson 61: The body 身体 — Page 282
Lesson 62: The face 脸 — Page 286
Lesson 63: Actions 动作 — Page 290
Lesson 64: Time 时间 — Page 294

| Test 16 | Lesson 61 - 64 | Page 298 |

Lesson 65: Tastes 味觉 — Page 300
Lesson 66: Condiments 调味料 — Page 304
Lesson 67: At a restaurant 在餐厅 — Page 308
Lesson 68: Tableware 餐具 — Page 312

| Test 17 | Lesson 65 - 68 | Page 316 |

Lesson 69: Kitchenware 厨房用品 — Page 318
Lesson 70: Home appliances 家电 — Page 322
Lesson 71: Stationery 文具 — Page 326
Lesson 72: Computers 电脑 — Page 330

| Test 18 | Lesson 69 - 72 | Page 334 |

Lesson 73: Ocean life 海洋生物 — Page 336
Lesson 74: Europe 欧洲 — Page 340
Lesson 75: At a hotel 在饭店 — Page 344
Lesson 76: Furniture 家具 — Page 348

| Test 19 | Lesson 73 - 76 | Page 352 |

Lesson 77: Water activities 水上活动 Page 354
Lesson 78: Asia 亚洲 Page 358
Lesson 79: People 人们 Page 362
Lesson 80: On an airplane 在飞机上 Page 366

Test 20 | Lesson 77 - 80 Page 370

Lesson 81: At the post office 在邮局 Page 372
Lesson 82: Martial arts 武术 Page 376
Lesson 83: Toiletries 梳妆用品 Page 380
Lesson 84: Musical instruments 乐器 Page 384

Test 21 | Lesson 81 - 84 Page 388

Lesson 85: Birds 鸟类 Page 390
Lesson 86: At the bank 在银行 Page 394
Lesson 87: Household items 生活用品 Page 398
Lesson 88: The solar system 太阳系 Page 402

Test 22 | Lesson 85 - 88 Page 406

Lesson 89: Sporting equipment 运动器材   Page 408
Lesson 90: Small animals 小动物   Page 412
Lesson 91: In the forest 在森林里   Page 416
Lesson 92: Natural disasters 自然灾害   Page 420

| Test 23 | Lesson 89 - 92 | Page 424 |

Lesson 93: America 美洲   Page 426
Lesson 94: Beverages 饮料   Page 430
Lesson 95: At the beach 在海滩   Page 434
Lesson 96: Africa 非洲   Page 438

| Test 24 | Lesson 93 - 96 | Page 442 |

Lesson 97: Special days 特别的日子   Page 444
Lesson 98: At the amusement park 在游乐园   Page 448
Lesson 99: Dairy 乳制品   Page 452
Lesson 100: My job 我的工作   Page 456

| Test 25 | Lesson 97 - 100 | Page 460 |

| Answers | Test 1 - 25 | Page 462 |

Let's begin...

Lesson 1: My family

我的家人

| Section A | Words |

1. **mother**
   母亲
2. **grandmother**
   祖母
3. **sister**
   姐妹
4. **baby sister**
   妹妹
5. **aunt**
   阿姨

6. **father**
   父亲
7. **grandfather**
   祖父
8. **brother**
   兄弟
9. **baby brother**
   弟弟
10. **uncle**
    叔叔

| Section B | Make a sentence |

Who is <u>she</u>?

She is my <u>mother</u>.

Who is <u>he</u>?

He is my <u>father</u>.

Note: isn't = is not

Section C — Make a question

Is <u>she</u> your <u>mother</u>?
Yes, she is. / No, she isn't.

Is <u>he</u> your <u>father</u>?
Yes, he is. / No, he isn't.

Section D — Learn a verb

see – seeing – saw – seen 看

He **sees** my father on Fridays.

I will be **seeing** him this afternoon.

My brother **saw** you yesterday.

I haven't **seen** that movie yet.

Section E — Learn an idiom

Like one of the family

Meaning: To be like a person in one's family.

"Our dog is treated *like one of the family*."

| Section F | Write |

Trace and write the words

1. Who is she?

She is my mother.

2. Who _____ he?

He is my father.

3. Who _____ _____?

She _____ my grandmother.

4. Who _____ _____?

He _____ _____ grandfather.

5. Is she your sister?

Yes, she is.

6. Is _____ your brother?

No, he isn't.

7. Is she your mother?

Yes, _____ _____.

8. Is _____ _____ father?

_____, _____ _____.

Section G   Let's have fun

My family!

Find the words!

```
c i o b j t d c z b g g r o v k
o i j m w d o g f a j r k s s q
q d e g q l z t c b z a q c u o
u w n r c e o z s y i n t t t v
n f f a t h e r o b a d y s y r
c d l n b h j m u r x f d v t q
l z a d m g y e o x a c m n v
e h p (m o t h e r) t z t j y t f
f u e o v q q f d h e h b x s n
n z v t u x l w j e z e k o u v
t a a h s i s t e r o r y a l r
t o u e y v s h b r o t h e r j
j n n r u d o s x j v t y k y o
j b t y t d b a b y s i s t e r
```

~~mother~~   brother
father   baby sister
grandmother   baby brother
grandfather   aunt
sister   uncle

Lesson 2: My pencil case

我的铅笔盒

| Section A | Words |

1. **a pencil**
   铅笔
2. **an eraser**
   橡皮擦
3. **glue**
   胶水
4. **pencil sharpener**
   削铅笔机
5. **whiteout**
   立可白
6. **a pen**
   原子笔
7. **a ruler**
   尺
8. **tape**
   胶带
9. **a marker**
   马克笔
10. **a crayon**
    蜡笔

| Section B | Make a sentence |

What is this?

It is <u>a pencil</u>.

What are these?

They are <u>pens</u>.

16

Section C | Make a question

Is this <u>an eraser</u>?

Yes, it is. / No, it isn't.

Are these <u>rulers</u>?

Yes, they are. / No, they aren't.

Section D | Learn a verb

buy – buying – bought – bought 买

I will **buy** some pencils for you.

My sister was **buying** a new ruler.

My father **bought** an eraser.

My mother hasn't **bought** some glue yet.

Section E | Learn an idiom

Cross your fingers

Meaning: To wish for luck.

"*Cross your fingers* and hope this marker has ink."

Section F | Write

Trace and write the words

1. What is this?

It is a pencil.

2. What _____ these?

They are pens.

3. What _____ _____?

It _____ a ruler.

4. What _____ _____?

They _____ markers.

5. Is this an eraser?

Yes, it is.

6. Is _____ a pencil sharpener?

No, it isn't.

7. Is _____ a crayon?

No, _____ isn't.

8. _____ _____ rulers?

Yes, _____ _____.

Section G | Let's have fun

My pencil case!

Unscramble the words!

1. encpil   _pencil_
2. enp   _____
3. relru   _____
4. eugl   _____
5. reshrapne cpneli _____
6. arerse   _____
7. emrakr   _____
8. hwteituo   _____
9. yocarn   _____
10. ptae   _____

Lesson 3: In the classroom

在教室

> What are these?
> These are old books.

Section A — Words

1. **chair**
   椅子
2. **blackboard**
   黑板
3. **poster**
   海报
4. **globe**
   地球仪
5. **clock**
   时钟
6. **desk**
   书桌
7. **whiteboard**
   白板
8. **bookshelf**
   书架
9. **computer**
   电脑
10. **book**
    书

Section B — Make a sentence

What is this?

This is a <u>big</u> <u>chair</u>.

What are these?

These are <u>small</u> <u>desks</u>.

Learn: big, small, new, old

Section C — Make a question

Is the <u>blackboard</u> <u>big</u>?
Yes, it is. / No, it is <u>small</u>.

Are the <u>desks</u> <u>new</u>?
Yes, they are. / No, they are <u>old</u>.

Section D — Learn a verb

look – looking – looked – looked 看

Please **look** at the blackboard.

They are **looking** at the whiteboard.

My father **looked** at your bicycle yesterday.

We have already **looked** at many houses.

Section E — Learn an idiom

Class clown

Meaning: A student who often makes everyone laugh in the classroom.

"Peter is the *class clown*. Even the teacher laughs sometimes."

| Section F | Write |

Trace and write the words

1. What is this?

This is a big chair.

2. What _____ these?

These are small desks.

3. What _____ _____?

This is a _____ _____.

4. What _____ _____?

These are _____ _____.

5. Is the blackboard big?

Yes, it is.

6. Are _____ desks new?

No, they _____ old.

7. Is the _____ small?

No, it is big.

8. Are the _____ _____?

Yes, _____ _____.

Section G Let's have fun

In the classroom!

1. chair
2. desk
3. blackboard
4. whiteboard
5. poster
6. bookshelf
7. globe
8. computer
9. clock
10. book

Lesson 4: The weather

天气

| Section A | Words |

1. **snowy**
下雪的
2. **sunny**
晴朗的
3. **rainy**
多雨的
4. **windy**
有风的
5. **cloudy**
多云的

6. **hot**
热的
7. **cold**
冷的
8. **warm**
暖和的
9. **cool**
凉的
10. **freezing**
冷冻的

| Section B | Make a sentence |

How is the weather on <u>Monday</u>?

It is <u>snowy</u>.

It is not <u>hot</u>.

Learn: Sunday, Monday, Tuesday, Wednesday, Thursday, Friday, Saturday

Section C — Make a question

Is the weather <u>cold</u> on <u>Wednesday</u>?
Yes, it is. / No, it isn't. It is <u>hot</u>.

Is the weather <u>sunny</u>?
Yes, it is. / No, it isn't. It is <u>rainy</u>.

Section D — Learn a verb

feel – feeling – felt – felt 觉得

My sister always **feels** tired after school.

I'm not **feeling** well.

I **felt** something on the back of my neck.

I haven't **felt** this happy for a long time!

Section E — Learn an idiom

It's raining cats and dogs

Meaning: It's raining heavily.

"You can't play outside right now. *It's raining cats and dogs.*"

| Section F | Write |

Trace and write the words

1. How is the weather on Monday?

It is snowy.

2. How is the weather _____ Thursday?

It is cloudy. It _____ not rainy.

3. How is the _____ _____ Friday?

It is _____.

4. How is _____ _____ _____ Tuesday?

It is cold. It is _____ _____.

5. Is the _____ hot?

Yes, it _____.

6. Is _____ _____ windy on Wednesday?

No, it isn't. It is _____.

7. Is the _____ _____ on Saturday?

Yes, _____ _____.

8. Is the weather _____?

No, it _____. It is _____.

Section G — Let's have fun

The weather!

| snowy | sunny | rainy | windy | cloudy |
| hot | cold | warm | cool | freezing |

Write the words

Sunday	Monday	Tuesday	Wednesday	Thursday	Friday	Saturday
Ra_n_	W_n_y	Cl_u_y	S_n_y	C_ _d	H_ _	W_r_

Circle the correct answer

1. Is the weather cold on Thursday?

   Yes, it is.   No, it's not. It's hot.

2. Is the weather windy on Monday?

   Yes, it is.   No, it's not. It's hot.

3. Is the weather rainy on Wednesday?

   Yes, it is.   No, it's not. It's sunny.

4. Is the weather cold on Friday?

   Yes, it is.   No, it's not. It's hot.

| Test 1 | Lesson 1 - 4 |

Write the answer next to the letter "A"

A: ___ 1. Who ___ she? She is ___ mother.

a. is, my   b. are, her   c. am, his   d. is, me

A: ___ 2. ___ he your father? Yes, ___ is.

a. Is, she   b. Are, he   c. Is, he   d. Are, she

A: ___ 3. We ___ a movie now.

a. are seeing   b. seen   c. is seeing   d. saw

A: ___ 4. The housekeeper is one ___ the family.

a. off   b. is   c. from   d. of

A: ___ 5. What are ___? ___ are markers.

a. this, They   b. these, It   c. it, They   d. these, They

A: ___ 6. Are ___ rulers? No, ___ aren't.

a. it, these   b. them, it   c. these, they   d. this, it

A: ___ 7. I ___ a pencil yesterday.

a. buy   b. buying   c. bought   d. buys

A: ___ 8. Tom: "I hope I pass my test." Mary: " ___ your fingers."

a. Hold   b. Cross   c. Pull   d. Look at

A: ___ **9.** What ___ these? These are ___ posters.

a. are, those   b. is, small   c. is, old   d. are, big

A: ___ **10.** Is the ___ small? No, it is ___.

a. it, old   b. globe, big   c. chair, desk   d. this, new

A: ___ **11.** He is ___ at the whiteboard.

a. looks   b. looking   c. looked   d. look

A: ___ **12.** "Johnny is the class ___. He's so funny."

a. clown   b. clowned   c. clowning   d. clowns

A: ___ **13.** How is the ___ on Tuesday? It is ___. It is not hot.

a. weather, cold   b. rainy, sunny   c. cool, old   d. hot, rain

A: ___ **14.** Is the weather ___ on Friday? Yes, ___ is.

a. cold, it   b. cold, snowy   c. hot, sunny   d. it, cold

A: ___ **15.** She ___ feel cold.

a. very   b. isn't   c. doesn't   d. do

A: ___ **16.** "Look at the heavy rain. It's raining ___ and ___."

a. lots, water   b. dogs, cats   c. cat, dog   d. cats, dogs

Answers on page 462

Lesson 5: Places

地方

Where is he going?
He is going to the gym.

| Section A | Words |

1. **park**
   公园
2. **beach**
   海滩
3. **night market**
   夜市
4. **store**
   商店
5. **supermarket**
   超级市场
6. **restaurant**
   餐厅
7. **swimming pool**
   游泳池
8. **department store**
   百货公司
9. **cinema** /movie theatre
   电影院
10. **gym**
    健身房

| Section B | Make a sentence |

Where is <u>she</u> going?

She is going to the <u>park</u>.

Where is <u>he</u> going?

He is going to the <u>beach</u>.

| Section C | Make a question |

Is he going to the store?
Yes, he is. / No, he isn't.

Is she going to the supermarket?
Yes, she is. / No, she isn't.

| Section D | Learn a verb |

walk – walking – walked – walked 走路

I **walk** at the park on Sundays.

She will be **walking** to the store tomorrow morning.

My grandmother **walked** to the supermarket last week.

I've never **walked** to the night market before.

| Section E | Learn an idiom |

Have a change of heart

Meaning: To change your mind about something.

"I've *had a change of heart* about this place. Let's go to another restaurant."

Section F   Write

Trace and fill in the words

1. Where is she going?

   She is going to the park.

2. Where is he going?

   He is going to the beach.

3. Where is _____ _____?

   She is going to the _____.

4. Where is _____ _____?

   He is _____ to the _____.

5. Is he going to the store?

   Yes, he is.

6. Is she going to the gym?

   No, she isn't.

7. Is he going to the _____?

   Yes, _____ is.

8. Is she going to the _____?

   No, _____ _____.

Section G | Let's have fun

Places!

1. Where is he going?

He is going to the department store.

2. Where is she going?

_____

3. Where is he going?

_____

4. Where is she going?

_____

5. Where is he going?

_____

Lesson 6: Sports

运动

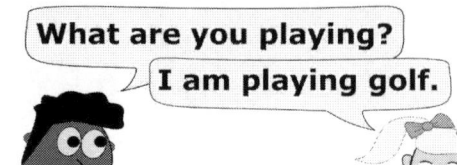

| Section A | Words |

1. **basketball**
   篮球
2. **soccer**
   足球
3. **badminton**
   羽毛球
4. **golf**
   高尔夫球
5. **hockey**
   曲棍球
6. **cricket**
   板球
7. **tennis**
   网球
8. **baseball**
   棒球
9. **volleyball**
   排球
10. **football**
    美式足球

| Section B | Make a sentence |

What are you playing?

I am playing <u>basketball</u>.

What are they playing?

They are playing <u>soccer</u>.

Note: aren't = are not / I'm = I am

Section C | Make a question

Are <u>you</u> playing <u>basketball</u>?
Yes, I am. / No, I'm not.

Are <u>they</u> playing <u>soccer</u>?
Yes, they are. / No, they aren't.

Section D | Learn a verb

play – playing – played – played 玩

I **play** basketball at the park on the weekends.

She will be **playing** tennis in the school competition.

My brother and I **played** badminton last night.

My grandfather has **played** golf for a long time.

Section E | Learn an idiom

A good sport

Meaning: Someone who can accept losing or be made fun of.

"We made fun of Johnny, but he was *a good sport* and laughed with us."

Section F | Write

Trace and fill in the words

1. What are you playing?

I am playing basketball.

2. What is she playing?

She is playing tennis.

3. What are they _____?

They are playing _____.

4. What _____ they _____?

_____ are playing _____.

5. Are you playing volleyball?

Yes, I am.

6. Is she playing football?

No, she isn't.

7. Are they playing _____?

Yes, _____ are.

8. Are we playing _____?

No, _____ _____.

Section G | Let's have fun

Sports!

Connect the sentences

What are you playing? •   • We are playing soccer.

What are they playing? •   • I am playing tennis.

What are you playing? •   • He is playing basketball.

What is he playing? •   • They are playing baseball.

Are you playing golf? •   • No, she isn't.

Is she playing hockey? •   • Yes, they are.

Is he playing football? •   • Yes, I am.

Are they playing volleyball? •   • No, he isn't.

Lesson 7: At the zoo

在动物园

How many lions are there?
There are two lions.

Section A — Words

1. monkey
   猴子
2. lion
   狮子
3. tiger
   老虎
4. rhino
   犀牛
5. bear
   熊
6. penguin
   企鹅
7. giraffe
   长颈鹿
8. elephant
   大象
9. kangaroo
   袋鼠
10. crocodile
    鳄鱼

Section B — Make a sentence

How many <u>monkeys</u> are there?

There is <u>one</u> monkey.

There are <u>three</u> <u>monkeys</u>.

Learn: one, two, three, four, five, six, seven, eight, nine, ten

Note: there's = there is

Section C — Make a question

Is there one <u>rhino</u>?
Yes, there is. / No, there isn't.

Are there five <u>bears</u>?
Yes, there are. / No, there aren't.

Section D — Learn a verb

like – liking – liked – liked 喜欢

I **like** the kangaroo.

The penguins are **liking** the new fish.

We **liked** the lions best at the zoo yesterday.

The bear hasn't **liked** any of the food we prepared.

Section E — Learn an idiom

Let the cat out of the bag

Meaning: To let someone know a secret.

"He *let the cat out of the bag* about the surprise party."

Section F | Write

Trace and fill in the words

1. How many monkeys are there?

There is one monkey.

2. How many penguins are there?

There _____ five penguins.

3. How many _____ are there?

There _____ one _____.

4. How many _____ are there?

There _____ six _____.

5. Is there one rhino?

Yes, there is.

6. Are there four bears?

No, there aren't.

7. Is there one _____?

Yes, there _____.

8. Are there four _____?

No, _____ _____.

Section G | Let's have fun

At the zoo!

Read and write

ANIMAL	AMOUNT
Monkey	6
Giraffe	
Lion	
Tiger	
Penguin	
Elephant	
Bear	
Kangaroo	
Crocodile	

1. How many monkeys are there?
   There are six monkeys.

2. How many giraffes are there?
   There are four giraffes.

3. How many lions are there?
   There is one lion.

4. How many penguins are there?
   There are seven penguins.

5. How many elephants are there?
   There are two elephants.

6. How many bears are there?
   There is one bear.

7. How many kangaroos are there?
   There are three kangaroos.

8. How many crocodiles are there?
   There is one crocodile.

9. How many tigers are there?
   There are four tigers.

Lesson 8: Colors

颜色

What is your favorite color?
My favorite color is red.

| Section A | Words |

1. red
   红色
2. blue
   蓝色
3. orange
   橙色
4. pink
   粉红色
5. black
   黑色
6. yellow
   黄色
7. green
   绿色
8. purple
   紫色
9. brown
   棕色
10. white
    白色

| Section B | Make a sentence |

What color is this?

It is <u>red</u>.

What is your favorite color?

My favorite color is <u>yellow</u>.

Note: it's = it is

Section C — Make a question

Is this <u>pencil</u> <u>purple</u>?
Yes, it is. / No, it's <u>blue</u>.

Is your favorite color <u>green</u>?
Yes, it is. / No, it isn't.

Section D — Learn a verb

draw – drawing – drew – drawn 画

My uncle can **draw** a green crocodile.

She is **drawing** a black bear.

The teacher **drew** a pink elephant on the blackboard.

I had first **drawn** a brown monkey, but didn't like it.

Section E — Learn an idiom

Feeling blue

Meaning: Feeling unhappy.

"He's *feeling blue* today because he lost the game."

| Section F | Write |

Trace and fill in the words

1. What color is this?

It is green.

2. What _____ your favorite color?

My favorite color is purple.

3. What color is _____?

It is _____.

4. What is your favorite _____?

My _____ color is _____.

5. Is this pencil blue?

Yes, it is.

6. Is your favorite color pink?

No, it isn't.

7. Is this eraser _____?

No, it's _____.

8. Is your favorite color _____?

Yes, it _____.

Section G   Let's have fun

Colors!

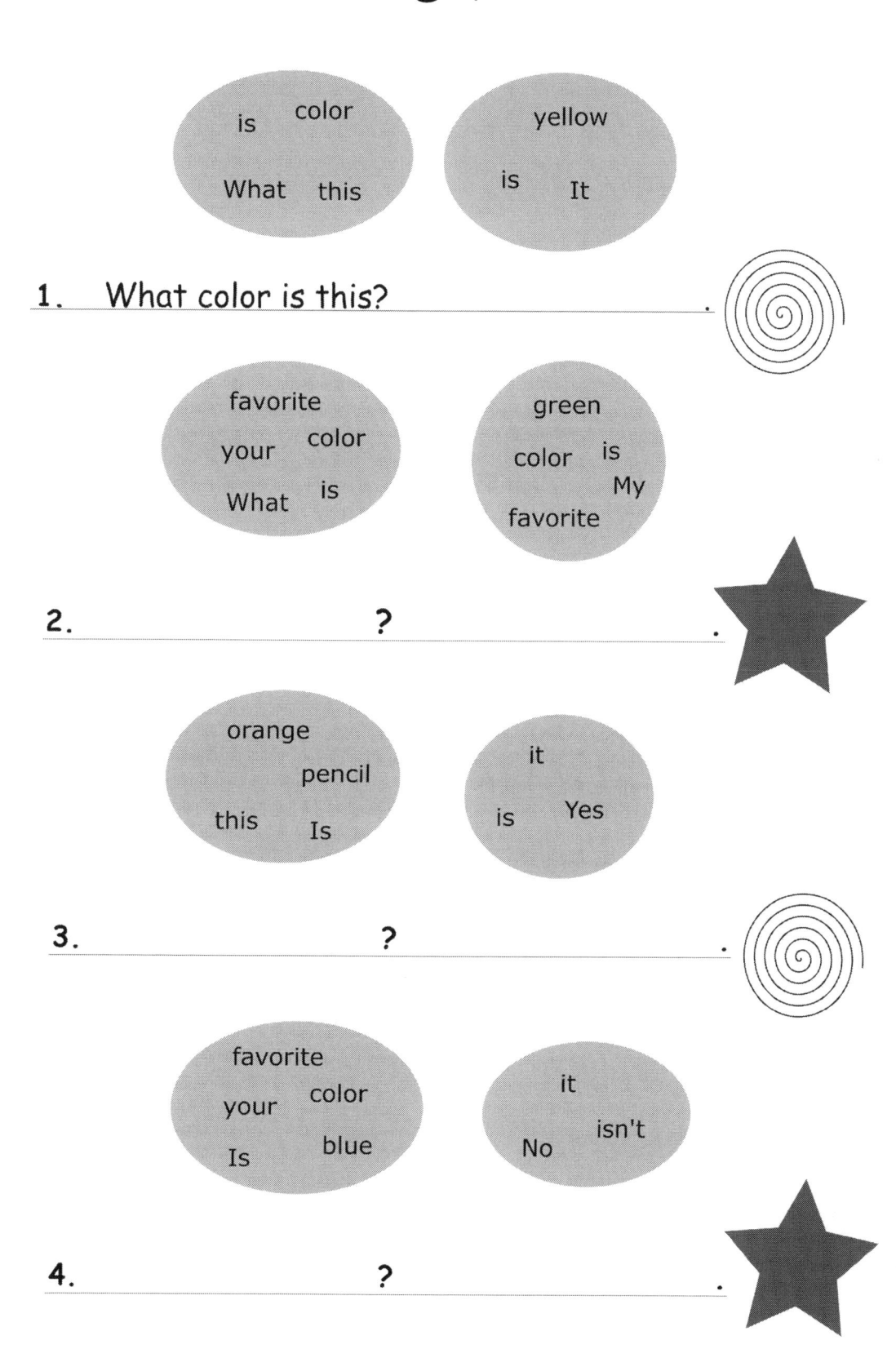

1. What color is this? _____ It is yellow.

2. What is your favorite color? _____ My favorite color is green.

3. Is this an orange pencil? _____ Yes, it is.

4. Is your favorite color blue? _____ No, it isn't.

Test 2   Lesson 5 - 8

Write the answer next to the letter "A"

A: ___ **1.** Where ___ she going? She is ___ to the beach.

a. does, going   b. is, going   c. are, go   d. is, go

A: ___ **2.** Is ___ going to the store? Yes, she ___.

a. we, can   b. her, is   c. she, is   d. he, is

A: ___ **3.** Yesterday, they ___ to the cinema.

a. are walk   b. walk   c. walked   d. walking

A: ___ **4.** "I changed my mind about going. I had a change of ___."

a. eyes   b. think   c. clothes   d. heart

A: ___ **5.** What are ___ playing? We ___ playing tennis.

a. you, are   b. we, is   c. they, can   d. she, are

A: ___ **6.** ___ you playing soccer? No, ___ not.

a. Is, she's   b. Are, I'm   c. Can, can   d. Are, he's

A: ___ **7.** They want to ___ baseball.

a. played   b. playing   c. plays   d. play

A: ___ **8.** "We laughed at John, but he was a ___ sport."

a. well   b. good   c. easy   d. difficult

46

A: ___ **9.** How many ___ are there? There ___ two tigers.

a. tiger, are   b. number, is   c. tiger, is   d. tigers, are

A: ___ **10.** Is ___ one kangaroo? No, there ___.

a. there, isn't   b. number, isn't   c. this, is   d. this, aren't

A: ___ **11.** He ___ the penguins.

a. like   b. liking   c. likes   d. was like

A: ___ **12.** "He told everyone my secret and let the cat ___ the bag."

a. out from   b. into   c. out of   d. out

A: ___ **13.** What is your ___ color? My favorite color ___ purple.

a. best, is   b. best, are   c. favorite, are   d. favorite, is

A: ___ **14.** Is this desk ___? Yes, ___ is.

a. red, they   b. color, pink   c. green, it   d. yellow, he

A: ___ **15.** She can ___ a yellow lion.

a. drawing   b. draw   c. draws   d. drew

A: ___ **16.** "I'm pretty unhappy today. I'm feeling ___."

a. red   b. green   c. color   d. blue

Answers on page 462

Lesson 9: Activities

活动

What do you like to do?
I like to read books.

Section A   Words

1. **play piano**
   弹钢琴
2. **read books**
   看书
3. **play video games**
   打电动
4. **surf the internet**
   上网
5. **take photos**
   拍照
6. **watch TV**
   看电视
7. **sing songs**
   唱歌
8. **study English**
   读英文
9. **play cards**
   玩牌
10. **go shopping**
    去购物

Section B   Make a sentence

What do you like to do?

I like to <u>play piano</u>.

What don't you like to do?

I don't like to <u>sing songs</u>.

Note: don't = do not

| Section C | Make a question |

Do you like to <u>play video games</u>?
Yes, I do. / No, I don't.

Don't you like to <u>read books</u>?
Yes, I do. / No, I don't.

| Section D | Learn a verb |

read – reading – read – read 读

I can **read** English books.

My sister was **reading** the newspaper this morning.

I **read** a really interesting article last week.

My brother hasn't **read** this book yet.

| Section E | Learn an idiom |

Shop around

Meaning: To shop at different stores to find the best price.

"You should *shop around* before you buy this piano."

Section F | Write

Trace and fill in the words

1. What do you like to do?

I like to read books.

2. What don't you like to do?

I don't like to _____ cards.

3. What do you _____ to do?

I like to _____ _____.

4. What don't you like to _____?

I don't like to _____ _____.

5. Do you like to take photos?

No, I _____.

6. Don't you like to go shopping?

Yes, I do.

7. Do you like to _____ _____?

Yes, I _____.

8. Don't you like to _____ _____?

No, I _____.

| Section G | Let's have fun |

Activities!

Unscramble the sentences!

> like to / video games / I / play

1. _____.

> I / like to / read books / don't

2. _____.

> I / study English / like / to

3. _____.

> don't / go shopping / I / like to

4. _____.

> like / take / I / photos / to

5. _____.

> the / don't / I / to / like / internet / surf

6. _____.

Lesson 10: Food & Drinks

食物和饮料

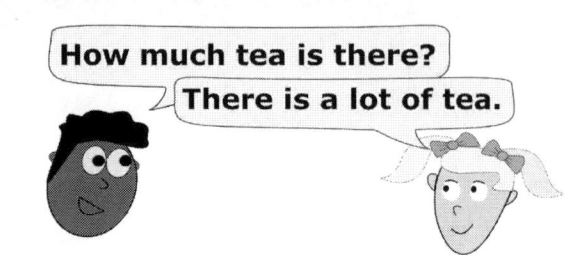

How much tea is there?
There is a lot of tea.

| Section A | Words |

1. cake
   蛋糕
2. cheese
   起司
3. milk
   牛奶
4. tea
   茶
5. soda
   汽水
6. pizza
   比萨
7. water
   水
8. juice
   果汁
9. coffee
   咖啡
10. pie
    馅饼

| Section B | Make a sentence |

How much <u>cake</u> is there?

There is <u>a little</u> cake.

How much <u>pizza</u> is there?

There is <u>a lot of</u> pizza.

Learn: a little, a lot of

Section C — Make a question

Is there a lot of <u>juice</u>?
Yes, there is. / No, there isn't.

Is there a little <u>water</u>?
Yes, there is. / No, there isn't.

Section D — Learn a verb

want – wanting – wanted – wanted 要

I **want** a lot of tea.
Wanting to improve your English takes practice.
They **wanted** a cheese cake, but the shop didn't have one.
My father has **wanted** to eat pizza all week.

Section E — Learn an idiom

Put food on the table

Meaning: To make money for the household expenses.

"I need this job to *put food on the table*."

Section F | Write

Trace and fill in the words

1. How much juice is there?

There is a little juice.

2. How much coffee is there?

There _____ a lot of coffee.

3. How much _____ is there?

There is a _____ _____.

4. How much _____ is there?

There is a _____ of _____.

5. Is there a lot of cheese?

Yes, there is.

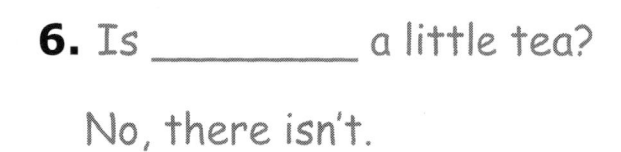

6. Is _____ a little tea?

No, there isn't.

7. Is there a _____ of _____?

Yes, there _____.

8. Is _____ a little _____?

No, _____ _____.

| Section G | Let's have fun |

Food + Drinks!

Circle the odd word

1. cake   pizza   cheese   (soda)   pie
2. soda   tea   cake   juice   milk
3. pizza   coffee   cheese   pie   cake
4. pie   soda   water   tea   coffee
5. cheese   cake   tea   pie   pizza
6. pizza   milk   coffee   juice   water
7. cake   juice   cheese   pie   pizza
8. water   soda   milk   juice   cheese

Write the word

1.
2.
3.
4.
5.
6.
7.
8.

Lesson 11: At the fruit market

在水果市场

What do you want?
I want an apple.

| Section A | Words |

1. **orange**
   橙子
2. **pear**
   梨子
3. **watermelon**
   西瓜
4. **strawberry**
   草莓
5. **cherry**
   樱桃
6. **lemon**
   柠檬
7. **banana**
   香蕉
8. **grape**
   葡萄
9. **pineapple**
   鳳梨
10. **apple**
    蘋果

| Section B | Make a sentence |

What do you want?

I want an <u>orange</u>.

What don't you want?

I don't want a <u>lemon</u>.

Note: Say *an* for all nouns that begin with a, e, i, o, u.

Section C — Make a question

Is there <u>one</u> <u>pear</u>?
Yes, there is. / No, there isn't.

Are there <u>five</u> <u>grapes</u>?
Yes, there are. / No, there aren't.

Section D — Learn a verb

need – needing – needed – needed 需要

I **need** two watermelons for the picnic.

People **needing** vitamin C should eat more oranges.

Yesterday, I **needed** to buy some apples.

I haven't **needed** to use the heater this year.

Section E — Learn an idiom

A bad apple

Meaning: The one bad person in a good group.

"He is *a bad apple* on this basketball team."

Section F   Write

Trace and fill in the words

1. What do you want?

I want an apple.

2. What don't you want?

I don't _____ a cherry.

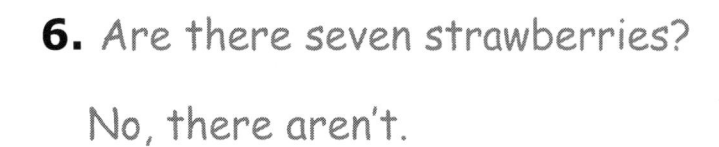

3. What _____ you want?

I want a _____.

4. What _____ you _____?

I don't _____ a _____.

5. Is there one grape?

Yes, there is.

6. Are there seven strawberries?

No, there aren't.

7. Is _____ one _____?

No, _____ isn't.

8. Are _____ three _____?

Yes, _____ _____.

Section G | Let's have fun

At the fruit market!

| orange | lemon | pear | strawberry | banana |
| watermelon | grape | pineapple | cherry | apple |

1. _orange_
- lemon
- pear
- strawberry
- pineapple
- watermelon
- apple
- cherry
- banana
- grape

2. _____
- apple
- orange
- strawberry
- banana
- pear
- lemon
- grape
- pineapple
- cherry

3. _____
- strawberry
- apple
- orange
- watermelon
- pineapple
- pear
- cherry
- banana
- grape

4. _____
- lemon
- pear
- strawberry
- orange
- watermelon
- apple
- cherry
- banana
- pineapple

5. _____
- lemon
- grape
- strawberry
- pineapple
- watermelon
- apple
- cherry
- orange
- banana

6. _____
- pear
- orange
- watermelon
- banana
- strawberry
- apple
- cherry
- lemon
- grape

7. _____
- grape
- pear
- orange
- pineapple
- watermelon
- apple
- banana
- cherry
- lemon

8. _____
- lemon
- pear
- strawberry
- cherry
- watermelon
- banana
- orange
- pineapple
- grape

Lesson 12: Shapes

形状

Section A — Words

1. **square**
   正方形
2. **circle**
   圆形
3. **star**
   星形
4. **heart**
   心形
5. **octagon**
   八角形
6. **triangle**
   三角形
7. **rectangle**
   长方形
8. **oval**
   椭圆形
9. **diamond**
   菱形
10. **pentagon**
    五角形

Section B — Make a sentence

What color is <u>this square</u>?

This is a <u>red</u> square.

What color is <u>that triangle</u>?

That is a <u>blue</u> triangle.

Section C — Make a question

Is this circle green?
Yes, it is. / No, it isn't. It's **blue**.

Is that rectangle orange?
Yes, it is. / No, it isn't. It's **purple**.

Section D — Learn a verb

find – finding – found – found 找到

I can't **find** my keys.

The teacher is **finding** many mistakes in my homework.

I **found** my grandfather's watch.

He still hasn't **found** his workbook.

Section E — Learn an idiom

Be out of shape

Meaning: To be unfit or overweight.

"He can't climb this mountain. He *is* really *out of shape*!"

Section F   Write

Trace and fill in the words

1. What color is this rectangle?

This is a yellow rectangle.

2. What color is that oval?

_____ is a green oval.

3. What _____ is _____ diamond?

This is a _____ diamond.

4. _____ color _____ that _____?

_____ _____ a _____ heart.

5. Is this circle purple?

Yes, it is.

6. _____ that octagon blue?

No, _____ _____. It's pink.

7. Is this _____ _____?

Yes, _____ _____.

8. _____ that _____ red?

No, _____ _____. It's _____.

| Section G | Let's have fun |

Shapes!

1. What color is this rectangle?

   <u>This is a blue rectangle.</u>   .

   blue

2. What color is this star?

   _____.

   red

3. What color is this circle?

   _____.

   gray

4. What color is this oval?

   _____.

   purple

5. What color is this diamond?

   _____.

   black

6. What color is this square?

   _____.

   blue

7. What color is this pentagon?

   _____.

   green

8. What color is this triangle?

   _____.

   pink

Test 3 Lesson 9 - 12

Write the answer next to the letter "A"

A: ___ **1.** What ___ you like to do? I like to ___ piano.

a. does, do   b. is, play   c. are, go   d. do, play

A: ___ **2.** Don't ___ like to play cards? Yes, I ___.

a. we, can   b. you, do   c. he, am   d. you, can

A: ___ **3.** He ___ comic books.

a. read   b. reading   c. see   d. reads

A: ___ **4.** "I think I can find a cheaper price. I'm going to ___ around."

a. buy   b. play   c. shop   d. cost

A: ___ **5.** How ___ pizza is there? There is ___ pizza.

a. many, big   b. much, a lot of   c. small, many   d. much, all

A: ___ **6.** Is ___ a lot of coffee? No, ___ isn't.

a. there, there   b. this, lot   c. them, she   d. it, he

A: ___ **7.** My grandmother ___ a lot of soda.

a. want   b. wanting   c. wants   d. doesn't

A: ___ **8.** "I need that job to put ___ on the table."

a. food   b. money   c. meat   d. milk

64

A: ___ **9.** What ___ you want? I don't ___ a banana.

a. do, try   b. can't, want   c. can, have   d. don't, want

A: ___ **10.** ___ there seven cherries? No, there ___.

a. Is, isn't   b. Our, aren't   c. Are, aren't   d. Have, hasn't

A: ___ **11.** We ___ eight pineapples.

a. needing   b. needs   c. need   d. is need

A: ___ **12.** "He's not a nice guy. He's really a bad ___."

a. tomato   b. orange   c. lemon   d. apple

A: ___ **13.** What color is ___ oval? That ___ a purple oval.

a. that, is   b. this, are   c. an, can   d. purple, has

A: ___ **14.** Is this ___ blue? Yes, it ___.

a. circle, can   b. heart, does   c. square, is   d. star, blue

A: ___ **15.** I can't ___ an orange octagon.

a. finding   b. found   c. find   d. be found

A: ___ **16.** "He really needs to get healthy. He's really ___ shape."

a. into   b. taking   c. losing   d. out of

Answers on page 462

Lesson 13: At the supermarket

在超级市场

What do you want to buy?
I want to buy some bread.

Section A — Words

1. milk
   牛奶
2. juice
   果汁
3. meat
   肉
4. drinks
   饮料
5. vegetables
   蔬菜
6. ice cream
   冰淇淋
7. fruit
   水果
8. bread
   面包
9. fish
   鱼
10. pizza
    比萨

Section B — Make a sentence

What do you want to buy?

I want to buy some <u>milk</u>.

What don't you want to buy?

I don't want to buy any <u>ice-cream</u>.

Learn: some, any

Section C | Make a question

Do you want to buy some <u>juice</u>?
Yes, I do. / No, I don't.

Do you want to buy some <u>fruit</u>?
Yes, I do. / No, I don't.

Section D | Learn a verb

get – getting – got – gotten 得到

I **get** my bread at the supermarket.
He is **getting** some bananas from the fruit market.
Last night, she **got** a pizza for dinner.
We haven't **gotten** any vegetables yet.

Section E | Learn an idiom

A rip off

Meaning: Something is too expensive.

"The supermarket around the corner is *a rip off*."

| Section F | Write |

Trace and fill in the words

1. What do you want to buy?

I want to buy some fruit.

2. What don't you want _____ buy?

I don't want to buy any bread.

3. What _____ you want to _____?

I want to _____ some _____.

4. What _____ you _____ to buy?

I don't want to _____ any _____.

5. Do you want to buy some fish?

Yes, I _____.

6. Do you want to buy some milk?

No, I don't.

7. Do you _____ to buy _____ _____?

Yes, I _____.

8. Do you want to _____ some _____?

No, I _____.

| Section G | Let's have fun |

At the supermarket!

Read the conversation

Max: What do you want to buy?

Julie: I want to buy some milk.

Max: What don't you want to buy?

Julie: I don't want to buy any meat.

Max: What do you want to buy?

Julie: I want to buy some fruit.

Max: What do you want to buy?

Julie: I want to buy some bread.

Max: What don't you want to buy?

Julie: I don't want to buy any fish.

Max: What do you want to buy?

Julie: I want to buy some vegetables.

Circle the things Julie wants

meat   milk   fruit   fish   vegetables

ice cream   bread   pizza   drinks   juice

Write the things she wants in the shopping cart

1. _____
2. _____
3. _____
4. _____

Lesson 14: At the ice cream shop

在冰淇淋店

Which flavor do you like?
I like mint flavor.

Section A — Words

1. **chocolate**
   巧克力
2. **strawberry**
   草莓
3. **mint**
   薄荷
4. **raspberry**
   覆盆子
5. **cherry**
   樱桃
6. **vanilla**
   香草
7. **coffee**
   咖啡
8. **almond**
   杏仁
9. **caramel**
   焦糖
10. **coconut**
    椰子

Section B — Make a sentence

Which flavor do you like?

I like <u>chocolate</u> flavor.

I don't like <u>almond</u> flavor.

Which flavor does he like?

He likes <u>vanilla</u> flavor.

He doesn't like <u>raspberry</u> flavor.

Section C — Make a question

Do you like <u>strawberry</u> ice cream?
Yes, I do. / No, I don't.

Does she like <u>mint</u> ice cream?
Yes, she does. / No, she doesn't.

Section D — Learn a verb

have/has – having – had – had 有

She **has** coffee ice cream in her refrigerator.

I am **having** mint ice cream instead.

My sister **had** almond ice cream last time.

My father hasn't **had** caramel ice cream yet.

Section E — Learn an idiom

Flavor of the month

Meaning: Something is suddenly popular for a short time.

"This song is just the *flavor of the month*."

| Section F | Write |

Trace and fill in the words

1. Which flavor do you like?

   I like coconut flavor.

2. Which flavor does he like?

   He _____ chocolate flavor.

3. Which _____ do you _____?

   I like _____ _____.

4. Which _____ does she _____?

   She _____ _____ _____.

5. Do you like vanilla ice cream?

   No, I don't.

6. Does she like coffee ice cream?

   Yes, she does.

7. Do you _____ _____ ice cream?

   Yes, I _____.

8. Does he _____ _____ ice cream?

   No, _____ _____.

Section G   Let's have fun

At the ice cream shop!

| don't | raspberry | do | like | you | flavor | she | does |

1. Which _____ do you like? I _____ chocolate flavor.

2. Which flavor _____ you like? I like _____ flavor.

3. Which flavor _____ she like? _____ likes mint flavor.

4. Do _____ like vanilla flavor? No, I _____.

Do or Does?

1. What flavor _____ she like?

2. What flavor _____ they like?

3. What flavor _____ he like?

4. What flavor _____ you like?

5. _____ you like strawberry flavor?

6. _____ he like vanilla flavor?

7. _____ they like vanilla flavor?

8. _____ she like vanilla flavor?

9. Yes, they _____.

10. No, she _____ not.

Lesson 15: In the refrigerator

在冰箱裡

What do you want to eat?
I want to eat rice.

Section A — Words

1. rice
   米
2. salad
   沙拉
3. toast
   吐司
4. soup
   汤
5. dumplings
   水饺
6. tea
   茶
7. cola
   可乐
8. eggs
   鸡蛋
9. water
   水
10. ice
    冰块

Section B — Make a sentence

What do you want to <u>eat</u>?

I want to eat <u>rice</u>.

I don't want to eat <u>dumplings</u>.

What does he want to <u>drink</u>?

He wants to drink <u>tea</u>.

He doesn't want to drink <u>cola</u>.

Section C — Make a question

Do you want to <u>eat</u> <u>salad</u>?
Yes, I do. / No, I don't.

Does she want to <u>drink</u> <u>juice</u>?
Yes, she does. / No, she doesn't.

Section D — Learn a verb

sell – selling – sold – sold 卖

They **sell** eggs at the supermarket.

He was **selling** delicious dumplings at the market last night.

Last week, they **sold** me some cheap rice.

The supermarket has never **sold** ice.

Section E — Learn an idiom

Be as cold as ice

Meaning: To describe someone who is very unfriendly.

"The teacher *was as cold as ice* after she caught me cheating on the science test."

Section F Write

Trace and fill in the words

1. What do you want to drink?

I want to drink water.

2. What does he want to eat?

He _____ to eat soup.

3. What _____ you want to _____?

I want to eat _____.

4. What _____ she _____ to drink?

She wants to _____ _____.

5. Do you want to eat toast?

Yes, I do.

6. Does he want to drink tea?

No, he doesn't.

7. Do you _____ to drink _____?

Yes, I _____.

8. Does _____ want to eat _____?

No, she _____.

| Section G | Let's have fun |

In the refrigerator!

1	2	3	4	5	6	7	8	9	10	11	12	13
a	b	c	d	e	f	g	h	i	j	k	l	m
14	15	16	17	18	19	20	21	22	23	24	25	26
n	o	p	q	r	s	t	u	v	w	x	y	z

Write the words using the code above

1. 19-15-21-16 ___ ___ ___ ___ **2.** 20-15-1-19-20 ___ ___ ___ ___ ___

3. 19-1-12-1-4 ___ ___ ___ ___ ___ **4.** 18-9-3-5 ___ ___ ___ ___

5. 23-1-20-5-18 ___ ___ ___ ___ ___ **6.** 3-15-12-1 ___ ___ ___ ___

This man's refrigerator has no food! Help him write a shopping list!

Shopping list

1. _____dumplings_____
2. _____
3. _____
4. _____
5. _____
6. _____
7. _____
8. _____

Lesson 16: Jobs

工作

| Section A | Words |

1. doctor
   医生
2. cook
   厨师
3. nurse
   护士
4. police officer
   警察
5. taxi driver
   计程车司机
6. teacher
   老师
7. farmer
   农夫
8. salesclerk
   店员
9. firefighter
   消防队员
10. builder
    建筑者

What is her job?
She is a salesclerk.

| Section B | Make a sentence |

What is her job?

She is a <u>doctor</u>.

She isn't a <u>nurse</u>.

What is his job?

He is a <u>teacher</u>.

He isn't a <u>salesclerk</u>.

Section C — Make a question

Is he a <u>farmer</u>?
Yes, he is. / No, he isn't.

Are they <u>teachers</u>?
Yes, they are. / No, they aren't.

Section D — Learn a verb

work – working – worked – worked 工作

I **work** on a farm every day.

She wasn't **working** at the hospital last year.

My mother **worked** at the police station yesterday.

He hasn't **worked** for two years.

Section E — Learn an idiom

Keep up the good work

Meaning: To encourage someone to keep doing well.

"You're doing a great job. *Keep up the good work.*"

Section F — Write

Trace and fill in the words

1. What is his job?

He is a cook.

2. What is _____ job?

She is a teacher.

3. What _____ his _____?

_____ is a _____.

4. What is _____ job?

She _____ a _____.

5. Is she a builder?

No, she isn't.

6. Are they doctors?

No, they aren't.

7. Is _____ a _____?

Yes, she _____.

8. Are we _____?

Yes, _____ _____.

Section G Let's have fun

Jobs!

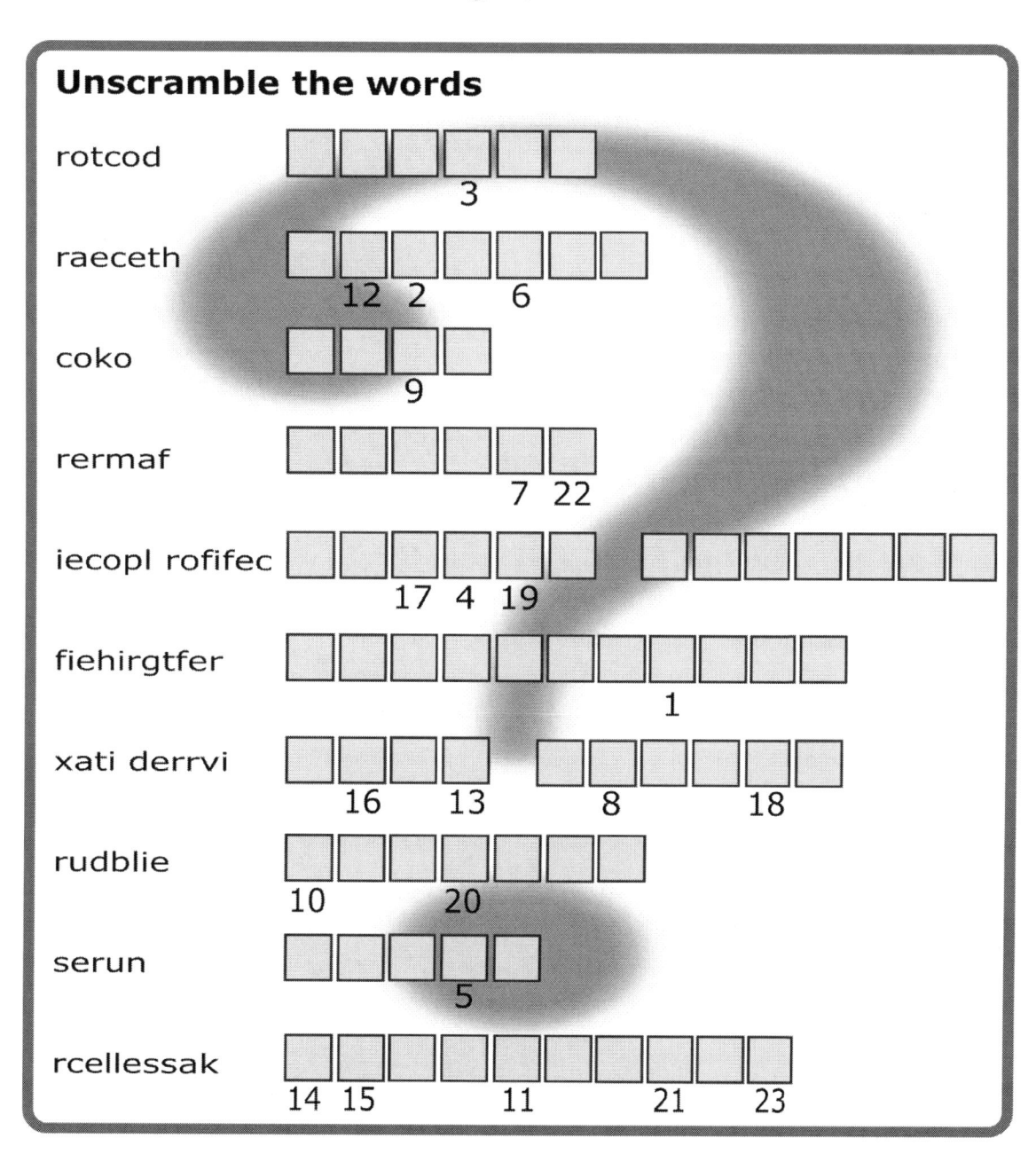

Unscramble the words

rotcod ☐☐☐☐☐☐
          3

raeceth ☐☐☐☐☐☐
        12 2   6

coko ☐☐☐☐
       9

rermaf ☐☐☐☐☐☐
            7 22

iecopl rofifec ☐☐☐☐☐ ☐☐☐☐☐☐☐
                17 4 19

fiehirgtfer ☐☐☐☐☐☐☐☐☐☐
                   1

xati derrvi ☐☐☐☐ ☐☐☐☐☐
             16 13   8   18

rudblie ☐☐☐☐☐☐
         10 20

serun ☐☐☐☐☐
         5

rcellessak ☐☐☐☐☐☐☐☐☐
            14 15 11 21 23

Write the sentence using the information above

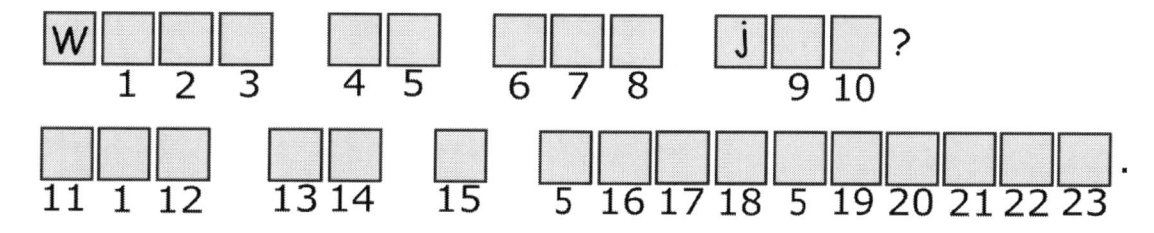

W☐☐ ☐☐ ☐☐☐ j☐☐ ?
1 2 3 4 5 6 7 8 9 10

☐☐☐ ☐☐ ☐ ☐☐☐☐☐☐☐☐☐ .
11 1 12 13 14 15 5 16 17 18 5 19 20 21 22 23

Test 4   Lesson 13 - 16

Write the answer next to the letter "A"

A: ___ 1. What does he want to ___? He ___ to buy some milk.

a. buys, want   b. buy, have   c. buys, wants   d. buy, wants

A: ___ 2. Do you ___ to buy some ___? Yes, I do.

a. wants, meat   b. want, bread   c. want, apple   d. wants, drinks

A: ___ 3. She ___ the vegetables at the supermarket.

a. get   b. getting   c. got   d. is get

A: ___ 4. "That was too expensive. What a rip ___."

a. of   b. over   c. off   d. curl

A: ___ 5. Which flavor ___ he like? He ___ mint flavor.

a. do, like   b. can, like   c. does, like   d. does, likes

A: ___ 6. ___ you like chocolate ice cream? Yes, I ___.

a. Does, does   b. Can, does   c. Do, like   d. Do, do

A: ___ 7. They didn't ___ almond ice cream.

a. have   b. has   c. having   d. had

A: ___ 8. "That new book is just the ___ of the month."

a. taste   b. word   c. ice cream   d. flavor

A: ___ **9.** What ___ she want to drink? She wants to ___ cola.

a. do, try   b. does, drink   c. can, have   d. don't, want

A: ___ **10.** Do ___ want to eat salad? No, I ___.

a. he, doesn't   b. you, don't   c. you, not like   d. we, haven't

A: ___ **11.** They are ___ coffee.

a. sell   b. sells   c. selling   d. sold

A: ___ **12.** "She wasn't friendly. She was as ___ as ice."

a. melted   b. cold   c. dry   d. mean

A: ___ **13.** What is ___ job? She ___ a taxi driver.

a. she, is   b. hers, can   c. she's, be   d. her, is

A: ___ **14.** ___ they teachers? No, they ___.

a. Are, don't   b. Do, don't   c. Have, haven't   d. Are, aren't

A: ___ **15.** They ___ at a school.

a. work   b. works   c. working   d. has worked

A: ___ **16.** "You're doing well. Keep ___ the good work."

a. into   b. on   c. going   d. up

Answers on page 462

Lesson 17: Names

名字

What's her name?
Her name is Helen.

Section A — Words

1. **John**
   约翰
2. **Matthew**
   马修
3. **Jason**
   贾森
4. **Helen**
   海伦
5. **Mary**
   玛丽
6. **Kevin**
   凯文
7. **Tom**
   汤姆
8. **Emily**
   艾米莉
9. **Jessica**
   洁西卡
10. **Susan**
    苏珊

Section B — Make a sentence

What's your name?

My name is John.

What's her name?

Her name is Susan.

Learn: my, your, his, her

Note: What's = What is

Section C — Make a question

Is <u>his</u> name <u>Jason</u>?
Yes, it is. / No, it isn't.

Is <u>her</u> name <u>Emily</u>?
Yes, it is. / No, it isn't.

Section D — Learn a verb

call – calling – called – called 打电话

You can **call** him Jason.

I will be **calling** you tomorrow at 9:30 A.M.

Kevin **called** Mary yesterday.

Helen hasn't **called** Matthew back yet.

Section E — Learn an idiom

A household name

Meaning: To describe someone famous who everyone knows.

"The actor became *a household name* after he won an Oscar for his performance."

Section F — Write

Trace and fill in the words

1. What's your name?

My name is Susan.

2. What's his name?

His name _____ Tom.

3. What's _____ name?

My _____ is _____.

4. What's _____ _____?

Her name _____ _____.

5. Is his name John?

Yes, it is.

6. Is her name Jessica?

No, it isn't.

7. Is _____ name _____?

Yes, it _____.

8. Is _____ _____ Kevin?

No, _____ isn't.

Section G | Let's have fun

Names!

1	2	3	4	5
M	T	S	J	K

Write their names

1. __ __ __ __

2. __ __ __

3. __ __ __ __ __

4. __ __ __ __

5. __ __ __ __ __

What's your name?

_____

Answer the questions

1. What is her name?

   Her name is Mary.

2. What is his name?

   _____

3. What is her name?

   _____

4. What is his name?

   _____

5. What is his name?

   _____

Lesson 18: More places

更多地方

Where did you go yesterday?
I went to school.

Section A — Words

1. **the library**
   图书馆
2. **school**
   学校
3. **the hospital**
   医院
4. **the train station**
   火车站
5. **the police station**
   警察局
6. **the office**
   办公室
7. **the factory**
   工厂
8. **the clinic**
   诊所
9. **the bus stop**
   公车站
10. **the fire station**
    消防局

Section B — Make a sentence

Where did you go <u>yesterday</u>?

I went to <u>the library</u>.

Where did they go <u>last week</u>?

They went to <u>the office</u>.

Learn: yesterday, last week, last night, last month

Note: didn't = did not

| Section C | Make a question |

Did she go to <u>school</u> <u>last night</u>?
Yes, she did. / No, she didn't.

Did you go to <u>the factory</u> <u>yesterday</u>?
Yes, I did. / No, I didn't.

| Section D | Learn a verb |

go – going – went – gone 去

I will **go** to the library after school.

When I was **going** to the office, I saw my friend.

Matthew **went** to the clinic this morning.

Mary hasn't **gone** to school yet.

| Section E | Learn an idiom |

Heart is in the right place

Meaning: To mean well and try to do the right thing.

"He makes a lot of mistakes, but his *heart is in the right place*."

Section F   Write

Trace and fill in the words

1. Where did you go yesterday?

I went to the police station.

2. Where _____ they go last night?

They went to _____ clinic.

3. Where _____ we _____ last week?

_____ went to the _____.

4. Where did _____ go _____?

She _____ to the _____.

5. Did he go to the bus stop yesterday?

Yes, he did.

6. Did you _____ to the train station last night?

No, I _____.

7. Did _____ go to the _____ last week?

Yes, _____ _____.

8. Did she _____ to the _____ last night?

No, _____ _____.

90

Section G Let's have fun

More places!

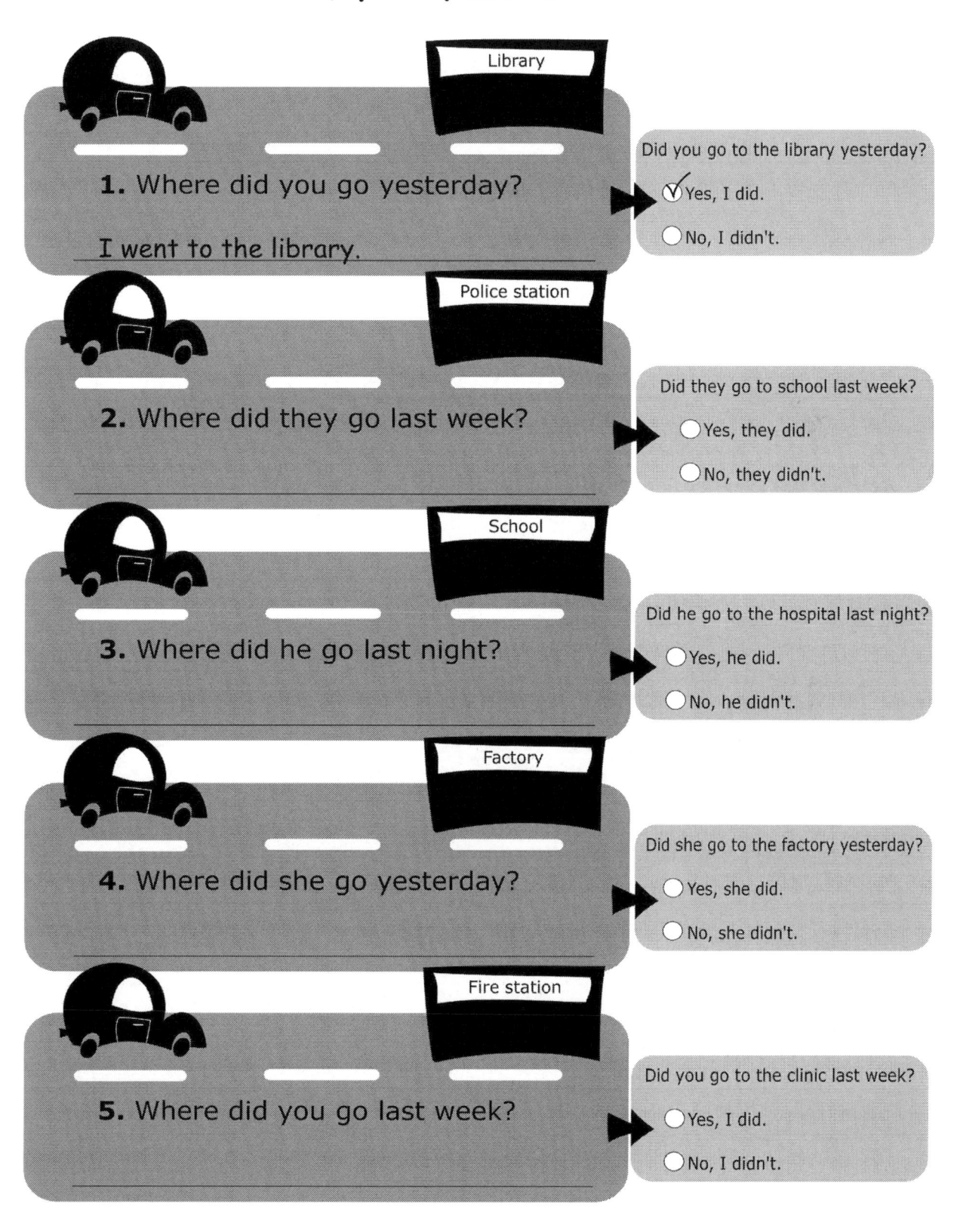

1. Where did you go yesterday?
I went to the library.

Library

Did you go to the library yesterday?
- ✓ Yes, I did.
- ○ No, I didn't.

2. Where did they go last week?

Police station

Did they go to school last week?
- ○ Yes, they did.
- ○ No, they didn't.

3. Where did he go last night?

School

Did he go to the hospital last night?
- ○ Yes, he did.
- ○ No, he didn't.

4. Where did she go yesterday?

Factory

Did she go to the factory yesterday?
- ○ Yes, she did.
- ○ No, she didn't.

5. Where did you go last week?

Fire station

Did you go to the clinic last week?
- ○ Yes, I did.
- ○ No, I didn't.

Lesson 19: Meats

肉類

> What did he eat for lunch?
> He ate chicken.

Section A — Words

1. **beef**
   牛肉
2. **pork**
   猪肉
3. **bacon**
   培根
4. **fish**
   鱼肉
5. **salami**
   义大利香肠
6. **chicken**
   鸡肉
7. **lamb**
   羊肉
8. **ham**
   火腿
9. **sausage**
   香肠
10. **shrimp**
    虾子

Section B — Make a sentence

What did he eat for <u>lunch</u>?

He ate <u>beef</u>.

He didn't eat <u>chicken</u>.

Learn: breakfast, lunch, dinner

Section C — Make a question

Did they eat <u>ham</u> for <u>breakfast</u>?
Yes, they did. / No, they didn't.

Did you eat <u>fish</u> for <u>dinner</u>?
Yes, I did. / No, I didn't.

Section D — Learn a verb

eat – eating – ate – eaten 吃

I **eat** bacon for breakfast every Sunday.

They're not **eating** meat.

We **ate** a sandwich with cheese and salami yesterday.

I had never **eaten** German sausages until I went there.

Section E — Learn an idiom

Beef up

Meaning: To strengthen something or somebody.

"We need to *beef up* our efforts if we are going to do well this year."

Section F Write

Trace and fill in the words

1. What did she eat for lunch?

She ate ham. She didn't eat fish.

2. What did they eat for dinner?

They ate pork. They didn't _____ shrimp.

3. What _____ he eat _____ lunch?

_____ ate _____. He didn't _____ beef.

4. _____ did you _____ for breakfast?

I _____ fish. _____ didn't eat _____.

5. Did we eat sausage for lunch?

Yes, we _____.

6. Did you eat lamb for dinner?

No, I _____.

7. Did _____ eat _____ for lunch?

Yes, he _____.

8. Did they _____ bacon for _____?

No, _____ _____.

Section G — Let's have fun

Meats!

Find the words!

```
f e p l x e m s x h e m d b o h z a l u
e p r n y l o q u y m x y r w g r p g d
i c r l y o i q d z m a u a p f q b s g
r v b k v y b n e z i x x q d r e c b h
r y u o r w l j g d s n z u u s l l z z
l h (b e e f) k w v q n b j e g f b w c m
c i b k b s q x b g m o i g n k n d r p
f q x b q a e k m f j o c b l s p k h n
m x j t o u n z z m f f s a l a m i y y
v i r m i a k e s k r g e k b u m z a e
w n p w n k q z r v h p h e s s n b l p
q o h n s t q u c n w u z l r a d f u v
a p s i g e l b o b q f x w s g n d e w
l b k p j c g n n c x o i z q e t e r i
s g n s x v w q l o x h k y k b q q y y
j k a x e h x a s z y p a c k r e v t r
j o w n g q v f i s h r i m p n o f m p
o a d h o b i e t h o h c q z n c p b m
y k o b m l v h v i c r q i k b c o f i
f i q a m x g l q k z w s n a w t n w w
```

~~beef~~ shrimp
pork bacon
ham sausage
fish lamb
chicken salami

Lesson 20: Vegetables

蔬菜

What will you cook tonight?
I will cook pumpkin.

| Section A | Words |

1. **pumpkin**
   南瓜
2. **potato**
   马铃薯
3. **carrot**
   胡萝卜
4. **asparagus**
   芦笋
5. **broccoli**
   花椰菜
6. **corn**
   玉米
7. **cabbage**
   高丽菜
8. **spinach**
   菠菜
9. **mushroom**
   蘑菇
10. **onion**
    洋葱

| Section B | Make a sentence |

What will he cook <u>tonight</u>?

He will cook <u>pumpkin</u>.

What won't she cook <u>tomorrow</u>?

She won't cook <u>onion</u>.

Learn: tonight, tomorrow, later, next week

Note: won't = will not

| Section C | Make a question |

Will we cook <u>carrot</u> <u>later</u>?
Yes, we will. / No, we won't.

Will you cook <u>asparagus</u> <u>tomorrow</u>?
Yes, I will. / No, I won't.

| Section D | Learn a verb |

cook – cooking – cooked – cooked 煮

She always **cooks** onions with the potatoes.

Mary will be **cooking** dinner for us tonight.

John **cooked** a delicious meal for us last weekend.

I've **cooked** cabbage and mushroom a lot lately.

| Section E | Learn an idiom |

Carrot on a stick

Meaning: A reward that is promised upon completion of a task.

"The coach gave his players a *carrot on a stick* and promised to take them all out for dinner if they win the game."

| Section F | Write |

Trace and fill in the words

1. What will he cook tonight?

He will cook corn.

2. What won't she cook tomorrow?

She won't _____ spinach.

3. What _____ he _____ later?

_____ will _____ onion. He won't cook _____.

4. What will _____ cook tonight?

She _____ cook _____.

5. Will they cook carrot tomorrow?

Yes, they _____.

6. Will you cook asparagus tomorrow?

No, I _____.

7. Will she _____ mushroom _____?

Yes, _____ will.

8. Will _____ cook _____ tomorrow?

No, we _____.

Section G   Let's have fun

Vegetables!

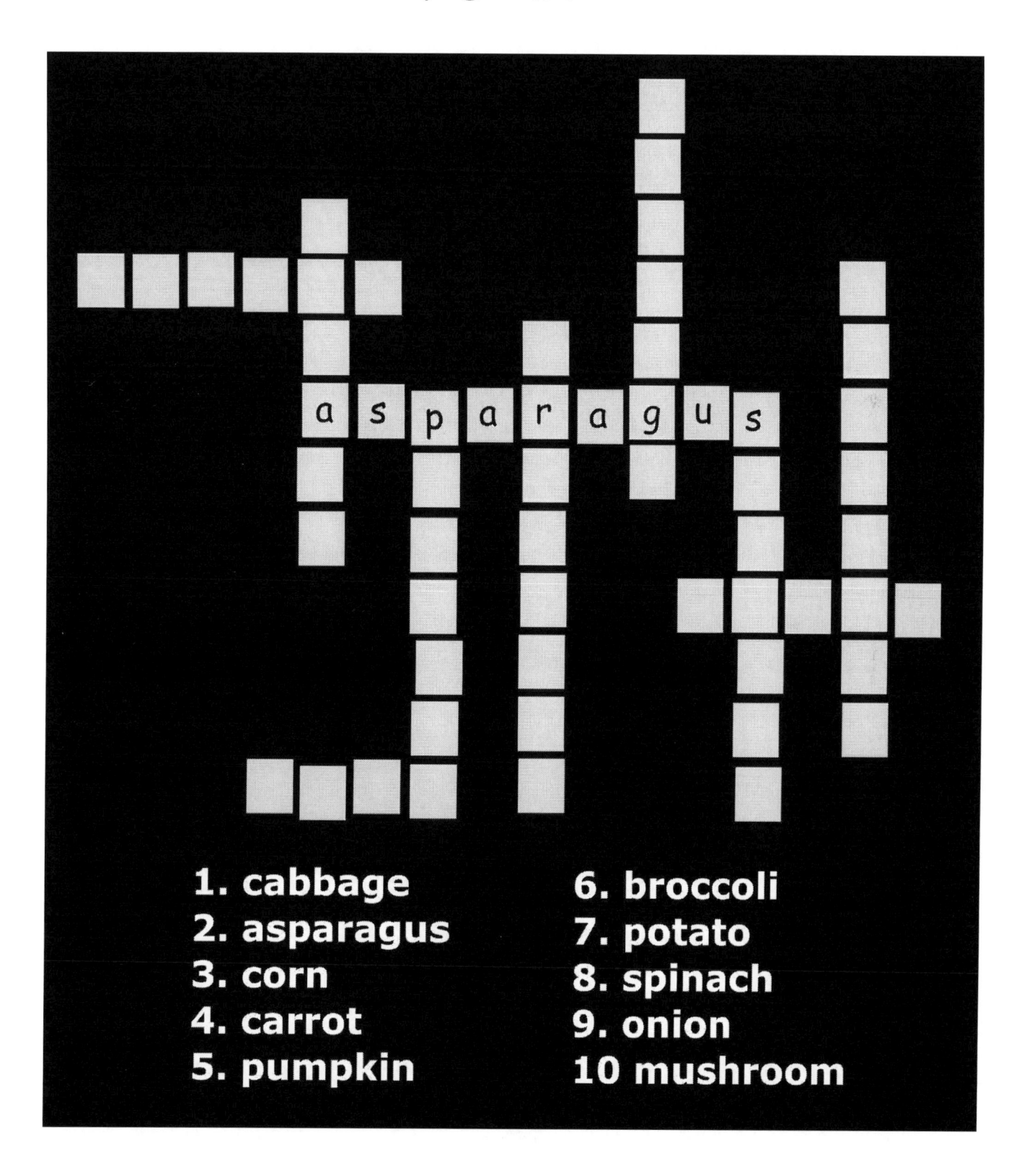

1. cabbage
2. asparagus
3. corn
4. carrot
5. pumpkin
6. broccoli
7. potato
8. spinach
9. onion
10 mushroom

Test 5 — Lesson 17 - 20

Write the answer next to the letter "A"

A: ___ 1. What's her ___? ___ name is Helen.

a. name, Her b. name, She's c. names, Her d. name, She

A: ___ 2. ___ his name Kevin? Yes, ___ is.

a. Is, it b. Is, he c. Can, it d. Does, it

A: ___ 3. Yesterday, Matthew ___ a green marker.

a. has b. is having c. had d. did had

A: ___ 4. "She's really famous. She's a ___ name."

a. homely b. household c. real d. star

A: ___ 5. Where ___ you go yesterday? I ___ to the clinic.

a. do, go b. did, go c. does, went d. did, went

A: ___ 6. ___ she go to the office last night? Yes, she ___.

a. Does, go b. Can, does c. Did, goes d. Did, did

A: ___ 7. I ___ to the train station every week.

a. gone b. go c. going d. goes

A: ___ 8. "He means well. His ___ is in the right place."

a. heart b. words c. mind d. smile

A: ___ **9.** What ___ he eat for dinner? He ___ eat pork.

a. does, didn't   b. is, is   c. didn't, didn't   d. did, was

A: ___ **10.** ___ they eat sausage for lunch? No, they ___.

a. Were, weren't   b. Did, don't   c. Like, not like   d. Did, didn't

A: ___ **11.** She has ___ all of the ham.

a. eat   b. ate   c. eaten   d. eating

A: ___ **12.** "He wants to get stronger. He said he wants to beef ___."

a. out   b. up   c. on   d. in

A: ___ **13.** What ___ he cook later? He will ___ broccoli.

a. is, cook   b. will, cooks   c. has, cook   d. will, cook

A: ___ **14.** ___ we cook asparagus tonight? ___, we will.

a. Can, Can   b. Don't, Do   c. Will, Yes   d. Are, Yes

A: ___ **15.** She will ___ vegetables tomorrow.

a. cook   b. cooks   c. cooking   d. cooked

A: ___ **16.** "I think the reward is like a ___ on a stick."

a. potato   b. pumpkin   c. carrot   d. mushroom

Answers on page 462

Lesson 21: At school

在学校

Where is the art room?
The art room is next to the gym.

Section A — Words

1. **classroom**
   教室
2. **office**
   办公室
3. **nurse's office**
   保健室
4. **gym**
   體育館
5. **hall**
   大厅
6. **computer lab**
   电脑教室
7. **art room**
   美术教室
8. **music room**
   音乐教室
9. **science lab**
   自然教室
10. **lunchroom**
    午餐室

Section B — Make a sentence

Where is the <u>classroom</u>?

The classroom is <u>across from</u> the <u>office</u>.

Where is the <u>computer lab</u>?

The computer lab is <u>between</u> the <u>gym</u> and the <u>hall</u>.

Learn: across from, next to, between

Section C — Make a question

Is the <u>art room</u> <u>next to</u> the <u>music room</u>?
Yes, it is. / No, it's <u>next to</u> the <u>science lab</u>.

Is the <u>nurse's office</u> <u>next to</u> the <u>office</u>?
Yes, it is. / No, it's <u>across from</u> the <u>computer lab</u>.

Section D — Learn a verb

put – putting – put – put 放

You can **put** the guitar in the music room.

We are **putting** the chairs in the new office.

The students already **put** the books in the computer lab.

She hasn't **put** any food in the lunchroom yet.

Section E — Learn an idiom

Old school

Meaning: To do something the old-fashioned way.

"We're going to do this *old school* and use a hammer and nails."

Section F　　　Write

Trace and fill in the words

1. Where is the office?

    The office is next to the lunchroom.

2. Where _____ the gym?

    The gym is _____ the art room and the science lab.

3. Where _____ the _____ room?

    The music room is across from the _____.

4. _____ is the _____ lab?

    The science lab is _____ the lunchroom and the _____.

5. Is the art room next to the music room?

    Yes, it is.

6. Is the computer lab _____ to the hall?

    No, it's _____ the gym and the art room.

7. _____ the nurse's office next to the _____?

    Yes, it is.

8. Is the hall across _____ the classroom?

    No, it's _____ the _____ and the office.

Section G | Let's have fun

At school!

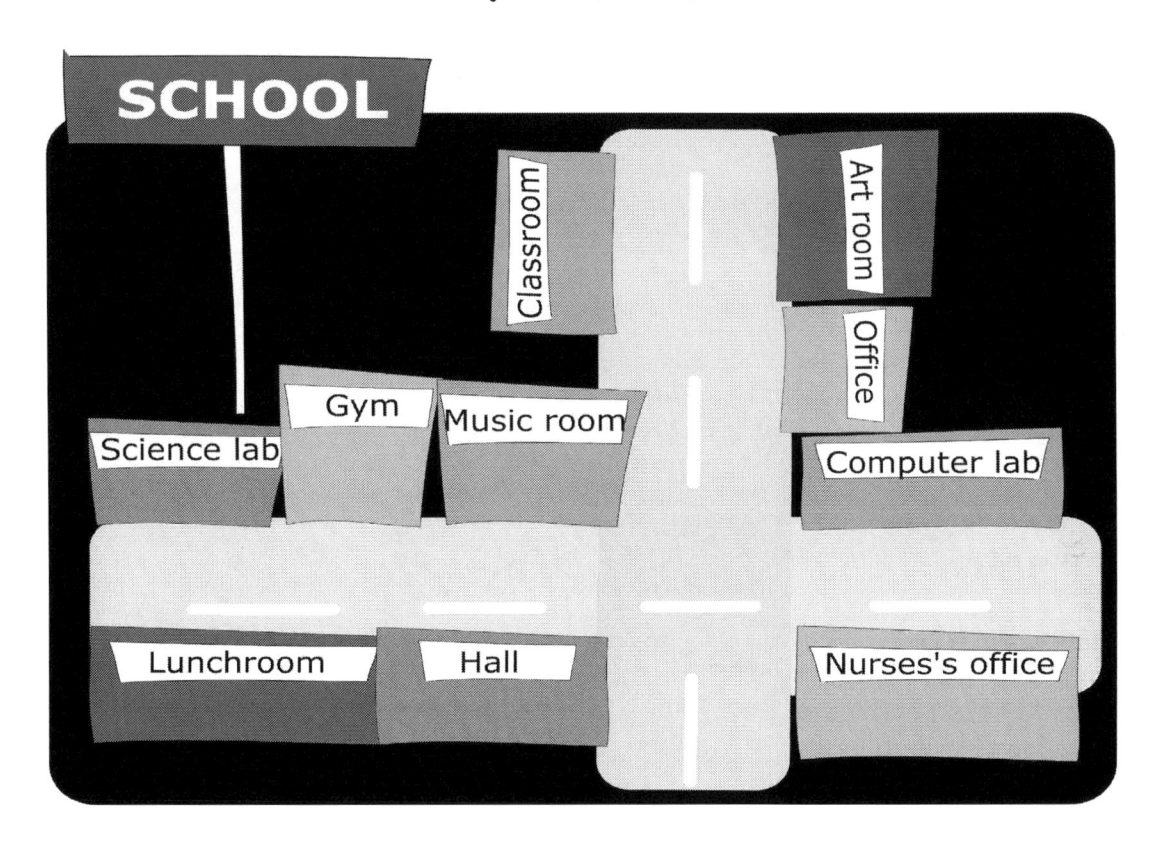

SCHOOL

Classroom | Art room | Office
Gym | Music room
Science lab | Computer lab
Lunchroom | Hall | Nurses's office

Answer the questions

1. Where is the gym?

   _____.

2. Where is the classroom?

   _____.

3. Where is the nurse's office?

   _____.

4. Is the lunchroom next to the hall?

   _____.

5. Is the science lab across from the office?

   _____.

Lesson 22: School subjects

学校科目

What class do you have after math?
I have an art class after math.

Section A | Words

1. **science**
   自然
2. **English**
   英文
3. **P.E.**
   体育课
4. **geography**
   地理
5. **social studies**
   社会
6. **math**
   数学
7. **art**
   美术
8. **music**
   音乐
9. **history**
   历史
10. **computer**
    电脑课

Section B | Make a sentence

What class do you have <u>after</u> <u>science</u>?

I have a <u>geography</u> class after science.

What class does he have <u>before</u> <u>science</u>?

He has a <u>history</u> class before science.

Learn: after, before / have, has

Section C — Make a question

Do you have a <u>math</u> class after <u>history</u>?
Yes, I do. / No, I have a <u>music</u> class.

Does he have a <u>math</u> class before <u>English</u>?
Yes, he does. / No, he has a <u>computer</u> class.

Section D — Learn a verb

do – doing – did – done 做

He couldn't **do** most of the questions on the math test.

They are **doing** the science project now.

John **did** really well on his English test last semester.

I will have already **done** the history homework by Sunday.

Section E — Learn an idiom

Cut class

Meaning: To miss class on purpose.

"Jenny *cut class* after she realized she didn't do her math homework."

Section F — Write

Trace and fill in the words

1. What class do you have after math?

I have an English class after math.

2. What class does she have before art?

She has a music _____ before art.

3. What _____ do you have _____ history?

I _____ a geography class before _____.

4. What class does _____ have after _____?

She _____ a science class _____ P.E.

5. Do you _____ a math class after history?

Yes, I _____.

6. Does he have a science _____ after English?

No, he _____ a computer class.

7. Do _____ have an art class before _____?

Yes, you _____.

8. Does _____ have a P.E. class _____ Music?

No, she _____ an _____ class.

Section G Let's have fun

School Subjects!

I have a geography class after science.
I have an English class before science.
I have a math class before English.
I have a history class after geography.
I have a computer class before math.

Fill out the School Schedule using the information above

School Schedule

9am _____

10am _____

11am _____

1pm ____science class_____

2pm _____

3pm _____

True or False? Circle the answer

1. You have a science class before geography. **True   False**

2. You have a computer class after math. **True   False**

3. You have a history class after geography. **True   False**

4. You have an English class after science. **True   False**

Lesson 23: Chores

家事

> What do you need to do today?
> I need to feed the pets.

Section A — Words

1. **wash the dishes**
   洗碗
2. **feed the pets**
   喂宠物
3. **vacuum the carpet**
   吸地毯
4. **take out the trash**
   丢垃圾
5. **clean the bedroom**
   整理卧室
6. **mop the floor**
   擦地板
7. **cook dinner**
   做晚餐
8. **do the laundry**
   洗衣服
9. **iron the clothes**
   烫衣服
10. **make the beds**
    铺床

Section B — Make a sentence

What do you need to do <u>this morning</u>?

This morning, I need to <u>wash the dishes</u>.

What does he need to do <u>this afternoon</u>?

This afternoon, he needs to <u>mop the floor</u>.

Learn: this morning, this afternoon, this evening, today

Section C | Make a question

Do you need to <u>make the beds</u> <u>this morning</u>?
Yes, I do. / No, I don't.

Does he need to <u>iron the clothes</u> <u>this afternoon</u>?
Yes, he does. / No, he doesn't.

Section D | Learn a verb

know – knowing – knew – known 知道

I don't **know** what to feed the pets.

There is no way of **knowing** which chores have been done.

Mary **knew** the trash hadn't been taken out yet.

I hadn't **known** at the time that nobody did the laundry.

Section E | Learn an idiom

All in a day's work

Meaning: A normal day without a change in routine.

"Taking out the trash before school is *all in a day's work*."

Section F | Write

Trace and fill in the words

1. What do you need to do this afternoon?

This afternoon, I need to do the laundry.

2. What does he _____ to do this morning?

This morning, he _____ to make the beds.

3. _____ do you need to do this _____?

This afternoon, _____ need to feed the _____.

4. What _____ she _____ to do today?

Today, _____ needs to do the _____.

5. Do you need to iron the clothes this evening?

Yes, I _____.

6. Does he need to _____ the beds this morning?

No, he _____.

7. Do _____ need to _____ the carpet today?

No, I _____.

8. Does she need to cook _____ this evening?

Yes, she _____.

Section G | Let's have fun

Chores!

Connect the sentences

What do you need to do this morning? • — • This morning, she needs to do the dishes.

What does he need to do this afternoon? • — • This morning, I need to wash the clothes.

What does she need to do this morning? • — • This evening, they need to cook dinner.

What do they need to do this evening? • — • This afternoon, we need to make the beds.

What do we need to do this afternoon? • — • This afternoon, he needs to feed the pets.

Unscramble the sentences

wash the / morning / need to / I / this / dishes

1. _____.

she / the pets / needs to / this afternoon / feed

2. _____.

to / the laundry / need / they / do / this evening

3. _____.

this afternoon / the trash / he / needs to / take out

4. _____.

Lesson 24: At the toy store

在玩具店

What are you playing with?
I'm playing with my ball.

| Section A | Words |

1. **doll**
   洋娃娃
2. **teddy bear**
   泰迪熊
3. **car**
   车子
4. **airplane**
   飞机
5. **dinosaur**
   恐龙
6. **robot**
   机器人
7. **ball**
   球
8. **jump rope**
   跳绳
9. **board game**
   桌游
10. **blocks**
    积木

| Section B | Make a sentence |

What are you playing with?

I am playing with <u>my</u> <u>doll</u>.

What is he playing with?

He is playing with <u>his</u> <u>robot</u>.

Learn: my, your, his, her, their, our, its

Note: I'm = I am

| Section C | Make a question |

Are you playing with <u>your</u> <u>teddy bear</u>?
Yes, I am. / No, I'm not.

Is she playing with <u>her</u> <u>ball</u>?
Yes, she is. / No, she isn't.

| Section D | Learn a verb |

borrow – borrowing – borrowed – borrowed 借来

You can **borrow** my ball.
She will be **borrowing** the board game for tonight.
I **borrowed** a book about cars from the library yesterday.
They haven't **borrowed** these books yet.

| Section E | Learn an idiom |

Like a kid with a new toy

Meaning: To be really happy with something.

"He was *like a kid with a new toy* when he drove the car for the first time."

Section F — Write

Trace and fill in the words

1. What are you playing with?

I am playing with my teddy bear.

2. What is she playing _____?

She _____ playing with her ball.

3. What are _____ playing _____?

We _____ _____ with our board game.

4. What is he _____ with?

_____ is playing with his _____.

5. Are you playing _____ your car?

Yes, I am.

6. Is he playing with _____ airplane?

No, he isn't.

7. _____ you _____ with your jump rope?

_____, I'm _____.

8. _____ she playing _____ her dinosaur?

Yes, _____ _____.

Section G | Let's have fun

Toys!

Circle the toys

1.	cool	geography	bag	(doll)	sister
2.	desk	blocks	math	father	milk
3.	teddy bear	history	classroom		beef
4.	pen	science	water	ball	gym

Write the word

1. _____

2. _____

3. _____

4. _____

Write the answer using the information above

1. What is she playing with? _____.

2. What is he playing with? _____.

3. Is she playing with her teddy bear? _____.

4. Is he playing with his robot? _____.

Test 6   Lesson 21 - 24

Write the answer next to the letter "A"

A: ___ 1. ___ is the office? It's ___ to the gym.

a. There, next   b. Where, next   c. How, near   d. This, next

A: ___ 2. ___ the hall across from the office? Yes, ___ is.

a. Does, it   b. Is, it   c. Are, they   d. Can, he

A: ___ 3. They will ___ the art room later.

a. find   b. found   c. finding   d. finds

A: ___ 4. "We did it the old-fashioned way. We did it old ___."

a. way   b. time   c. man   d. school

A: ___ 5. What class ___ you ___ after science?

a. are, have   b. does, has   c. do, have   d. can, has

A: ___ 6. ___ we have math class after art? Yes, we ___.

a. Can, are   b. Does, do   c. Do, do   d. Are, are

A: ___ 7. They ___ gym class earlier today.

a. has   b. having   c. are had   d. had

A: ___ 8. "She ___ class because she didn't do her homework."

a. put   b. cut   c. lost   d. made

A: ___ **9.** This morning, I ___ to ___ the pets.

a. need, feed	b. am, take	c. can, walk	d. need, make

A: ___ **10.** ___ we need to ___ the beds this morning?

a. Does, take	b. Are, open	c. Do, mop	d. Do, make

A: ___ **11.** He ___ to do the laundry before lunch.

a. needs	b. need	c. needing	d. is need

A: ___ **12.** "Cleaning the room after school is all in a day's ___."

a. time	b. work	c. travel	d. test

A: ___ **13.** What are you ___ with? I'm playing ___ my robot.

a. play, with	b. playing, with	c. plays, by	d. play, on

A: ___ **14.** Is he playing with ___ jump rope? Yes, he ___.

a. him, can	b. he, is	c. his, is	d. him, has

A: ___ **15.** She doesn't like to ___ with dinosaurs.

a. plays	b. playing	c. play	d. played

A: ___ **16.** "He was so happy, he was like a kid with a new ___."

a. car	b. bike	c. toy	d. ball

Answers on page 462

Lesson 25: In the kitchen

在厨房

What was he cleaning?
He was cleaning the stove.

Section A — Words

1. **refrigerator**
   冰箱
2. **coffee maker**
   咖啡壶
3. **microwave oven**
   微波炉
4. **stove**
   瓦斯炉
5. **blender**
   果汁机
6. **cupboard**
   碗柜
7. **rice cooker**
   电锅
8. **dish rack**
   碗架
9. **pan**
   平底锅
10. **toaster**
    烤面包机

Section B — Make a sentence

What was he cleaning?

He was cleaning the <u>refrigerator</u>.

What were they cleaning?

They were cleaning the <u>cupboard</u>.

Note: weren't = were not, wasn't = was not

Section C | Make a question

Was she cleaning the <u>coffee maker</u>?
Yes, she was. / No, she wasn't.

Were they cleaning the <u>toaster</u>?
Yes, they were. / No, they weren't.

Section D | Learn a verb

clean – cleaning – cleaned – cleaned 清洗

He **cleans** the gas stove every day.

We are **cleaning** the refrigerator.

My mother **cleaned** the toaster this morning.

I've already **cleaned** the blender, so you can use it now.

Section E | Learn an idiom

Too many cooks in the kitchen

Meaning: When too many people try to take control.

"We couldn't find a solution because there were *too many cooks in the kitchen*."

Section F   **Write**

Trace and fill in the words

1. What was she cleaning?

She was cleaning the cupboard.

2. What were they cleaning?

They were _____ the coffee maker.

3. What _____ he cleaning?

_____ was _____ the pan.

4. _____ were _____ cleaning?

They _____ cleaning the toaster.

5. Was he cleaning the microwave oven?

No, he wasn't.

6. Were we cleaning the gas stove?

No, we _____.

7. Was _____ cleaning the _____?

Yes, she _____.

8. _____ they _____ the blender?

Yes, _____ _____.

Section G — Let's have fun

In the kitchen!

Write the missing words

| wasn't was you were pan cleaning she the |

1. What _____ he cleaning? He was _____ the microwave.

2. What _____ they cleaning? They were cleaning _____ stove.

3. What was _____ cleaning? She was cleaning the _____.

4. Were _____ cleaning the blender? No, I _____.

Was or Were?

1. What _____ she cleaning?

   She _____ cleaning the blender.

2. What _____ they cleaning?

   They _____ cleaning the toaster.

3. What _____ you cleaning?

   I _____ cleaning the refrigerator.

4. _____ he cleaning the cupboard?

   Yes, he _____.

5. _____ they cleaning the rice cooker?

   No, they _____ not.

Lesson 26: In the toolbox

在工具箱里

What were you using to fix the chair?
I was using the electric drill.

Section A — Words

1. **hammer**
   榔头
2. **electric drill**
   电钻
3. **screwdriver**
   螺丝起子
4. **paintbrush**
   油漆刷
5. **shovel**
   铲子
6. **tape measure**
   卷尺
7. **axe**
   斧头
8. **pliers**
   钳子
9. **ladder**
   梯子
10. **wrench**
    扳手

Section B — Make a sentence

What were you using to fix the <u>table</u>?

I was using the <u>hammer</u>.

What was she using to fix the <u>fence</u>?

She was using the <u>pliers</u>.

Learn: table, chair, fence, roof, door, cupboard

Section C — Make a question

Was he using the <u>electric drill</u> to <u>fix the chair</u>?
Yes, he was. / No, he wasn't.

Were they using the <u>ladder</u> to <u>fix the roof</u>?
Yes, they were. / No, they weren't.

Section D — Learn a verb

use – using – used – used 用

She **uses** the shovel to do the gardening.
They were **using** the wrench last week.
My father **used** the screwdriver earlier today.
My brother has never **used** an electric drill.

Section E — Learn an idiom

Tools of the trade

Meaning: Things that are needed for a specific job.

"My cell phone, diary and calculator are all *tools of the trade*."

Section F — Write

Trace and fill in the words

1. What were you using to fix the table?

I was using the electric drill.

2. What was she _____ to fix the chair?

She _____ using the screwdriver.

3. What _____ you _____ to fix the door?

_____ was using the _____.

4. What was _____ using to _____ the roof?

He _____ _____ the ladder.

5. Was she using the pliers to fix the cupboard?

No, she wasn't.

6. Were they using the shovel to fix the fence?

No, _____ weren't.

7. Was _____ using the pliers to fix the _____?

Yes, he _____.

8. Were you using the hammer to fix the chair?

Yes, _____ _____.

Section G Let's have fun

In the toolbox!

Was or Were?

He _____ using the electric drill to fix the cupboard.

She _____ using the hammer to fix the fence.

They _____ using the tape measure to fix the door.

We _____ using the ladder to fix the roof.

I _____ using the pliers to fix the table.

John _____ using the screwdriver to fix the chair.

What was fixed?

1. _____   4. _____

2. _____   5. _____

3. _____   6. _____

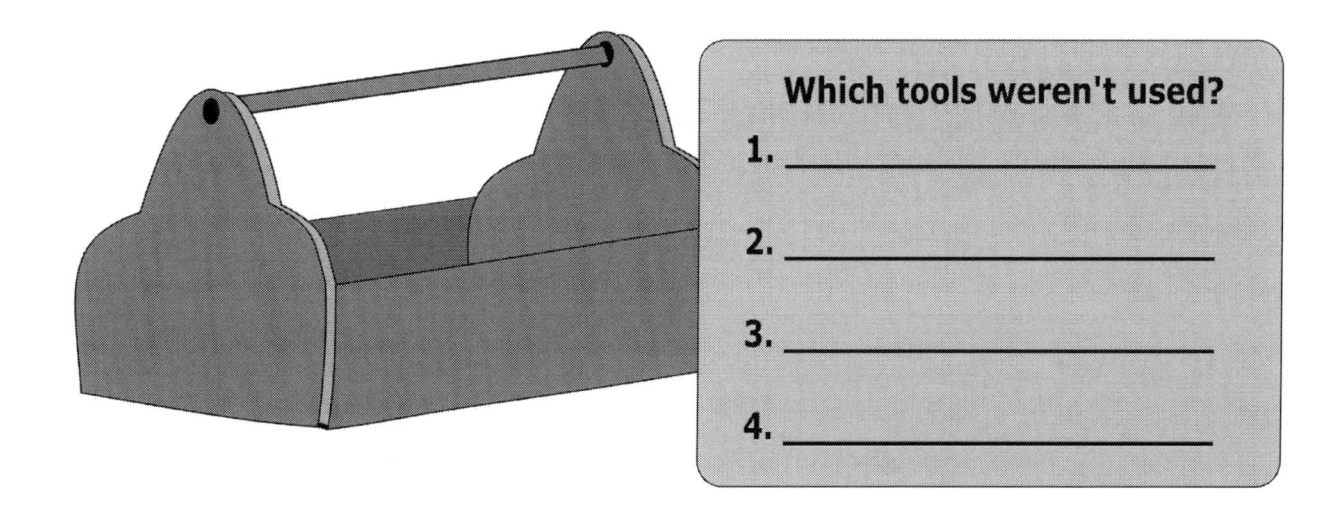

Which tools weren't used?

1. _____

2. _____

3. _____

4. _____

Lesson 27: Transportation

运输工具

How will you be going to Rome?
I will be taking a bus.

| Section A | Words |

1. **catch a bus**
   坐公车
2. **take a taxi**
   坐计程车
3. **take a ferry**
   坐渡轮
4. **ride a motorcycle**
   骑摩托车 (大的)
5. **take the subway**
   坐地铁

6. **take a train**
   坐火车
7. **drive a car**
   开车
8. **ride a scooter**
   骑摩托车 (小的)
9. **ride a bicycle**
   骑脚踏车
10. **take an airplane**
    坐飞机

| Section B | Make a sentence |

How will you be going to New York?

I will be catching a bus there.

Learn: New York, Sydney, Vancouver, Rome, London, Shanghai, Hong Kong, Paris, Berlin, Cape town, Buenos Aires, Venice

Note: I'll = I will

Section C — Make a question

Will you be <u>taking a ferry</u> to <u>Hong Kong</u>?
Yes, I will be. / No, I'll be <u>taking an airplane</u>.

Will you be <u>riding a bicycle</u> to <u>Sydney</u>?
Yes, I will be. / No, I'll be <u>catching a bus</u>.

Section D — Learn a verb

take – taking – took – taken 拿 / 坐

You can **take** the subway to work.

She will be **taking** a taxi to the restaurant.

We **took** a ferry to the Hong Kong airport last year.

I hadn't **taken** an airplane until I went to Rome.

Section E — Learn an idiom

Lose <u>one's</u> train of thought

Meaning: To forget what you were thinking about.

"I'm sorry, I *lost* my *train of thought*. What were we talking about?"

Section F   Write

Trace and fill in the words

1. How will you be going to Sydney?

I will be taking a train there.

2. How will he be _____ to Vancouver?

He will _____ driving a car.

3. How _____ we be going to Rome?

_____ will be _____ a scooter there.

4. How will _____ be _____ to Paris?

They _____ be _____ an airplane.

5. Will you be riding a motorcycle to Berlin?

No, I'll be riding a bicycle.

6. Will _____ be _____ a ferry to Hong Kong?

No, they'll be taking an airplane.

7. Will _____ be _____ the subway to Venice?

No, he'll _____ catching a bus.

8. Will she _____ _____ a train to London?

Yes, _____ _____ _____.

Section G Let's have fun

Transportation!

Unscramble the words and write

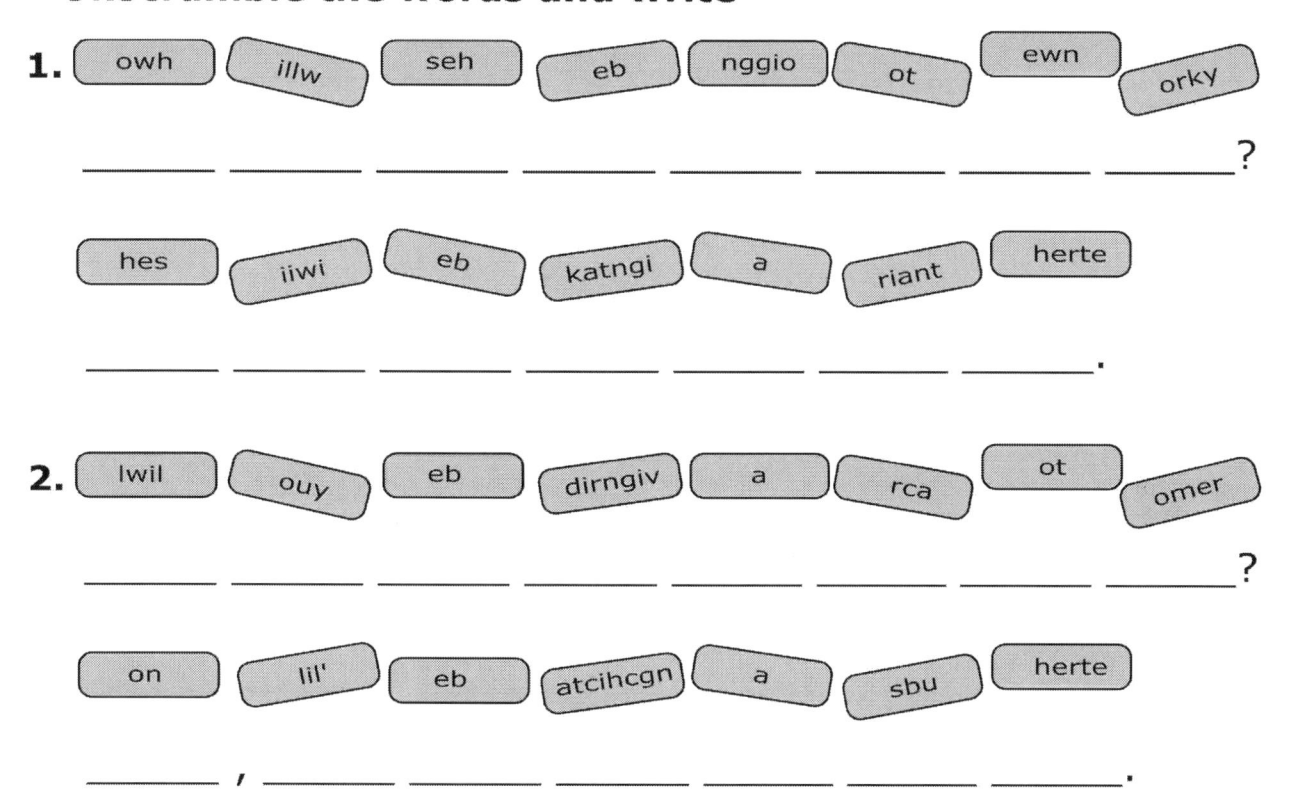

1. owh | illw | seh | eb | nggio | ot | ewn | orky

   How will she be going to New York?

   hes | iiwi | eb | katngi | a | riant | herte

   She will be taking a train there.

2. lwil | ouy | eb | dirngiv | a | rca | ot | omer

   Will you be driving a car to Rome?

   on | lil' | eb | atcihcgn | a | sbu | herte

   _No_, _I'll be catching a bus there_.

Connect the words

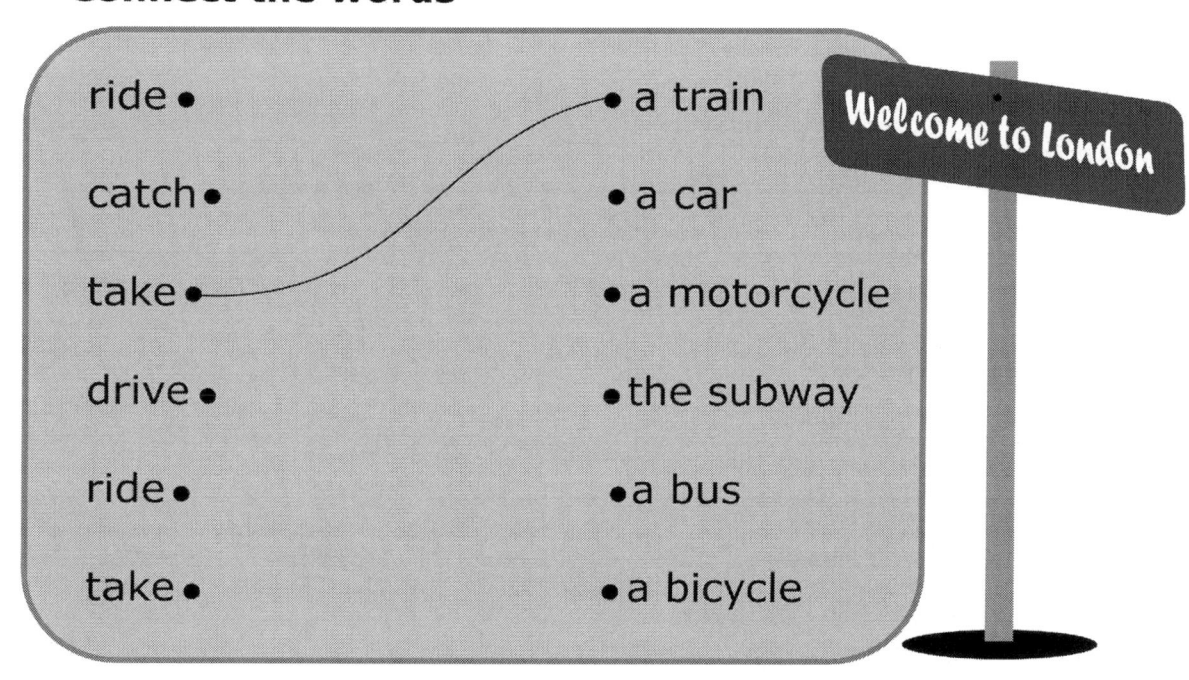

ride •   • a train

catch •   • a car

take •   • a motorcycle

drive •   • the subway

ride •   • a bus

take •   • a bicycle

Welcome to London

Lesson 28: Clothes

衣服

> Whose jacket is that?
> It's mine.

Section A | Words

1. **T-shirt**
   T恤衫
2. **blouse**
   女衬衫
3. **scarf**
   围巾
4. **coat**
   外套
5. **dress**
   洋装
6. **hat**
   帽子
7. **sweater**
   毛衣
8. **jacket**
   夹克
9. **skirt**
   裙子
10. **necktie**
    领带

Section B | Make a sentence

Whose T-shirt is this?

It's mine.

Whose hat is that?

It's yours.

Learn: mine, yours, his, hers, theirs, ours

Section C | Make a question

Is this your sweater?
Yes, it is. / No, it isn't.

Is this her blouse?
Yes, it is. / No, it isn't.

Section D | Learn a verb

wear – wearing – wore – worn 穿

You should **wear** a jacket today.

I don't like **wearing** a necktie.

She **wore** a skirt to school yesterday.

My sister hasn't **worn** a dress for a long time.

Section E | Learn an idiom

Wear <u>somebody</u> out

Meaning: To make someone tired.

"My boss completely *wore* me *out* today."

| Section F | Write |

Trace and fill in the words

1. Whose hat is this?

It's mine.

2. Whose blouse _____ that?

It's hers.

3. Whose sweater _____ this?

_____ his.

4. _____ scarf _____ that?

_____ ours.

5. Is this your jacket?

No, _____ isn't.

6. Is this your coat?

_____, it is.

7. _____ this his jacket?

No, _____ _____.

8. _____ that her _____?

Yes, _____ _____.

Section G — Let's have fun

Clothes!

- skirt
- T-shirt
- necktie
- jacket

Write the answer

1. Whose skirt is this? _____.

2. Whose T-shirt is that? _____.

3. Whose necktie is this? _____.

4. Whose jacket is that? _____.

Complete the words

j__ck__t

bl__u__e

__o__t

sk__r__

d__e__s

swe__t__r

n__c__t__e

Is or Are?

1. _____ this your sweater?

Yes, it _____.

2. _____ that her T-shirt?

No, it _____ not.

3. _____ these his shoes?

Yes, they _____.

4. _____ those their jackets?

No, they _____ not.

Test 7 Lesson 25 - 28

Write the answer next to the letter "A"

A: ___ 1. What ___ he cleaning? He was ___ the blender.

a. is, clean　　b. can, cleans　　c. was, cleaning　　d. is, cleaned

A: ___ 2. ___ they cleaning the cupboard? Yes, ___ were.

a. Are, we　　b. Can, there　　c. Were, they　　d. Do, they

A: ___ 3. They ___ the stove yesterday morning.

a. clean　　b. cleaned　　c. cleans　　d. is cleaning

A: ___ 4. "It's difficult because there are too many ___ in the kitchen."

a. cooks　　b. cook　　c. cooking　　d. cooked

A: ___ 5. She was ___ a hammer to fix the fence.

a. use　　b. using　　c. uses　　d. used

A: ___ 6. Was he ___ the axe to fix the tree? No, he ___.

a. using, wasn't　　b. use, can't　　c. uses, doesn't　　d. used, isn't

A: ___ 7. He ___ the pliers every Thursday.

a. use　　b. using　　c. uses　　d. was use

A: ___ 8. "These important things are all my ___ of the trade."

a. work　　b. stuff　　c. jobs　　d. tools

136

A: ___ **9.** How will he be ___ to New York?

a. go　　　　b. goes　　　　c. went　　　　d. going

A: ___ **10.** ___ you be ___ a taxi to Sydney? Yes, I will be.

a. Can, take　　b. Are, riding　　c. Will, taking　　d. Do, takes

A: ___ **11.** They ___ a ferry to Hong Kong last night.

a. took　　　b. taken　　　c. taking　　　d. takes

A: ___ **12.** "I wasn't thinking clearly, I lost my ___ of thought."

a. taxi　　　b. mind　　　c. train　　　d. take

A: ___ **13.** ___ blouse is this? It's ___.

a. Who, my　　b. Whose, mine　　c. Wear, on　　d. Who is, my

A: ___ **14.** Is that ___ jacket? Yes, ___ is.

a. she, it　　b. her, it　　c. him, this　　d. his, they

A: ___ **15.** She was ___ a skirt at school yesterday.

a. wear　　　b. wore　　　c. wears　　　d. wearing

A: ___ **16.** "Doing my homework was tiring. It wore me ___.

a. over　　　b. on　　　c. in　　　d. out

Answers on page 462

Lesson 29: More clothes

更多衣服

Section A Words

1. **pants**
   裤子
2. **shorts**
   短裤
3. **shoes**
   鞋子
4. **dresses**
   洋装
5. **shirts**
   衬衫
6. **jeans**
   牛仔裤
7. **socks**
   袜子
8. **gloves**
   手套
9. **pajamas**
   睡衣
10. **boots**
    靴子

Section B Make a sentence

Whose <u>pants</u> are these?

They're <u>mine</u>.

Whose <u>jeans</u> are those?

They're <u>hers</u>.

Note: They're = They are

| Section C | Make a question |

Are these <u>shoes</u> <u>yours</u>?
Yes, they are. / No, they aren't.

Are those <u>socks</u> <u>his</u>?
Yes, they are. / No, they aren't.

| Section D | Learn a verb |

lend – lending – lent – lent 借出

I will **lend** my shirt to you.

He is **lending** me his gloves.

My mother **lent** her eraser to me.

I have **lent** my shovel to him before.

| Section E | Learn an idiom |

Fits like a glove

Meaning: Something is the right size.

"The new shirt you bought me *fits like a glove*."

Section F — Write

Trace and fill in the words

1. Whose jeans are these?

They're mine.

2. Whose shorts _____ those?

_____ hers.

3. Whose socks are _____?

_____ his.

4. _____ shoes _____ those?

_____ hers.

5. Are these gloves yours?

No, they aren't.

6. _____ _____ dresses hers?

_____, they _____.

7. _____ _____ bags his?

Yes, _____ _____.

8. _____ those _____ mine?

No, _____ _____.

Section G — Let's have fun

More clothes!

Write the answer

1. Whose dresses are those? _____.
2. Whose pants are these? _____.
3. Whose skirts are those? _____.
4. Whose shoes are these? _____.

Connect the words

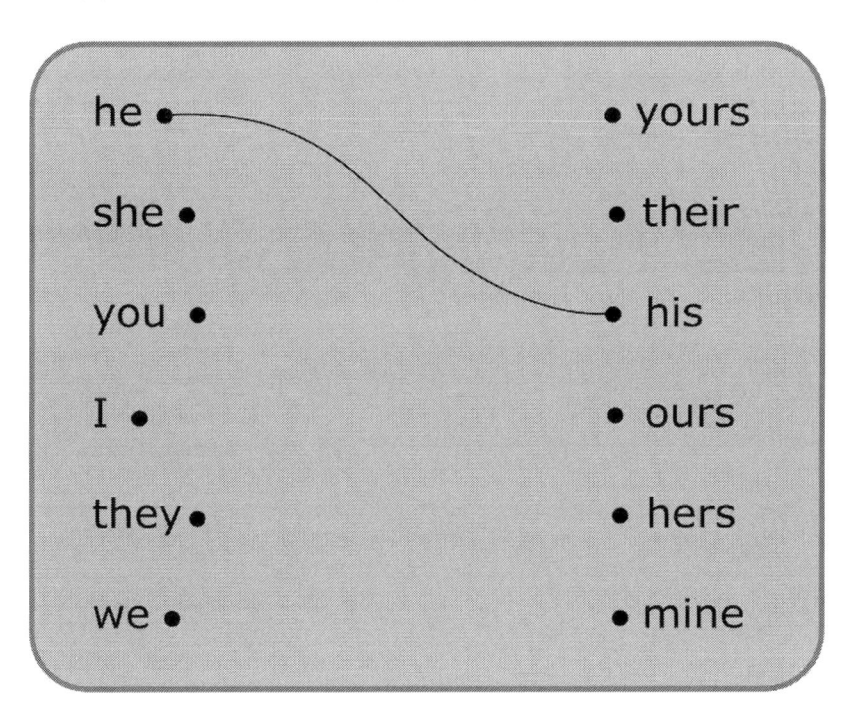

he • — • yours
she • — • their
you • — • his
I • — • ours
they • — • hers
we • — • mine

Complete the words

p___nts

sh___rt___

s___o___s

sk___rt

dre___s___s

g___ov___s

bo___ts

Lesson 30: In the living room

在客厅

Where is the coffee table?
It's in front of the sofa.

| Section A | Words |

1. **bookcase**
   书柜
2. **television**
   电视
3. **clock**
   时钟
4. **coffee table**
   茶几
5. **armchair**
   扶手椅
6. **painting**
   画
7. **TV stand**
   电视柜
8. **rug**
   地毯
9. **sofa**
   沙发
10. **vase**
    花瓶

| Section B | Make a sentence |

Where is the <u>bookcase</u>?

It's <u>next to</u> the <u>sofa</u>.

Where are the <u>books</u>?

They're <u>under</u> the <u>vase</u>.

Learn: in front of, behind, next to, on, under

Section C — Make a question

Is there a <u>vase</u> on the <u>coffee table</u>?
Yes, there is. / No, there isn't.

Are there <u>pens</u> behind the <u>TV stand</u>?
Yes, there are. / No, there aren't.

Section D — Learn a verb

move – moving – moved – moved 移动

After dinner, I will **move** the coffee table.
They are **moving** the armchair next to the sofa.
Dad **moved** the television to the bedroom last night.
We still haven't **moved** the bookcase to the living room.

Section E — Learn an idiom

A race against the clock

Meaning: To not have too much time left to complete a task.

"It's *a race against the clock* to finish this project."

| Section F | Write |

Trace and fill in the words

1. Where is the television?

It's in front of the sofa.

2. Where _____ the paintings?

They're next _____ the armchair.

3. _____ is the _____?

_____ behind the _____.

4. _____ _____ the vases?

_____ in front of the _____.

5. Is there a cup on the bookcase?

No, there isn't.

6. Are _____ pencils on the coffee table?

No, there aren't.

7. _____ _____ a notebook on the _____?

Yes, _____ _____.

8. _____ _____ books _____ the rug?

Yes, _____ _____.

Section G   Let's have fun

In the living room!

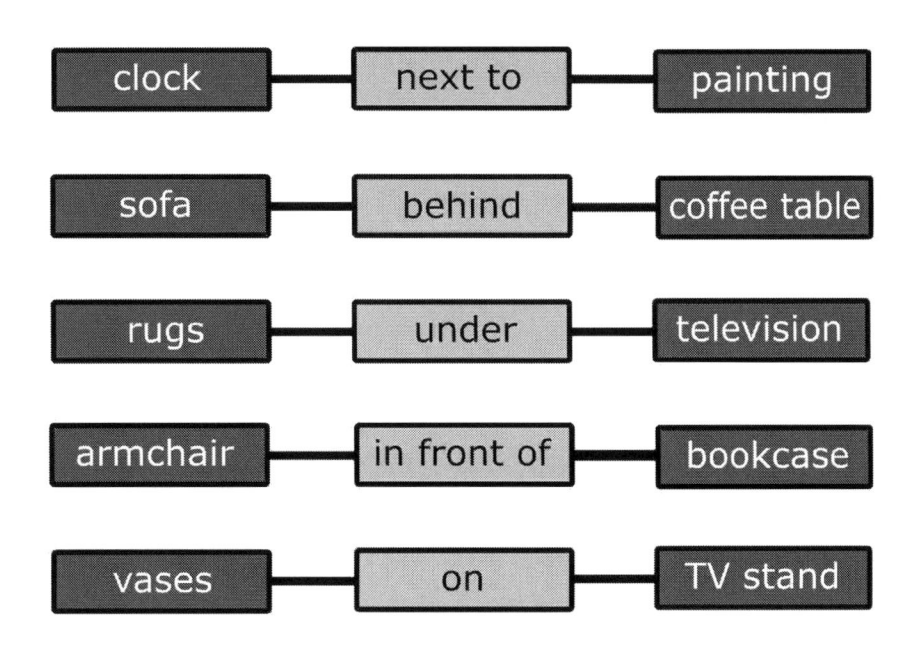

clock	next to	painting
sofa	behind	coffee table
rugs	under	television
armchair	in front of	bookcase
vases	on	TV stand

Answer the questions

1. Where is the clock?
_____.

2. Where is the sofa?
_____.

3. Where are the rugs?
_____.

4. Where is the armchair?
_____.

5. Where are the vases?
_____.

Choose the correct answer

1. Is there a clock next to the painting?

   ✓ Yes, there is.   ◯ No, there isn't.

2. Is there a sofa behind the coffee table?

   ◯ Yes, there is.   ◯ No, there isn't.

3. Are there rugs under the bookcase?

   ◯ Yes, there are.   ◯ No, there aren't.

4. Is there an armchair in front of the sofa?

   ◯ Yes, there is.   ◯ No, there isn't.

5. Are there vases on the TV stand?

   ◯ Yes, there are.   ◯ No, there aren't.

Lesson 31: In the bathroom

在浴室

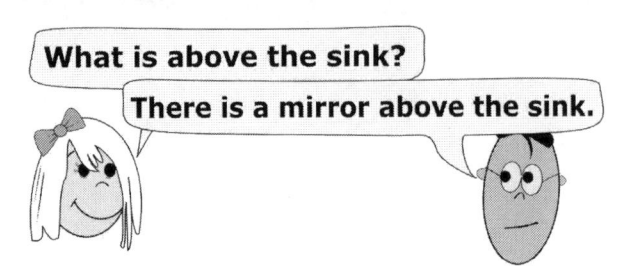

What is above the sink?
There is a mirror above the sink.

Section A Words

1. mirror
   镜子
2. bath towel
   浴巾
3. shower
   淋浴
4. toilet paper
   卫生纸
5. bath mat
   脚踏垫
6. shelf
   架子
7. sink
   洗脸台
8. toilet
   马桶
9. bathtub
   浴缸
10. soap
    香皂

Section B Make a sentence

What is <u>beside</u> the <u>bathtub</u>?

There is a <u>bath mat</u> beside the bathtub.

There isn't any <u>toilet paper</u> in the bathroom.

What are <u>on</u> the <u>shelf</u>?

There are some <u>towels</u> on the shelf.

There aren't any <u>bath towels</u> in the bathroom.

Section C — Make a question

Is there a <u>shelf</u> <u>below</u> the <u>mirror</u>?
Yes, there is. / No, there isn't.

Is there <u>toilet paper</u> <u>beside</u> the <u>toilet</u>?
Yes, there is. / No, there isn't.

Section D — Learn a verb

wash – washing – washed – washed 洗

She **washes** the sink every day.
He was **washing** his hands with the new soap.
Kevin **washed** the bath towel this morning.
I won't have **washed** the bath mat by tomorrow.

Section E — Learn an idiom

Throw in the towel

Meaning: To give up or quit.

"After trying three times, he decided to *throw in the towel*."

| Section F | Write |

Trace and fill in the words

1. What is below the mirror?

There is a sink below the mirror.

2. What _____ beside the bath mat?

There is a bathtub _____ the bath mat.

3. _____ is _____ the toilet?

There _____ a shelf beside the _____.

4. What _____ above _____ faucet?

_____ is a shelf _____ the _____.

5. Is there a showerhead above the faucet?

No, _____ isn't.

6. Is there a mirror above _____ toilet?

Yes, there is.

7. Is _____ a bath towel next to the _____?

_____, _____ isn't.

8. _____ _____ a sink beside the _____?

_____, _____ is.

Section G   Let's have fun

In the bathroom!

There is a mirror above the sink.
There are some bath towels on the shelf.
There aren't any towels in the bathroom.
There is a toilet beside the bathtub.
There isn't any soap in the bathroom.
There is a bath mat under the sink.

Read the information above. Choose the correct answer

1. Is there a mirror above the sink?   ☑Yes, there is   ◯No, there isn't

2. Are there bath towels on the shelf?   ◯Yes, there are ◯No, there aren't

3. Are there any towels in the bathroom?   ◯Yes, there are ◯No, there aren't

4. Is there a toilet beside the bathtub?   ◯Yes, there is   ◯No, there isn't

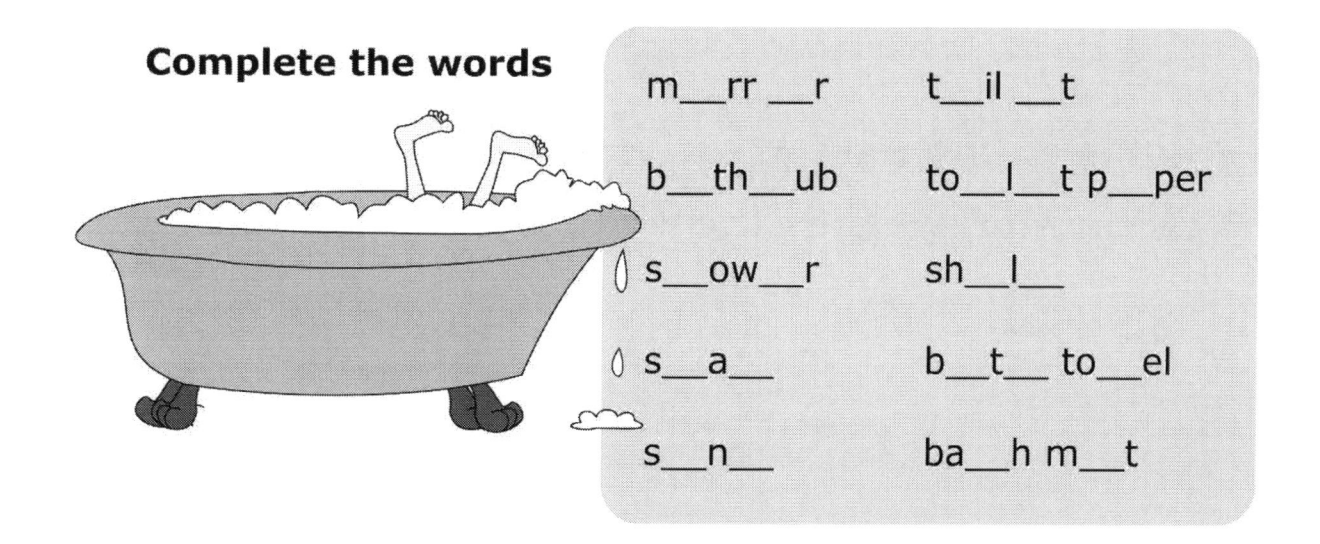

5. Is there any soap in the bathroom?   ◯Yes, there is   ◯No, there isn't

6. Is there a bath mat under the sink?   ◯Yes, there is   ◯No, there isn't

Complete the words

m__rr __r   t__il __t

b__th__ub   to__l__t p__per

s__ow__r   sh__l__

s__a__   b__t__ to__el

s__n__   ba__h m__t

Lesson 32: In the bedroom

在卧室

> What is on the left of the bed?
> There is a lamp on the left of the bed.

Section A — Words

1. **bed**
   床
2. **pillow**
   枕头
3. **mattress**
   床垫
4. **blanket**
   毯子
5. **drawers**
   五斗柜
6. **lamp**
   台灯
7. **alarm clock**
   闹钟
8. **wardrobe**
   衣橱
9. **bed sheets**
   床单
10. **nightstand**
    床头柜

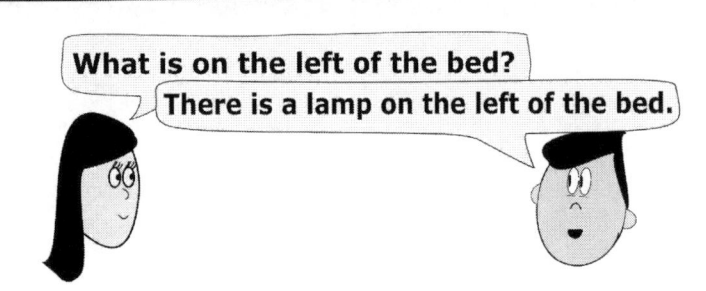

Section B — Make a sentence

What is <u>on the left of</u> the <u>bed</u>?

There is a <u>lamp</u> on the left of the bed.

What is <u>on the right of</u> the <u>wardrobe</u>?

There are <u>drawers</u> on the right of the wardrobe.

Learn: on the left of, on the right of

Section C | Make a question

Is there a <u>nightstand</u> <u>on the left of</u> the <u>bed</u>?
Yes, there is. / No, there isn't.

Are there <u>pillows</u> <u>on the left of</u> the <u>blanket</u>?
Yes, there are. / No, there aren't.

Section D | Learn a verb

change – changing – changed – changed 改变

My brother needs to **change** his bed sheets soon.
We will be **changing** our mattress for a harder one.
I **changed** my pillow last night and slept much better.
I haven't **changed** the light bulb in this lamp for two years.

Section E | Learn an idiom

Get up on the wrong side of the bed

Meaning: To describe somebody who is in a bad mood.

"Mom's in a really bad mood. I think she *got up on the wrong side of the bed*."

Section F   Write

Trace and fill in the words

1. What is on the right of the bed?

There is a pillow on the right of the bed.

2. What is on the _____ of the nightstand?

_____ is a book on the left of the _____.

3. _____ is on the right of the _____?

_____ is a chair on the _____ of the wardrobe.

4. _____ _____ on the left of the bed?

There _____ a pillow on the left of the _____.

5. Is _____ a nightstand on the right of the bed?

No, there isn't.

6. _____ there blankets on the left of the mattress?

Yes, _____ are.

7. _____ there a _____ on the right of the drawers?

No, _____ _____.

8. Are there _____ on the left of the _____?

Yes, _____ _____.

Section G | Let's have fun

In the bedroom!

Write the answers

| alarm clock | bed | drawers |

1. What is on the left of the bed?

_____.

2. Are the drawers on the right of the bed?

_____.

| blanket | mattress | pillow |

1. What is on the right of the mattress?

_____.

2. Is the pillow on the left of the mattress?

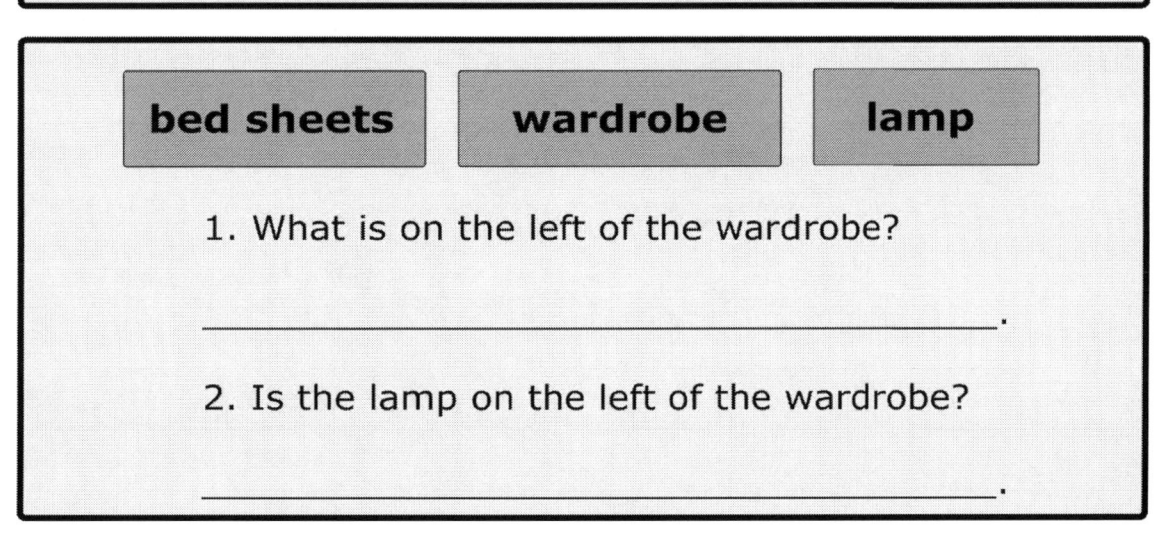

_____.

| bed sheets | wardrobe | lamp |

1. What is on the left of the wardrobe?

_____.

2. Is the lamp on the left of the wardrobe?

_____.

Test 8   Lesson 29 - 32

Write the answer next to the letter "A"

A: ___ 1. ___ jeans are those? Those jeans are ___.

a. Whose, hers   b. Who, her   c. Wear, on   d. Whose, her

A: ___ 2. ___ those gloves his? Yes, ___ are.

a. Are, there   b. Are, they   c. Were, them   d. Do, they

A: ___ 3. Can you ___ me your boots?

a. lent   b. lending   c. lend   d. has lent

A: ___ 4. "The new shirt fits perfectly. It fits like a ___."

a. hat   b. sock   c. boot   d. glove

A: ___ 5. Where ___ the books? ___ under the vase.

a. is, They   b. do, It's   c. are, They're   d. put, It's

A: ___ 6. Is ___ a vase on the coffee table? No, there ___.

a. it, wasn't   b. there, isn't   c. there, doesn't   d. he, isn't

A: ___ 7. He hasn't ___ that new television yet.

a. move   b. moving   c. moves   d. moved

A: ___ 8. "We don't have much time. We have to race against the ___."

a. clock   b. watch   c. car   d. team

A: ___ **9.** There ___ a bathmat ___ the bathtub.

a. are, above   b. have, on   c. be, in   d. is, beside

A: ___ **10.** Are ___ towels beside the mirror? No, there ___.

a. them, can't   b. there, aren't   c. have, hasn't   d. it, isn't

A: ___ **11.** He ___ the sink every Saturday afternoon.

a. wash   b. washing   c. washes   d. is wash

A: ___ **12.** "After failing many times, I decided to throw in the ___."

a. towel   b. quit   c. anger   d. ball

A: ___ **13.** There ___ drawers on the ___ of the wardrobe.

a. have, top   b. is, side   c. can, right   d. are, left

A: ___ **14.** Is ___ a lamp on the left of the bed? Yes, there ___.

a. it, have   b. there, is   c. they're, are   d. his, can

A: ___ **15.** We will ___ the blankets tomorrow.

a. changes   b. changing   c. change   d. changed

A: ___ **16.** "He's grumpy. I think he got up on the wrong side of the ___."

a. bed   b. lamp   c. happy   d. clock

Answers on page 462

Lesson 33: Around the house

在房子周围

Section A — Words

1. **work in the garage**
   在车库工作
2. **fix the mailbox**
   修理信箱
3. **fix the gate**
   修理大门
4. **work in the garden**
   在花园工作
5. **clean the pool**
   清理游泳池
6. **work in the yard**
   在后院工作
7. **fix the fence**
   修理篱笆
8. **clean the balcony**
   清理阳台
9. **clean the outdoor furniture**
   清理户外家具
10. **clean the barbecue**
    清理烤肉架

Section B — Make a sentence

What will he be doing <u>this weekend</u>?

He will be <u>working in the garage</u>.

What won't she be doing <u>this weekend</u>?

She won't be <u>fixing the mailbox</u>.

Note: won't be = will not be, he'll = he will, she'll = she will

Section C — Make a question

Will he be working in the garage tomorrow?
Yes, he will be. / No, he won't be.

Will you be having a barbecue tomorrow?
Yes, I will be. / No, I won't be.

Section D — Learn a verb

fix – fixing – fixed – fixed 修理

He **fixes** the fence every year.

My father is **fixing** the gate right now.

My uncle **fixed** our mailbox after the big storm last week.

I still haven't **fixed** the grammar mistakes in my report.

Section E — Learn an idiom

On the house

Meaning: To get something for free.

"The waiter apologized and gave him the meal *on the house*."

Section F | Write

Trace and fill in the words

1. What will she be doing this weekend?

She will be working in the yard.

2. What will _____ be _____ this weekend?

He _____ be fixing the fence.

3. What _____ they be doing this _____?

_____ will be cleaning the balcony.

4. _____ will _____ be doing this _____?

He _____ _____ fixing the gate.

5. Will he be working in the garden tomorrow?

No, he won't _____.

6. Will we _____ cleaning the pool tomorrow?

Yes, _____ will _____.

7. _____ you be working in the garden _____?

Yes, _____ _____ _____.

8. Will they _____ having a barbecue _____?

No, _____ _____ _____.

Section G | Let's have fun

Around the house!

doing	weekend	this	
be	will	the	working

Write the words

What _____ she be doing this weekend?

She will _____ cleaning the balcony.

What will they be _____ this _____?

They will be fixing _____ fence.

What will you be doing _____ weekend?

I will be _____ in the yard.

don't, doesn't, didn't, won't, isn't, aren't, wasn't, weren't?

do not = __don't__

did not = _____

will not = _____

is not = _____

were not = _____

are not = _____

does not = _____

was not = _____

Lesson 34: Hobbies

嗜好

What do you enjoy doing on the weekend?
I enjoy going hiking.

Section A — Words

1. **do gardening**
   做园艺
2. **go hiking**
   爬山
3. **take photographs**
   拍照
4. **play video games**
   玩电动
5. **listen to music**
   听音乐
6. **go camping**
   去露营
7. **play chess**
   下棋
8. **watch movies**
   看电影
9. **go fishing**
   去钓鱼
10. **sing karaoke**
    唱卡拉 OK

Section B — Make a sentence

What <u>do</u> you enjoy doing on the weekend?

I <u>enjoy</u> <u>doing gardening</u> on the weekend.

What <u>does</u> he enjoy doing on the weekend?

He <u>enjoys</u> <u>going camping</u> on the weekend.

Section C — Make a question

Do you enjoy <u>going hiking</u> on the weekend?
Yes, I do. / No, I enjoy <u>playing chess</u>.

Does he enjoy <u>watching movies</u> on the weekend?
Yes, he does. / No, he enjoys <u>going fishing</u>.

Section D — Learn a verb

enjoy – enjoying – enjoyed – enjoyed 享受

He **enjoys** doing the gardening in spring.

My aunt is **enjoying** the book you lent her.

I really **enjoyed** the movie we watched last night.

You would have **enjoyed** the video game we played today.

Section E — Learn an idiom

Face the music

Meaning: To face the consequences of one's actions.

"You need to own up to your mistake and *face the music*."

| Section F | Write |

Trace and fill in the words

1. What do you enjoy doing on the weekend?

I enjoy going camping on the weekend.

2. What does _____ enjoy doing on the _____?

She _____ going hiking on the weekend.

3. _____ do they enjoy _____ on the weekend?

_____ enjoy singing karaoke on the _____.

4. What _____ he enjoy _____ on the _____?

_____ _____ playing chess on the _____.

5. Do you enjoy playing video games on the weekend?

No, I enjoy listening to music.

6. _____ he enjoy taking photographs on the weekend?

_____, _____ does.

7. _____ they _____ going hiking on the _____?

No, _____ enjoy _____ _____.

8. _____ she enjoy _____ chess on the _____?

Yes, _____ _____.

Section G — Let's have fun

Hobbies!

Connect the words

listen • • hiking

take • • movies

go • • chess

play • • karaoke

watch • • photographs

sing • • to music

Enjoy or Enjoys?

1. He _____ listening to music on the weekend.

2. They _____ watching movies on the weekend.

3. We _____ going hiking on the weekend.

4. My brother _____ playing chess on the weekend.

5. She _____ taking photographs on the weekend.

6. I _____ playing video games on the weekend.

Answer the questions

1. What do you enjoy doing on the weekend?
   _____.

2. What does your friend enjoy doing on the weekend?
   _____.

Lesson 35: Countries

国家

Which countries have you been to?
I have been to Brazil and Mexico.

Section A — Words

1. **Japan**
   日本
2. **Canada**
   加拿大
3. **Brazil**
   巴西
4. **Australia**
   澳洲
5. **South Africa**
   南非
6. **China**
   中国
7. **Mexico**
   墨西哥
8. **Argentina**
   阿根廷
9. **New Zealand**
   纽西兰
10. **Kenya**
    肯亚

Section B — Make a sentence

Which countries have you been to?

I have been to <u>Japan</u> and <u>China</u>.

Which countries has she been to?

She has been to <u>Canada</u> and <u>Mexico</u>.

Note: haven't = have not / hasn't = has not

Section C — Make a question

Have you been to <u>Brazil</u>?
Yes, I have. / No, I haven't.

Has he been to <u>Argentina</u>?
Yes, he has. / No, he hasn't.

Section D — Learn a verb

write – writing – wrote – written 写

I always **write** homework on the weekend.

She is **writing** a new book about South Africa.

My father **wrote** a letter to his friend in Japan last week.

He has already **written** four emails to the factory in China.

Section E — Learn an idiom

Second to none

Meaning: To describe something that is the best.

"The mountains in Canada are *second to none* for skiing."

Section F — Write

Trace and fill in the words

1. Which countries have you been to?

I have been to Canada and Mexico.

2. Which _____ has he been to?

He has _____ to Brazil and Argentina.

3. _____ countries _____ we been to?

We _____ been to _____ and _____.

4. Which _____ has she _____ _____?

_____ _____ been to _____ and _____.

5. Have you been to New Zealand?

Yes, I have.

6. Has _____ been _____ Australia?

_____, she hasn't.

7. _____ they _____ to China?

Yes, _____ _____.

8. _____ he _____ _____ Kenya?

No, _____ _____.

Section G — Let's have fun

Countries!

Write the missing words

| hasn't | they | has | been |
| to | countries | Which | haven't |

1. Which _____ have you been to?

I have _____ to Japan and China.

2. _____ countries has he been to?

He _____ been to Mexico and Canada.

3. Has she been _____ South Africa?

No, she _____.

4. Have _____ been to New Zealand?

No, they _____.

Has or Have?

1. _____ she been to Canada?

Yes, she _____.

2. _____ they been to Mexico?

No, they _____ not.

3. Which countries _____ you been to?

I _____ been to Argentina and Brazil.

4. Which countries _____ he been to?

He _____ been to Kenya and China.

Lesson 36: Landscapes

自然景观

> What had you prepared for yesterday's English class?
> I had prepared a video about lakes.

Section A | Words

1. **river**
   河
2. **beach (es)**
   海滩
3. **mountain**
   山
4. **volcano (es)**
   火山
5. **forest**
   森林
6. **lake**
   湖
7. **waterfall**
   瀑布
8. **island**
   岛
9. **ocean**
   海洋
10. **jungle**
    丛林

Section B | Make a sentence

What had you prepared for yesterday's <u>geography</u> class?
I had prepared a <u>poster</u> about <u>river</u>s.

What had they prepared for yesterday's <u>Chinese</u> class?
They had prepared an <u>article</u> about <u>lake</u>s.

Learn: poster, speech, video, article, presentation

Note: hadn't = had not

Section C — Make a question

Had you prepared anything for yesterday's <u>English</u> class?
Yes, I had prepared a <u>speech</u>. / No, I hadn't.

Had you prepared anything for yesterday's <u>science</u> class?
Yes, I had prepared a <u>video</u>. / No, I hadn't.

Section D — Learn a verb

prepare – preparing – prepared – prepared 准备

I'll **prepare** some food for you to take to the mountains.
She'll be **preparing** some drinks for the picnic at the lake.
The teacher always **prepared** a quiz for the students before.
I wish I had **prepared** more for the geography test.

Section E — Learn an idiom

A drop in the ocean

Meaning: To only make a tiny impact.

"We donated money to the victims of the tsunami, but I'm afraid it is just *a drop in the ocean*."

Section F — Write

Trace and fill in the words

1. What had you prepared for yesterday's geography class?

I had prepared an article about beaches.

2. What had he _____ for yesterday's _____ class?

He _____ prepared a speech _____ waterfalls.

3. What had they _____ for _____ _____ class?

They _____ _____ a video about mountains.

4. What had you _____ for _____ geography class?

_____ _____ _____ a poster about islands.

5. Had he prepared anything for yesterday's math class?

No, he hadn't.

6. Had you prepared _____ for yesterday's art class?

Yes, I _____ _____ a poster.

7. Had she _____ anything for _____ science class?

No, _____ _____.

8. Had he prepared anything for yesterday's English class?

Yes, _____ had _____ a _____.

Section G   Let's have fun

Landscapes!

Unscramble the words and write

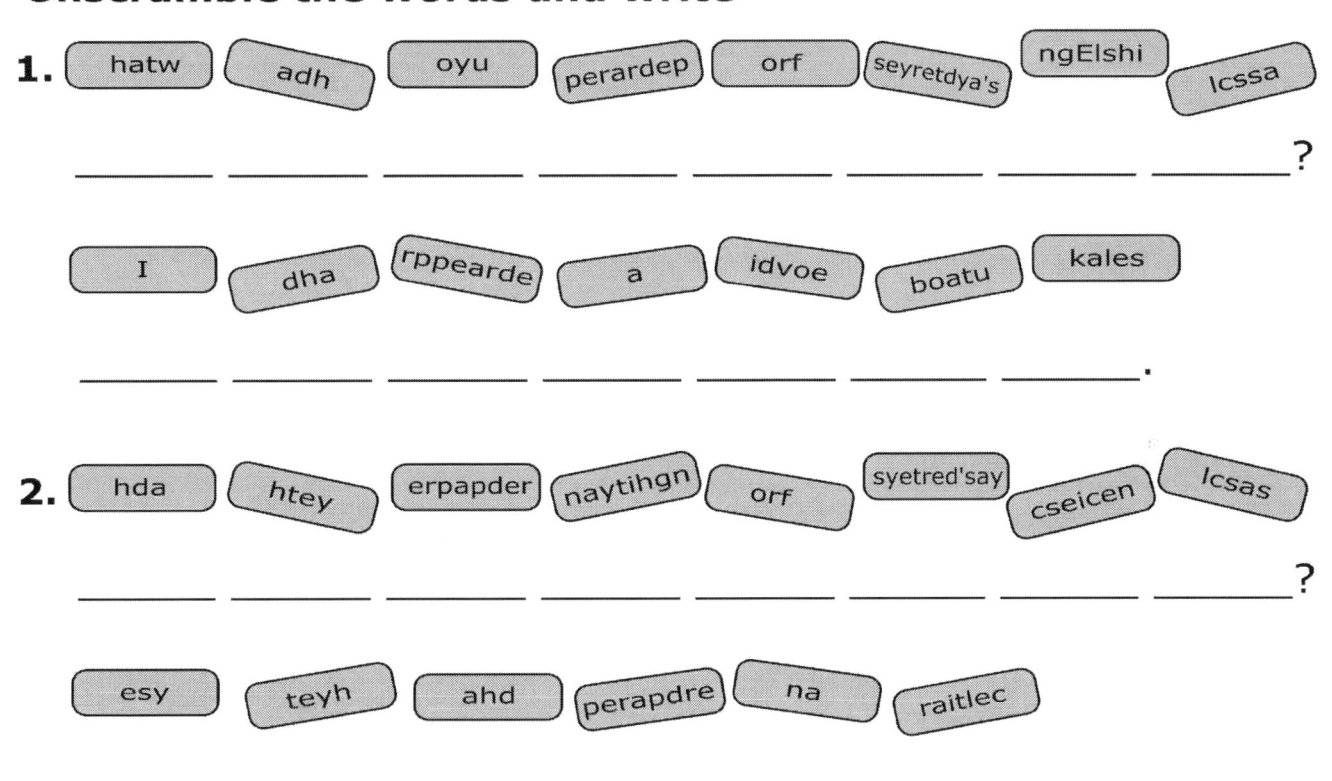

1. hatw | adh | oyu | perardep | orf | seyretdya's | ngElshi | lcssa

    ___ ___ ___ ___ ___ ___ ___ ___?

    I | dha | rppearde | a | idvoe | boatu | kales

    ___ ___ ___ ___ ___ ___ ___.

2. hda | htey | erpapder | naytihgn | orf | syetred'say | cseicen | lcsas

    ___ ___ ___ ___ ___ ___ ___ ___?

    esy | teyh | ahd | perapdre | na | raitlec

    ___ / ___ ___ ___ ___ ___.

Complete the words

r__v__r   j__ng__e

v__l__a__o   i__la__d

m__un__a__n   f__r__ __t

be__c__   w__te__f__l__

o__e__n   l__k__

Test 9 — Lesson 33 - 36

Write the answer next to the letter "A"

A: ___ 1. ___ weekend, he will be ___ the mailbox.

a. On, clean   b. This, fixing   c. That, work   d. In, cleaning

A: ___ 2. ___ she be fixing the gate tonight? Yes, she ___.

a. Can, is   b. Won't, fix   c. Will, will   d. Will, fix

A: ___ 3. My mother ___ the barbecue last year.

a. fix   b. is fixing   c. fixed   d. will fixing

A: ___ 4. "This one's free. It's on the ___."

a. house   b. yard   c. gate   d. garage

A: ___ 5. He ___ fishing on the weekend.

a. enjoy going   b. is enjoy go   c. enjoys go   d. enjoys going

A: ___ 6. ___ he enjoy watching movies? No, he ___ playing chess.

a. Do, does   b. Is, isn't   c. Does, doesn't   d. Does, enjoys

A: ___ 7. She is ___ her new barbecue.

a. enjoying   b. enjoy   c. enjoys   d. enjoyed

A: ___ 8. "You should admit your mistake and face the ___."

a. sunshine   b. music   c. trouble   d. smile

A: ___ **9.** Which countries ___ you ___ to?

a. have, go   b. did, went   c. do, be   d. have, been

A: ___ **10.** ___ she been to Japan? No, she ___.

a. Has, hasn't   b. Have, don't   c. Is, hasn't   d. Is, can't

A: ___ **11.** He has ___ nine messages this week.

a. write   b. wrote   c. written   d. writes

A: ___ **12.** "Her English is the best. It's second to ___."

a. all   b. none   c. best   d. win

A: ___ **13.** They had ___ a speech for last week's geography class.

a. prepare   b. prepared   c. preparing   d. prepares

A: ___ **14.** ___ he prepared anything for English class? No, he ___.

a. Had, hadn't   b. Is, isn't   c. Does, don't   d. Has, haven't

A: ___ **15.** The teacher always ___ easy tests for his students.

a. prepare   b. preparing   c. prepares   d. are preparing

A: ___ **16.** "It had a very small effect. It was just a drop in the ___."

a. line   b. ball   c. water   d. ocean

Answers on page 462

Lesson 37: Everyday life

日常生活

> When will you have woken up by?
> I will have woken up by six o'clock.

Section A — Words

1. **woken up**
   醒来
2. **brushed my teeth**
   刷牙
3. **done homework**
   做家庭作业
4. **cooked dinner**
   做晚餐
5. **taken out the trash**
   丢垃圾
6. **eaten breakfast**
   吃早餐
7. **gone to school**
   去学校
8. **taken a shower**
   洗澡
9. **gone to sleep**
   睡觉
10. **gone shopping**
    去购物

Section B — Make a sentence

When will you have <u>woken up</u> by?
I will have woken up by <u>seven o'clock</u>.

When will he have <u>eaten breakfast</u> by?
He will have eaten breakfast by <u>half past eight</u>.

Learn: o'clock, half past, a quarter past, a quarter to

| Section C | Make a question |

Will you have <u>taken a shower</u> by <u>nine o'clock</u>?
Yes, I will have. / No, I won't have.

Will they have <u>done homework</u> by <u>a quarter to six</u>?
Yes, they will have. / No, they won't have.

| Section D | Learn a verb |

wake – waking – woke – woken 醒来

I **wake** up at seven o'clock every day.

The baby is **waking** up now.

You **woke** up late this morning.

I haven't **woken** up this early for years.

| Section E | Learn an idiom |

Hit the nail on the head

Meaning: To say something that is correct.

"I agree with what you said. You really *hit the nail on the head*."

Section F   Write

Trace and fill in the words

1. When will you have woken up by?

I will have woken up by a quarter past seven.

2. When will he have _____ his teeth by?

He _____ have brushed his teeth by half past nine.

3. When _____ you _____ gone to school _____?

I will _____ gone to _____ by ten _____.

4. When will _____ have _____ homework by?

She will _____ done _____ by _____ o'clock.

5. Will they have cooked dinner by six o'clock?

No, they won't _____.

6. Will _____ have gone to sleep by _____ past ten?

Yes, we _____ _____.

7. _____ she _____ gone shopping by nine o'clock?

No, _____ _____ have.

8. _____ you have brushed _____ teeth by one o'clock?

Yes, _____ _____ _____.

Section G — Let's have fun

Everyday life!

Unscramble the sentences

o'clock / gone / have / we / will / shopping / by / four

1. _____.

two / taken / have / they / will / a shower / by / half past

2. _____.

I / the trash / won't / one o'clock / have / by / taken out

3. _____.

o'clock / cooked dinner / have / he / won't / by / six

4. _____.

Connect the words

brushed • • out the trash

gone • • dinner

taken • • my teeth

done • • a shower

cooked • • homework

taken • • to sleep

Lesson 38: Languages

语言

How long have you been learning German?
I have been learning German for one year.

Section A — Words

1. **English**
   英语
2. **German**
   德文
3. **Portuguese**
   葡萄牙语
4. **Japanese**
   日文
5. **Vietnamese**
   越南语
6. **Spanish**
   西班牙语
7. **French**
   法文
8. **Chinese**
   中文
9. **Hindi**
   印度文
10. **Arabic**
    阿拉伯语

Section B — Make a sentence

How long have you been <u>learning</u> <u>English</u>?

I have been learning English for <u>three years</u>.

How long has he been <u>studying</u> <u>Spanish</u>?

He has been studying Spanish for <u>five months</u>.

Learn: learning, studying, speaking

Section C — Make a question

Have they been <u>studying</u> <u>French</u> for a long time?
Yes, they have been. / No, they haven't been.

Has she been <u>learning</u> <u>Japanese</u> for a long time?
Yes, she has been. / No, she hasn't been.

Section D — Learn a verb

speak – speaking – spoke – spoken 讲

He **speaks** three languages.

She is **speaking** to him in Japanese.

I **spoke** with my teacher about the German homework.

We haven't **spoken** to each other for over five years.

Section E — Learn an idiom

Speak the same language

Meaning: To share the same understanding and be in agreement.

"I agree with everything you are saying. I think we're *speaking the same language*."

| Section F | Write |

Trace and fill in the words

1. How long have you been _____ German?

I have been learning German for three years.

2. How _____ has _____ been studying French?

She has _____ studying _____ for six years.

3. How _____ have we _____ learning _____?

_____ have been _____ English for three years.

4. _____ long have _____ been _____ Hindi?

They _____ been learning _____ for one year.

5. _____ they been speaking Arabic for a long time?

Yes, they have _____.

6. Has he been _____ Japanese for a long time?

No, _____ hasn't _____.

7. Have _____ been _____ Arabic for a long time?

Yes, I _____ _____.

8. Has she _____ studying _____ for a long time?

No, _____ _____ _____.

Section G | Let's have fun

Languages!

Mexico   France   Scotland   Japan   Egypt

Write the Country, Question and Answer

[He] — [English] — [Three years] — [Scotland]

How long has he been learning English ?
He has been learning English for three years.

[They] — [Spanish] — [Ten years] — [ ]

_____?
_____.

[She] — [Arabic] — [Four years] — [ ]

_____?
_____.

[John] — [Japanese] — [One year] — [ ]

_____?
_____.

[Susan] — [French] — [Two years] — [ ]

_____?
_____.

How long have you been studying English?
_____.

Lesson 39: Pets

宠物

What is faster than a mouse?
A rabbit is faster than a mouse.

Section A — Words

1. dog
   狗
2. fish
   鱼
3. bird
   鸟
4. rabbit
   兔子
5. guinea pig
   天竺鼠
6. cat
   猫
7. turtle
   乌龟
8. mouse
   老鼠
9. hamster
   仓鼠
10. snake
    蛇

Section B — Make a sentence

What is <u>bigger</u> than a <u>mouse</u>?

A <u>dog</u> is <u>bigger</u> than a <u>mouse</u>.

What is <u>more expensive</u> than the <u>hamster</u>?

The <u>rabbit</u> is <u>more expensive</u> than the <u>hamster</u>.

Learn: faster, slower, bigger, smaller, more expensive, cheaper, more colorful, better, worse

Section C — Make a question

Is a <u>turtle</u> <u>slower</u> than a <u>rabbit</u>?
Yes, it is. / No, it's not. It's <u>faster</u>.

Is the <u>hamster</u> <u>more expensive</u> than the <u>snake</u>?
Yes, it is. / No, it's not. It's <u>cheaper</u>.

Section D — Learn a verb

feed – feeding – fed – fed 喂

You need to **feed** the dog every morning.

He is **feeding** the turtle some leaves.

I **fed** the mouse some cheese and it happily ate it.

My sister hasn't **fed** the pets today.

Section E — Learn an idiom

The teacher's pet

Meaning: A student whom the teacher favors.

"Her classmates are jealous of her because she is *the teacher's pet*."

Section F **Write**

Trace and fill in the words

1. What is bigger than a mouse?

   A rabbit is _____ than a mouse.

2. What is more _____ _____ the dog?

   The fish is _____ colorful than the _____.

3. _____ _____ slower than a _____?

   A turtle is _____ _____ a cat.

4. What is less _____ _____ the snake?

   _____ bird is _____ expensive than the _____.

5. Is the bird faster _____ the guinea pig?

   Yes, _____ _____.

6. Is the rabbit more _____ than the dog?

   No, _____ _____. It's cheaper.

7. _____ the turtle slower than the _____?

   _____, _____ is.

8. Is the cat slower _____ the hamster?

   No, it's _____. It's _____.

184

Section G | Let's have fun

Pets!

Write the animals

	Animal	Speed	Size
(rabbit)	_____	48 km/h	30 cm
(turtle)	_____	0.4 km/h	40 cm
(mouse)	_____	13 km/h	9 cm
(fish)	_____	5 km/h	15 cm

Answer the questions

1. What is bigger than a fish? _____.

2. What is faster than a mouse? _____.

3. Is the turtle faster than the fish? _____.

4. Is the mouse slower than the rabbit? _____.

5. What is bigger than a rabbit? _____.

6. What is smaller than a fish? _____.

7. Is the rabbit bigger than the turtle? _____.

8. Is the rabbit bigger than the fish? _____.

Lesson 40: Fast food

速食

What is the sweetest food?
The sweetest food is the pancake.

Section A — Words

1. **doughnut**
   甜甜圈
2. **cheeseburger**
   起司汉堡
3. **chicken nuggets**
   鸡块
4. **pancake**
   松饼
5. **taco**
   塔可
6. **french fries**
   薯条
7. **onion rings**
   洋葱圈
8. **hot dog**
   热狗
9. **fried chicken**
   炸鸡
10. **burrito**
    卷饼

Section B — Make a sentence

What is the <u>cheapest</u> food?

The <u>cheapest</u> food is the <u>doughnut</u>.

What is the <u>most expensive</u> food?

The <u>most expensive</u> food is the <u>burrito</u>.

Learn: most delicious, most expensive, cheapest, saltiest, sweetest, best, worst

| Section C | Make a question |

Is the <u>hot dog</u> the <u>most delicious</u>?
Yes, it is. / No, it's not.

Are the <u>French fries</u> the <u>cheapest</u>?
Yes, they are. / No, they aren't.

| Section D | Learn a verb |

try – trying – tried – tried 试试

He wants to **try** the cheeseburger at that restaurant.
I'm **trying** to decide whether to buy the taco or burrito.
My baby brother **tried** the pancake, but didn't like it.
We haven't **tried** the fried chicken here yet.

| Section E | Learn an idiom |

You are what you eat

Meaning: The food that you eat affects your health.

"Careful not to eat too much fast food. *You are what you eat.*"

Section F   Write

Trace and fill in the words

1. What is the cheapest food?

   The _____ food is the taco.

2. What is the best _____?

   The _____ food is the burrito.

3. _____ is the _____ delicious food?

   _____ most _____ food is the doughnut.

4. _____ _____ the worst food?

   _____ _____ food is _____ hot dog.

5. Is the most expensive food the cheeseburger?

   No, it _____. It's the cheapest.

6. _____ the saltiest food _____ french fries?

   Yes, _____ _____.

7. Is the most delicious _____ the fried chicken?

   Yes, _____ _____.

8. Is _____ worst _____ _____ pancake?

   No, it _____. It's _____ best.

Section G Let's have fun

Fast food!

Joe's Diner

doughnut	$2	french fries	$5
cheeseburger	$4	onion rings	$6
chicken nugget	$1	hot dog	$3
pancake	$6	fried chicken	$7
taco	$8	burrito	$9

Answer the questions

1. What is the most expensive food? _____.

2. What is the cheapest food? _____.

3. What is the saltiest food? _____.

4. What is the sweetest food? _____.

5. What is the most delicious food? _____.

6. Is the pancake the sweetest food? _____.

7. Is the taco the most delicious food? _____.

8. Are the french fries the saltiest food? _____.

Test 10 Lesson 37 - 40

Write the answer next to the letter "A"

A: ___ **1.** When ___ you have ___ to school by?

a. do, go   b. will, gone   c. can, went   d. will, go

A: ___ **2.** They will have ___ dinner by ___ six.

a. eat, o'clock   b. ate, past   c. eats, quarter   d. eaten, half past

A: ___ **3.** They haven't ___ with each other for two years.

a. spoken   b. spokes   c. speaking   d. speaks

A: ___ **4.** "You said it exactly right. You hit the ___ on the head."

a. hammer   b. work   c. nail   d. day

A: ___ **5.** How long ___ he ___ learning Arabic?

a. does, is   b. is, can   c. have, does   d. has, been

A: ___ **6.** No, ___ haven't been ___ Spanish for a long time.

a. I, learn   b. we, learned   c. they, learning   d. he, learns

A: ___ **7.** He ___ Chinese with the doctor last night.

a. spoke   b. is   c. was   d. speaks

A: ___ **8.** "I really agree with him. I think we ___ the same language."

a. speaks   b. speak   c. spoken   d. speaking

A: ___ **9.** What is ___ than a guinea pig?

a. cheaper   b. more cheap   c. more cheaper   d. cheapest

A: ___ **10.** Is the mouse ___ than the cat? No, it's ___.

a. slow, slower   b. big, smaller   c. slow, fast   d. slower, faster

A: ___ **11.** We haven't ___ the pets yet.

a. feed   b. fed   c. feeding   d. feeds

A: ___ **12.** "The teacher really loved him. He was the teacher's ___."

a. pets   b. petting   c. pet   d. best

A: ___ **13.** What is the ___ food on the menu?

a. more cheap   b. cheapest   c. most cheap   d. cheapen

A: ___ **14.** ___ the taco the ___ delicious?

a. Had, more   b. Is, more   c. Does, most   d. Is, most

A: ___ **15.** He usually ___ new food every weekend.

a. try   b. trying   c. tries   d. had try

A: ___ **16.** "You should eat healthier food. You ___ what you eat."

a. are   b. can   c. do   d. try

Answers on page 462

Lesson 41: At the cinema

在电影院

> What was the romance movie like?
> It was romantic.

Section A — Words

1. scary
   害怕的
2. exciting
   兴奋的
3. informative
   资讯充足的
4. romantic
   浪漫的
5. violent
   暴力的
6. boring
   无聊的
7. interesting
   有趣的
8. funny
   好笑的
9. enjoyable
   享受的
10. sad
    难过

Section B — Make a sentence

What was the <u>horror</u> movie like?

It was <u>scary</u>.

What was the <u>action</u> movie like?

It was <u>exciting</u>.

Learn: horror, comedy, action, romance, sci-fi, animation

Section C — Make a question

Was the <u>horror</u> movie as <u>exciting</u> as the <u>action</u> movie?
Yes, it was. / No, it wasn't.

Was the <u>sci-fi</u> movie as <u>funny</u> as the <u>comedy</u> movie?
Yes, it was. / No, it wasn't.

Section D — Learn a verb

teach – teaching – taught – taught 教

The movie **teaches** us about looking after the environment.
My father will be **teaching** me how to swim.
My history teacher **taught** us interesting things this year.
The teacher hasn't **taught** us anything informative yet.

Section E — Learn an idiom

A tough act to follow

Meaning: Someone who did so well that it would be hard to do better.

"He was so funny in this movie. It will be *a tough act to follow*."

| Section F | Write |

Trace and fill in the words

1. What was the comedy movie like?

It was really funny.

2. What _____ the romance movie _____?

_____ was romantic.

3. _____ _____ the sci-fi movie like?

_____ _____ really exciting.

4. What _____ _____ animation movie _____?

_____ _____ enjoyable.

5. Was the _____ movie as funny as the comedy movie?

No, it _____.

6. Was the action movie as _____ as the horror movie?

Yes, _____ _____.

7. _____ the animation movie as sad as the sci-fi movie?

_____, _____ wasn't.

8. Was the horror _____ as violent as the action movie?

_____, it _____.

Section G Let's have fun

At the cinema!

- What was the comedy movie like? — It was funny.
- What was the action movie like? — It was exciting.
- What was the sci-fi movie like? — It was interesting.
- What was the romance movie like? — It was boring.

True of False? Circle the answer

1. The comedy movie was funny.   True   False
2. The romance movie was informative.   True   False
3. The action movie was exciting.   True   False
4. The sci-fi movie was sad.   True   False

Complete the words

b__r__ng   i__fo__ma__i__e   e__jo__ab__e

i__t__r__s__in__   e__c__tin__   sc__r__

f__n__y   r__m__nt__c   v__o__en__

Lesson 42: Music

音乐

How does she play the violin?
She plays the violin gracefully.

Section A — Words

1. **beautifully**
   漂亮地
2. **quietly**
   安静地
3. **slowly**
   慢地
4. **gracefully**
   优雅地
5. **well**
   好地
6. **loudly**
   大声地
7. **quickly**
   快地
8. **terribly**
   可怕地
9. **correctly**
   正确地
10. **badly**
    不好地

Section B — Make a sentence

How does he <u>sing the song</u>?

He <u>sings the song</u> <u>beautifully</u>.

How do they <u>play the guitar</u>?

They <u>play the guitar</u> <u>loudly</u>.

Learn: sing the song, play the piano, play the violin, play the cello, play the drums, play the guitar

| Section C | Make a question |

Does she <u>play the violin</u> <u>gracefully</u>?
Yes, she does. / No, she doesn't.

Do you <u>play the drums</u> <u>well</u>?
Yes, I do. / No, I don't.

| Section D | Learn a verb |

notice – noticing – noticed – noticed 注意到

You will **notice** that my family speaks loudly.
I'm **noticing** more and more how well she speaks English.
I **noticed** you haven't done your homework correctly.
She hadn't **noticed** her friend looking at her.

| Section E | Learn an idiom |

Music to <u>one's</u> ears

Meaning: Something very pleasing to hear.

"It was *music to* my *ears* when I heard that the teacher cancelled the test!"

Section F Write

Trace and fill in the words

1. How does _____ play the piano?

She plays the _____ quickly.

2. _____ do we play the _____?

_____ play the violin terribly.

3. How _____ he play _____ cello?

He _____ the cello gracefully.

4. _____ _____ you play the drums?

_____ _____ the drums well.

5. Does he play the trumpet correctly?

Yes, _____ does.

6. _____ you sing the song beautifully?

No, _____ don't.

7. _____ she _____ the cello correctly?

Yes, _____ does.

8. _____ _____ play _____ guitar quietly?

No, they _____.

Section G — Let's have fun

Music!

Write the correct verb

1. **play/plays?** He _____ the piano beautifully.

2. **sing/sings?** She _____ the song quietly.

3. **play/plays?** They _____ the violin badly.

4. **play/plays?** We _____ the guitar well.

Write the sentences

1. plays the piano - quick

   She plays the piano quickly.

2. sings the song - beautiful

   _____.

3. plays the trumpet - loud

   _____.

4. plays the cello - bad

   _____.

Lesson 43: Feelings

感觉

How have you been feeling lately?
Lately, I've been feeling tired.

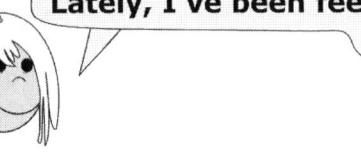

Section A Words

1. **sad**
   难过的
2. **tired**
   累的
3. **fine**
   好的
4. **bored**
   无聊的
5. **energetic**
   有活力的
6. **happy**
   快乐的
7. **sick**
   生病的
8. **angry**
   生气的
9. **excited**
   兴奋的
10. **frustrated**
    焦虑的

Section B Make a sentence

How have you been feeling lately?
Lately, I've been feeling <u>sad</u>.

How are you now?
I'm <u>happy</u>.

Note: I've = I have / she's = she has / he's = he has
they've = they have / we've = we have / you've = you have

Section C — Make a question

Have you been feeling <u>tired</u> lately?

Yes, I have. / No, I haven't.

Are you <u>angry</u>?

Yes, I am. / No, I'm not.

Section D — Learn a verb

think – thinking – thought – thought 想

I **think** she feels fine now. Thank you for your concern.

She's frustrated because she keeps **thinking** about work.

Peter **thought** about how excited his child was to see him.

I haven't **thought** about this before.

Section E — Learn an idiom

Mixed Feelings

Meaning: When you are not sure about how you feel about something.

"He had *mixed feelings* about moving to a new city."

Section F — Write

Trace and fill in the words

1. How have you been feeling lately?

Lately, I've been feeling tired.

2. How has she _____ feeling lately?

Lately, she's been _____ angry.

3. How _____ they been _____ lately?

Lately, they've _____ feeling bored.

4. How _____ he _____ feeling _____?

Lately, _____ been _____ _____.

5. Have you been feeling excited lately?

No, I haven't.

6. Has he been _____ energetic lately?

Yes, _____ _____.

7. Have _____ _____ feeling frustrated lately?

Yes, I _____.

8. _____ he been _____ sick _____?

No, _____ _____.

202

Section G Let's have fun

Feelings!

Match the face with the word

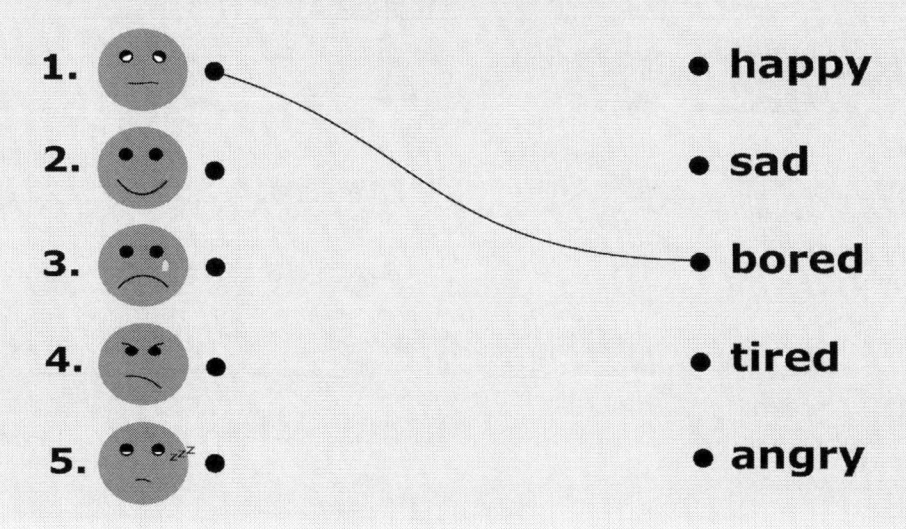

1. •   • happy
2. •   • sad
3. •   • bored
4. •   • tired
5. •   • angry

Answer the questions

1. How has he been feeling lately?
    <u>Lately, he's been feeling bored</u>.

2. How has she been feeling lately?
    _____.

3. How have they been feeling lately?
    _____.

4. Has she been feeling tired lately?
    _____.

5. Has he been feeling angry lately?
    _____.

How have you been feeling lately?

_____.

Lesson 44: The calendar

日历

When is your competition?
My competition is on the 2nd of May.

Section A　Words

1. **birthday**
   生日
2. **competition**
   比赛
3. **class**
   课
4. **speech**
   演说
5. **party**
   派对
6. **meeting**
   开会
7. **appointment**
   约会
8. **test**
   考试
9. **day off**
   放假
10. **recital**
    演奏会

Section B　Make a sentence

When is your <u>birthday</u>?

My birthday is on the <u>21st</u> of <u>February</u>.

Learn: January, February, March, April, May, June, July, August, September, October, November, December

1st 2nd 3rd 4th 5th 6th 7th 8th 9th 10th 11th 12th 13th 14th 15th 16th 17th 18th 19th 20th 21st 22nd 23rd 24th 25th 26th 27th 28th 29th 30th 31st

Section C — Make a question

Is your <u>meeting</u> on the <u>12th</u> of <u>November</u>?
Yes, it is. / No, it isn't.

Was your <u>party</u> on the <u>10th</u> of <u>June</u>?
Yes, it was. / No, it wasn't.

Section D — Learn a verb

organize – organizing – organized – organized 安排

She will **organize** a meeting for this Friday.
Fran is **organizing** a person to help me with the recital.
The teacher **organized** a speech competition at school.
She has **organized** many parties for the company.

Section E — Learn an idiom

Make a date

Meaning: To arrange a meeting with someone.

"We should *make a date* and discuss this further."

| Section F | Write |

Trace and fill in the words

1. When is your appointment?

My appointment is on the 22ⁿᵈ of September.

2. When _____ his competition?

His _____ is on the 31ˢᵗ of October.

3. When is their test?

_____ _____ is on the 11ᵗʰ of _____.

4. When _____ _____ party?

Her _____ is _____ _____ 12ᵗʰ of _____.

5. Is your recital on the 15ᵗʰ of November?

No, _____ isn't.

6. Was his speech _____ the 18ᵗʰ of _____?

No, it _____.

7. Is her day off _____ the _____ of _____?

Yes, _____ _____.

8. Was their class _____ the _____ _____ May?

_____, it _____.

Section G — Let's have fun

The calendar!

May

Monday	Tuesday	Wednesday	Thursday	Friday	Saturday	Sunday
	1st	2nd	3rd	4th Meeting	5th	6th
7th	8th Recital	9th	10th	11th	12th	13th
14th	15th	16th	17th Birthday	18th	19th	20th
21st	22nd Test	23rd	24th	25th	26th Party	27th
28th Day off	29th	30th	31st			

Answer the questions

1. When is your birthday?

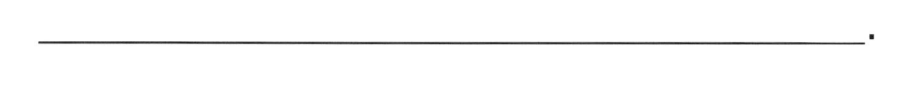

   _____.

2. When is your test?

   _____.

3. Is your party on the 26th of May?

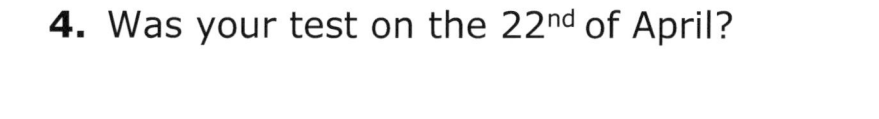

   _____.

4. Was your test on the 22nd of April?

   _____.

Test 11   Lesson 41 - 44

Write the answer next to the letter "A"

A: ___ **1.** ___ was the horror movie ___? It was scary.

a. How, like   b. When, see   c. Where, like   d. What, like

A: ___ **2.** Was the comedy as funny ___ the action movie?

a. movie   b. watch   c. like   d. as

A: ___ **3.** His mother ___ how to swim.

a. teach him   b. taught him   c. teaches he   d. learn him

A: ___ **4.** "Her speech was great. It will be a tough ___ to follow."

a. day   b. act   c. song   d. beat

A: ___ **5.** She ___ the piano ___ every Saturday night.

a. plays, well   b. play, quickly   c. playing, slowly   d. play, bad

A: ___ **6.** Does he ___ the drums ___ for this song?

a. play, correctly   b. play, good   c. plays, well   d. plays, badly

A: ___ **7.** He hadn't ___ his friend speaking Chinese to him.

a. notice   b. notices   c. noticed   d. noticing

A: ___ **8.** "It's such good news! It's ___ to my ears."

a. singing   b. dancing   c. sound   d. music

208

A: ___ **9.** Lately, she ___ been ___ happy.

a. have, feeling   b. is, felt   c. has, feeling   d. does, feels

A: ___ **10.** ___ you been feeling ___ lately? No, I haven't been.

a. Do, tired   b. Can, tired   c. Have, tired   d. Have, tire

A: ___ **11.** Todd wasn't ___ excited during gym class yesterday.

a. feeling   b. feel   c. feels   d. felt

A: ___ **12.** "He wasn't sure what to do. He had ___ feelings."

a. mixing   b. mixed   c. mix   d. mixes

A: ___ **13.** When is ___ birthday? His birthday is on ___ 10th of May.

a. him, it   b. he's, a   c. he's, one   d. his, the

A: ___ **14.** Is ___ recital on the 15th of November? No, it ___.

a. her, isn't   b. his, doesn't   c. your, can't   d. my, won't

A: ___ **15.** Fran is ___ a group of people to help us.

a. organize   b. organizing   c. organizes   d. organized

A: ___ **16.** "Let's arrange a meeting. We should make a ___."

a. meet   b. test   c. date   d. try

Answers on page 462

Lesson 45: World foods

世界食品

Where is sushi eaten?
Sushi is eaten in Japan.

Section A — Words

1. **pasta/Italy**
   面食/义大利
2. **rice/Vietnam**
   米/越南
3. **sushi/Japan**
   寿司/日本
4. **kimchi/South Korea**
   泡菜/韩国
5. **curry/India**
   咖喱/印度
6. **burritos/Mexico**
   卷饼/墨西哥
7. **meat pies/Australia**
   肉馅饼/澳大利亚
8. **sausages/Germany**
   香肠/德国
9. **dumplings/China**
   饺子/中国
10. **kebabs/Turkey**
    烤羊肉串/土耳其

Section B — Make a sentence

Where is <u>pasta</u> eaten?

<u>Pasta</u> is eaten in <u>Italy</u>.

Where are <u>burritos</u> eaten?

<u>Burritos</u> are eaten in <u>Mexico</u>.

Section C — Make a question

Is <u>rice</u> eaten in <u>Vietnam</u>?
Yes, it is. / No, it isn't.

Are <u>meat pies</u> eaten in <u>Australia</u>?
Yes, they are. / No, they aren't.

Section D — Learn a verb

convince – convincing – convinced – convinced 说服

He always **convinces** us to eat more pasta.
My teacher was **convincing** me to try the sushi in Japan.
Dad **convinced** me to join the competition.
We haven't **convinced** Mom and Dad to take us to Mexico.

Section E — Learn an idiom

Bite off more than <u>one</u> can chew

Meaning: To try to do more than one can handle.

"I think he *bit off more than* he *could chew* when he tried to cook Indian food by himself."

Section F — Write

Trace and fill in the words

1. Where _____ curry eaten?

Curry is eaten _____ India.

2. Where _____ meat pies eaten?

Meat _____ are _____ in Australia.

3. Where _____ kimchi _____?

Kimchi is eaten _____ South Korea.

4. Where _____ dumplings eaten?

_____ are _____ in China.

5. Is pasta _____ in Italy?

Yes, _____ is.

6. Are burritos eaten _____ Turkey?

No, they _____.

7. Is _____ eaten in Vietnam?

Yes, it _____.

8. Are kebabs _____ _____ Mexico?

No, _____ _____.

Section G | Let's have fun

World foods!

Unscramble the words and write

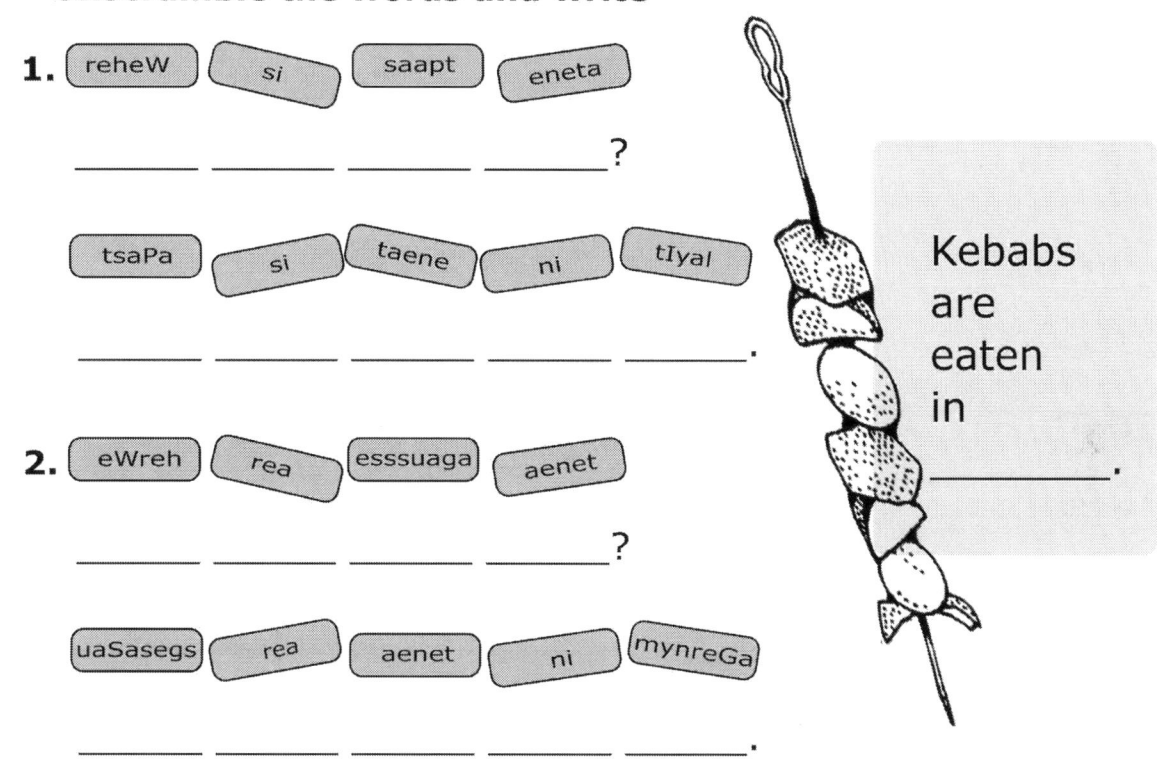

1. [reheW] [si] [saapt] [eneta]

   _____ _____ _____ _____ ?

   [tsaPa] [si] [taene] [ni] [tIyal]

   _____ _____ _____ _____ _____ .

2. [eWreh] [rea] [esssuaga] [aenet]

   _____ _____ _____ _____ ?

   [uaSasegs] [rea] [aenet] [ni] [mynreGa]

   _____ _____ _____ _____ _____ .

Kebabs are eaten in _____.

Connect the words

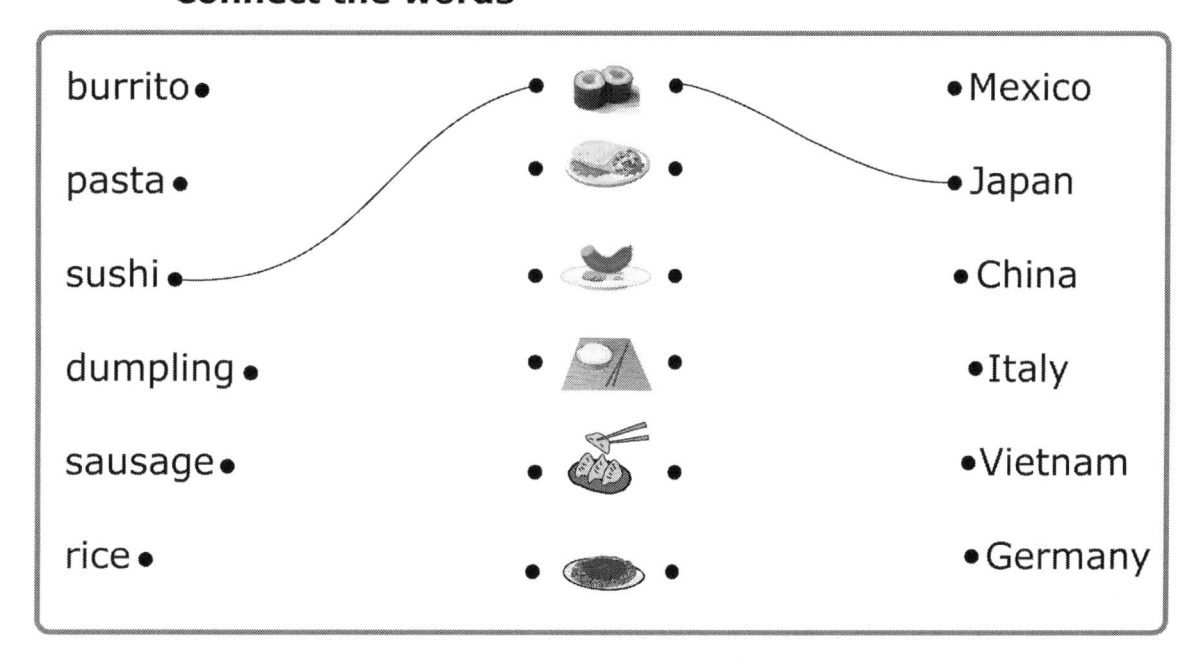

burrito • • Mexico
pasta • • Japan
sushi • • China
dumpling • • Italy
sausage • • Vietnam
rice • • Germany

Lesson 46: Desserts

甜品

> Who were the waffles prepared by?
> The waffles were prepared by her.

Section A — Words

1. **cake**
   蛋糕
2. **apple pie**
   苹果派
3. **ice cream**
   冰淇淋
4. **pudding**
   布丁
5. **cheesecake**
   起司蛋糕
6. **cookies**
   饼干
7. **brownies**
   布朗尼
8. **cupcakes**
   杯子蛋糕
9. **waffles**
   松饼
10. **pastries**
    酥皮糕点

Section B — Make a sentence

Who was the <u>pudding</u> made by?

The pudding was made by <u>him</u>.

Who were the <u>cookies</u> baked by?

The cookies were baked by <u>them</u>.

Learn: prepared, baked, made

Section C — Make a question

Was the <u>ice cream</u> prepared by <u>you</u>?
Yes, it was. / No, it wasn't.

Were the <u>cookies</u> baked by <u>her</u>?
Yes, they were. / No, they weren't.

Section D — Learn a verb

visit – visiting – visited – visited 拜访

She **visits** her parents every Sunday.

I will be **visiting** my friend tomorrow to try her cookies.

We **visited** the new bakery and bought some cupcakes.

My brother has **visited** us two times this month.

Section E — Learn an idiom

Food for thought

Meaning: To have something to think about.

"This book gave me *food for thought* about how to eat healthier."

Section F | **Write**

Trace and fill in the words

1. Who _____ the cake baked by?

The cake was _____ by her.

2. Who _____ the cupcakes made by?

The cupcakes were _____ _____ me.

3. Who was _____ ice cream _____ by?

_____ ice cream _____ prepared _____ them.

4. _____ _____ the pastries prepared _____?

The _____ _____ _____ by him.

5. Were _____ waffles prepared by her?

Yes, they _____.

6. Was the cheesecake made _____ you?

No, _____ wasn't.

7. Were _____ brownies baked _____ him?

Yes, they _____.

8. _____ _____ pudding made _____ them?

No, _____ _____.

Section G   Let's have fun

Desserts!

Circle the dessert

I baked some cookies.

I prepared the ice cream.

I baked a cake.

I made the cupcakes.

Write the answer using the information above

The ☐ were ☐ was made by ☐ him ☐ her.

The ☐ were ☐ was baked by ☐ him ☐ her.

The ☐ were ☐ was prepared by ☐ him ☐ her.

The ☐ were ☐ was baked by ☐ him ☐ her.

Lesson 47: Homework

家庭作业

When will the report be written by?
The report will be written by Tuesday.

Section A — Words

1. **essay** 散文
2. **quiz** 小测验
3. **poster** 海报
4. **speech** 演讲
5. **workbook** 练习簿
6. **science project** 科学项目
7. **presentation** 展示
8. **vocabulary words** 字汇
9. **report** 报告
10. **article** 文章

Section B — Make a sentence

When will the <u>essay</u> be <u>written</u> by?
The essay will be written by <u>Monday</u>.

When will the <u>science project</u> be <u>done</u> by?
The science project will be done by <u>Thursday</u>.

Learn: done, prepared, written, completed

| Section C | Make a question |

> **Will the <u>poster</u> be <u>prepared</u> by <u>Wednesday</u>?**
> Yes, it will be. / No, it won't be.
>
> **Will the <u>report</u> be <u>completed</u> by Friday?**
> Yes, it will be. / No, it won't be.

| Section D | Learn a verb |

fall – falling – fell – fallen 落下

Be careful not to **fall** during your presentation!
The poster had a picture of a boy **falling** down the hill.
The article was about a boy who **fell** off the bridge.
She had **fallen** off her bike, so she couldn't do her speech.

| Section E | Learn an idiom |

Do your homework

Meaning: To do research before making a decision.

"You'll need to *do your homework* if you really want to sail across the ocean."

| Section F | Write |

Trace and fill in the words

1. When will the report _____ written by?

The _____ will be written by Friday.

2. When _____ the speech _____ prepared by?

The _____ will be _____ by Tuesday.

3. When _____ the science project be completed _____?

_____ science _____ will be _____ by Monday.

4. When will _____ poster _____ done _____?

The _____ will _____ _____ _____ Tuesday.

5. Will the essay be written _____ Thursday?

Yes, it will _____.

6. Will _____ workbook _____ done by Wednesday?

No, _____ won't _____.

7. Will _____ quiz _____ prepared _____ Monday?

Yes, _____ _____ _____.

8. _____ _____ presentation _____ prepared _____ Monday?

No, _____ _____ _____.

220

| Section G | Let's have fun |

Homework!

When will the essay be written by?
The essay will be written by Monday.

When will the presentation be done by?
The presentation will be done by Wednesday.

When will the report be completed by?
The report will be completed by Friday.

When will the quiz be prepared by?
The quiz will be prepared by Tuesday.

Read the sentences above. Circle True or False?

The quiz will be prepared by Monday.	True	False
The report will be completed by Friday.	True	False
The presentation will be done by Sunday.	True	False
The essay will be written by Monday.	True	False

pr__se__tat__on   r__ __or__   **Which 2 are missing?**

q__ __ __   __rt__cl__   1_____

es__a__   s__e__c__   2_____

po__ __e__   wo__k__o__k

Lesson 48: At the hospital

在医院

> Who is the surgery being performed by?
> The surgery is being performed by the doctor.

Section A Words

1. **appointment/booked**
   预约/预订
2. **patient/checked**
   病人/检查
3. **medicine/taken**
   药物/服用
4. **surgery/performed**
   手术/执行
5. **temperature/checked**
   温度/检查
6. **floors/cleaned**
   地板/清洗
7. **bed sheets/changed**
   床单/更换
8. **X-rays/examined**
   X 光/检查
9. **babies/delivered**
   婴儿/接生
10. **operating tables/prepared**
    手术台/准备

Section B Make a sentence

Who is the <u>appointment</u> being <u>booked</u> by?

The appointment is being booked by the <u>nurse</u>.

Who are the <u>X-rays</u> being <u>examined</u> by?

The X-rays are being examined by the <u>doctor</u>.

Learn: nurse, doctor, janitor, patient

Section C | Make a question

Is the <u>patient</u> being <u>checked</u> by the <u>nurse</u>?
Yes, the patient is. / No, the patient isn't.

Are the <u>floors</u> being <u>cleaned</u> by the <u>janitor</u>?
Yes, the floors are. / No, the floors aren't.

Section D | Learn a verb

ride – riding – rode – ridden 骑

The janitor **rides** his motorcycle to work every day.

The patient was **riding** a bike when a car hit him.

The nurse **rode** a scooter to the hospital this morning.

The doctor has never **ridden** a horse before.

Section E | Learn an idiom

Just what the doctor ordered

Meaning: To be exactly what one needs.

"A day at the beach is *just what the doctor ordered* to help me relax."

Section F   **Write**

Trace and fill in the words

1. Who is the patient _____ checked by?

The patient _____ being checked by the nurse.

2. Who is the medicine _____ taken _____?

The medicine _____ being _____ by the patient.

3. Who are _____ floors _____ cleaned _____?

The floors _____ being _____ _____ the janitor.

4. _____ are the X-rays _____ examined _____?

The _____ _____ _____ _____ by the doctor.

5. Is the temperature being _____ by the janitor?

Yes, the temperature _____.

6. Are the _____ being delivered _____ the nurse?

No, _____ babies _____.

7. Is _____ appointment _____ booked _____ the doctor?

No, the _____ _____.

8. Are _____ bed sheets _____ _____ by the nurse?

Yes, _____ bed sheets _____.

Section G Let's have fun

At the hospital!

Connect the sentences

The appointment is being • — • booked by the nurse.

The surgery is being • • delivered by the doctor.

The medicine is being • • cleaned by the janitor.

The X-rays are being • • taken by the patient.

The babies are being • • performed by the doctor.

The operating table is being • • examined by the nurse.

The floors are being • • prepared by the nurse.

Finish the sentence using the information above

1. The floors are being cleaned by the _____.

2. The babies are being delivered by the _____.

3. The appointment is being booked by the _____.

Test 12 Lesson 45 - 48

Write the answer next to the letter "A"

A: ___ **1.** Where ___ sushi eaten? Sushi is ___ in Japan.

a. is, eat　　b. is, eaten　　c. was, eaten　　d. are, eaten

A: ___ **2.** ___ sausages eaten in Germany? Yes, ___ are.

a. Are, they　　b. Is, it　　c. Are, them　　d. Were, they

A: ___ **3.** Last night, my mom ___ me to try the meat pies in Australia.

a. convincing　　b. convince　　c. convinced　　d. convinces

A: ___ **4.** "I bit off more than I can ___ when I chose to do this project."

a. cook　　b. eat　　c. swallow　　d. chew

A: ___ **5.** The cupcakes ___ baked ___ me.

a. was, by　　b. were, by　　c. was, with　　d. were, be

A: ___ **6.** Was the ice cream prepared by ___? No, it ___.

a. her, wasn't　　b. she, wasn't　　c. him, weren't　　d. them, isn't

A: ___ **7.** I will be ___ my grandmother this Sunday.

a. visit　　b. visited　　c. visits　　d. visiting

A: ___ **8.** "What you said is very interesting and ___ for thought."

a. something　　b. information　　c. food　　d. fruit

226

A: ___ **9.** The babies ___ being ___ by the doctor.

a. was, checked   b. is, performed   c. are, delivered   d. are, booked

A: ___ **10.** Is the surgery being performed by the doctor? Yes, ___.

a. the surgery is   b. surgery is   c. the surgery are   d. surgery are

A: ___ **11.** I haven't ___ a bike for two years.

a. ride   b. riding   c. ridden   d. rode

A: ___ **12.** "It was really fun today. It's just what the doctor ___."

a. booked   b. needed   c. examined   d. ordered

A: ___ **13.** ___ will the quiz ___ completed by?

a. When, been   b. What, be   c. When, be   d. Who, been

A: ___ **14.** Will the article be written ___ Friday? No, it ___.

a. on, won't   b. by, don't be   c. at, won't be   d. by, won't be

A: ___ **15.** "You should do your ___ first before you buy this car."

a. homework   b. work   c. housework   d. school work

A: ___ **16.** I ___ off my bike two times when I was learning how to ride.

a. fell   b. falling   c. fallen   d. fall

Answers on page 462

Lesson 49: On the farm

在农场

What was being done on the farm last week?
The eggs were being collected.

Section A   Words

1. **corn/harvested**
   玉米/收获
2. **wheat/cut**
   小麦/切
3. **fence/fixed**
   围栏/固定
4. **cow/milked**
   母牛/挤奶
5. **tractor/driven**
   牵引几/驾车
6. **apples/picked**
   苹果/摘
7. **seeds/planted**
   种子/种植
8. **animals/fed**
   动物/喂
9. **eggs/collected**
   鸡蛋/收集
10. **fields/plowed**
    田/犁

Section B Make a sentence

What was being done on the farm <u>last month</u>?
The <u>corn</u> was being <u>harvested</u>.

What was being done on the farm <u>last week</u>?
The <u>apples</u> were being <u>picked</u>.

Learn: last week, last month, last year, last night

Section C — Make a question

Was the <u>fence</u> being <u>fixed</u> <u>last year</u>?
Yes, it was. / No, it wasn't.

Were the <u>animals</u> being <u>fed</u> <u>last night</u>?
Yes, they were. / No, they weren't.

Section D — Learn a verb

forget – forgetting – forgot – forgotten 忘记

I often **forget** to collect the eggs.

She is **forgetting** to do many things on the farm.

The farmer **forgot** to fix the fence.

Have you **forgotten** to milk the cows again?

Section E — Learn an idiom

A cash cow

Meaning: Something that continues to make a lot of money.

"His apple farm has been *a cash cow* for a long time."

Section F   Write

Trace and fill in the words

1. What _____ being done on the farm last week?

The fence was being _____.

2. What was _____ done on _____ farm last month?

The eggs _____ being _____.

3. What was _____ _____ on _____ farm last night?

The tractor _____ _____ _____.

4. What was _____ done on _____ _____ last year?

_____ fields _____ _____ _____.

5. Was the cow _____ milked this morning?

Yes, it was.

6. Were _____ apples _____ picked last week?

No, they _____.

7. _____ the wheat _____ cut yesterday?

Yes, _____ _____.

8. _____ _____ seeds being _____ today?

_____, _____ weren't.

230

Section G | Let's have fun

On the farm!

Farm Schedule

Monday ___fix fence___

Tuesday ___feed animals___

Wednesday ___harvest corn___

Thursday ___collect eggs___

Friday ___plow fields___

Saturday ___pick apples___

Answer the questions using the information above

1. What was being done on the farm last Wednesday?
_____

2. What was being done on the farm last Thursday?
_____

3. What was being done on the farm last Saturday?
_____

4. Were the animals being fed last Tuesday?
_____

5. Was the fence being fixed last Friday?
_____

Lesson 50: In the office

在办公室里

> Who will the email be being written by?
> The email will be being written by the director.

Section A — Words

1. presentation/given
   展示/给出
2. calls/made
   电话/打
3. interview/conducted
   采访/进行
4. email/written
   电子邮件/写
5. newsletter/prepared
   业务通讯/准备
6. advertisement/designed
   广告/设计
7. meeting/held
   会议/举办
8. copies/made
   拷贝/制作
9. training/taught
   培训/教
10. files/organized
    文件/安排

Section B — Make a sentence

Who will the <u>presentation</u> be being <u>given</u> by?

The <u>presentation</u> will be being <u>given</u> by <u>my co-worker</u>.

Who will the <u>interview</u> be being <u>conducted</u> by?

The interview will be being conducted by <u>the manager</u>.

Learn: co-worker, manager, secretary, director

Section C — Make a question

Will the <u>newsletter</u> be being <u>prepared</u> by the <u>secretary</u>?
Yes, it will be. / No, it won't be.

Will the <u>files</u> be being <u>organized</u> by the <u>director</u>?
Yes, they will be. / No, they won't be.

Section D — Learn a verb

replace – replacing – replaced – replaced 替换

The director will **replace** one co-worker next year.

We are **replacing** the newsletter with an email.

The secretary **replaced** the markers in the meeting room.

The manager will have **replaced** the computers by Monday.

Section E — Learn an idiom

Call a meeting

Meaning: To ask people to have a meeting.

"The director wants to *call a meeting* to discuss the problem."

Section F   Write

Trace and fill in the words

1. Who will the newsletter _____ being prepared by?

   The newsletter will be _____ prepared by the secretary.

2. Who _____ the training be being taught _____?

   The training will _____ being _____ by my co-worker.

3. Who will the meeting _____ _____ held _____?

   The _____ will be being held _____ the manager.

4. _____ will _____ calls be _____ made _____?

   The calls _____ _____ being made by the director.

5. Will the interview be _____ conducted by the manager?

   Yes, it _____ be.

6. Will the advertisement be being _____ by my co-worker?

   No, it _____ _____.

7. Will the email _____ _____ written by the secretary?

   Yes, _____ _____ _____.

8. _____ the presentation be _____ given _____ the director?

   No, _____ _____ _____.

Section G Let's have fun

In the office!

Circle the office words

1. corn   fence   apples   (calls)   eggs

2. medicine   email   doctor   surgery   floors

3. cake   cupcakes   interview   pudding   brownies

4. files   rice   curry   kebabs   sushi

5. birthday   class   training   recital   party

6. tired   meeting   excited   fine   bored

7. scary   newsletter   violent   funny   sad

8. well   badly   slowly   presentation   loudly

Write the word

1.
2.
3.
4.
5.
6.
7.
8.

Lesson 51: At the airport

在机场

> Have the passports already been stamped?
> No, they haven't been stamped yet.

Section A — Words

1. luggage/loaded
   行李/装载
2. ticket/printed
   票据/印刷
3. boarding pass/prepared
   登机证/准备
4. departure time/delayed
   出发时间/延迟
5. airplane/boarded
   飞机/登上
6. arrival times/updated
   到达时间/更新
7. flights/announced
   航班/公布
8. passports/stamped
   护照/盖章
9. bags/checked
   袋子/检查
10. gates/changed
    登机门/变更

Section B — Make a sentence

What has already been done?

The <u>luggage</u> has already been <u>loaded</u>.

What hasn't been done yet?

The <u>arrival times</u> haven't been <u>updated</u> yet.

Learn: already, yet

Section C — Make a question

Has the <u>boarding pass</u> already been <u>prepared</u>?
Yes, it has already been prepared. / No, it hasn't been prepared yet.

Haven't the <u>bags</u> been <u>checked</u> yet?
Yes, they have already been checked. / No, they haven't been checked yet.

Section D — Learn a verb

finish – finishing – finished – finished 完成

They will **finish** loading the luggage in ten minutes.
He was **finishing** his presentation at the airport.
The flight attendant **finished** checking the bags.
They have already **finished** announcing the flights.

Section E — Learn an idiom

In full flight

Meaning: To be in a state of high productivity.

"The project is now *in full flight* and we should be finished soon."

Section F   Write

Trace and fill in the words

1. What has already _____ done?

   The airplane _____ already been boarded.

2. What hasn't been _____ yet?

   The flights haven't _____ announced _____.

3. What has _____ _____ done?

   The ticket _____ already been _____.

4. _____ _____ been _____ yet?

   _____ passports _____ been stamped _____.

5. Has the luggage already _____ loaded yet?

   Yes, it has _____ been loaded.

6. Haven't _____ bags been checked _____?

   No, they haven't _____ yet.

7. Has _____ boarding pass already been _____?

   Yes, it has _____ _____ prepared.

8. Haven't _____ arrival times _____ updated yet?

   _____, _____ haven't been _____ _____.

238

Section G   Let's have fun

At the airport!

CROSSWORD PUZZLE

Across:
1. Haven't the _____ been checked yet?
2. The bags have already been _____.
3. The flights haven't been _____ yet.
4. The arrival times have already been _____.
5. The _____ pass has already been prepared.

Down:
6. The gates have already been _____.
7. The _____ hasn't been printed yet.
8. The _____ time hasn't been delayed yet.
9. The _____ have already been stamped.
10. Has the _____ already been loaded?

Lesson 52: Camping

露营

What had already been packed by them?
The plastic dishes had already been packed by them.

Section A — Words

1. **tent** 帐篷
2. **cooler** 冷藏箱
3. **barbecue** 烤肉
4. **gas bottle** 瓦斯瓶
5. **compass** 指南针
6. **fishing rods** 钓鱼竿
7. **plastic dishes** 塑胶盘
8. **binoculars** 双筒望远镜
9. **sleeping bags** 睡袋
10. **flashlights** 手电筒

Section B — Make a sentence

What had already been packed by <u>you</u>?

The <u>tent</u> had already been <u>packed</u> by me.

What still hadn't been packed by <u>her</u>?

The <u>sleeping bags</u> still hadn't been packed by her.

Learn: still, her, him, me, them, us

Section C — Make a question

Had the <u>cooler</u> already been packed?
Yes, it had already been packed. / No, it still hadn't been packed.

Hadn't the <u>binoculars</u> been packed yet?
Yes, they had already been packed. / No, they still hadn't been packed.

Section D — Learn a verb

search – searching – searched – searched 找

You can **search** on the internet for a cheaper tent.
We were **searching** the campsite for a barbecue.
We **searched** for animals at night using our flashlights.
I had **searched** for information about camping at that place.

Section E — Learn an idiom

Camp out

Meaning: To sleep somewhere temporarily.

"I had to *camp out* on the sofa because my bed was broken."

| Section F | Write |

Trace and fill in the words

1. What had already _____ packed by you?

   The gas bottle had _____ been packed by me.

2. What still hadn't _____ _____ by him?

   The binoculars _____ hadn't been packed _____ him.

3. What _____ _____ been _____ by her?

   The plastic dishes _____ already _____ packed _____ her.

4. _____ still _____ been packed _____ you?

   The cooler _____ hadn't _____ packed _____ me.

5. Had the sleeping bags already _____ packed?

   Yes, they had already been _____.

6. Hadn't _____ fishing rods _____ packed yet?

   No, they still _____ been packed.

7. Had _____ compass _____ been _____?

   Yes, it _____ already _____ packed.

8. Hadn't the tent _____ packed _____?

   No, _____ still _____ been _____.

Section G — Let's have fun

Camping!

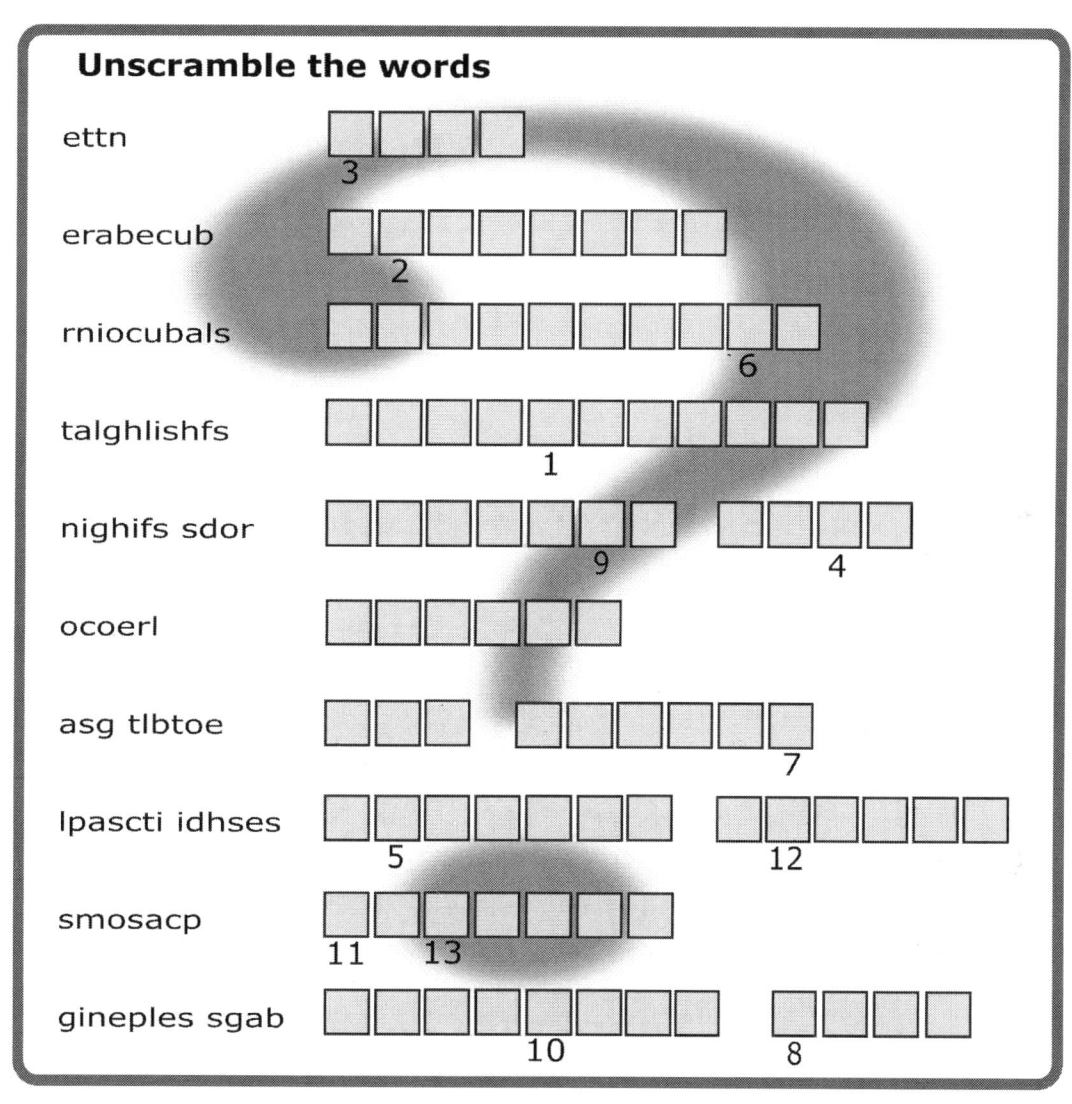

Unscramble the words

- ettn
- erabecub
- rniocubals
- talghlishfs
- nighifs sdor
- ocoerl
- asg tlbtoe
- lpascti idhses
- smosacp
- gineples sgab

Write the sentence using the information above

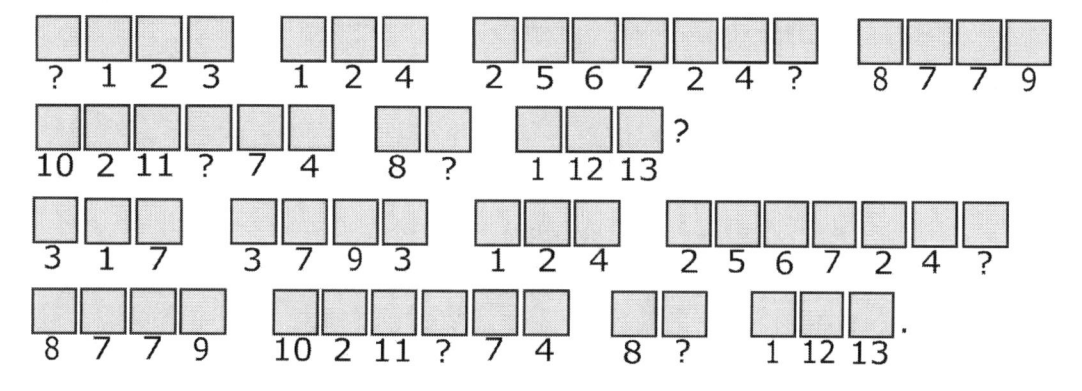

Test 13   Lesson 49 - 52

Write the answer next to the letter "A"

A: ___ **1.** The eggs ___ being ___ last week.

a. was, collected   b. were, collected   c. are, fried   d. is, delivered

A: ___ **2.** ___ the apples ___ picked last month?

a. Was, being   b. Are, being   c. Were, been   d. Were, being

A: ___ **3.** I ___ to bring my pencil. Can I please borrow yours?

a. forgot   b. forgets   c. forgotten   d. forgetting

A: ___ **4.** "His pizza restaurant is a ___ cow for him in summer."

a. money   b. cash   c. dollar   d. milk

A: ___ **5.** The training ___ being taught ___ the manager.

a. will, by   b. won't, for   c. will be, by   d. are, with

A: ___ **6.** Will the copies be being made by the secretary?

a. Yes, it will be.   b. Yes, they will be.   c. No, they won't.   d. No, it won't.

A: ___ **7.** We will have already ___ the old desks by Monday.

a. replacing   b. replaces   c. replace   d. replaced

A: ___ **8.** "The director wants to ___ a meeting for tomorrow afternoon."

a. calling   b. start   c. begin   d. call

A: ___ 9. What ___ already been ___?

a. has, done   b. have, done   c. hasn't, yet   d. hasn't, do

A: ___ 10. ___ the ticket been printed yet? No, ___ hasn't been printed yet.

a. Haven't, it   b. Hasn't, they   c. Hasn't, it   d. Did, it

A: ___ 11. He ___ the report now.

a. finish   b. have finished   c. is finishing   d. finishing

A: ___ 12. "The project is in ___ flight and will be finished this Friday."

a. high   b. full   c. busy   d. fast

A: ___ 13. The binoculars ___ hadn't ___ packed by him.

a. still, been   b. already, been   c. still, be   d. already, be

A: ___ 14. Had the barbecue been packed ___? Yes, it had ___ been packed.

a. already, already   b. yet, already   c. yet, still   d. still, already

A: ___ 15. I often ___ the internet for information.

a. searches   b. searching   c. searched   d. search

A: ___ 16. "You're welcome to camp ___ at my house for a week."

a. on   b. in   c. outside   d. out

Answers on page 462

Lesson 53: Birthday party

生日聚会

What won't have been completed for the party yet?
The room won't have been decorated.

Section A — Words

1. presents/wrapped
   礼物/包裹
2. games/organized
   游戏/组织
3. guests/invited
   客人/邀请
4. candles/lit
   蜡烛/点
5. balloons/blown up
   气球/充气
6. cake/baked
   蛋糕/烤
7. drinks/poured
   饮料/倒
8. table/set
   桌子/摆
9. candy/put out
   糖果/放
10. room/decorated
    房间/装饰

Section B — Make a sentence

What will have been completed for the party?

The <u>presents</u> will have been <u>wrapped</u>.

What won't have been completed for the party?

The <u>cake</u> won't have been <u>baked</u>.

Section C — Make a question

Will the <u>table</u> have been <u>set</u> for the party?
Yes, it will have. / No, it won't have.

Won't the <u>balloons</u> have been <u>blown up</u> for the party?
Yes, they will have. / No, they won't have.

Section D — Learn a verb

copy – copying – copied – copied 拷贝/影印

Please **copy** these notes down in your notebook for the test.
One student was **copying** my work in class today.
I **copied** some newsletters for the meeting tomorrow.
She had **copied** the price and pasted it into the email.

Section E — Learn an idiom

The life of the party

Meaning: Someone who brings a lot of energy to a social event.

"He was always fun at work because he was *the life of the party*."

Section F | Write

Trace and fill in the words

1. What _____ have been completed for the party?

   The balloons will _____ been blown up.

2. What won't have _____ completed _____ the party?

   The candles won't _____ been _____.

3. What will _____ been _____ for _____ party?

   _____ cake _____ have _____ baked.

4. _____ won't _____ been completed for _____ party?

   The drinks _____ have _____ _____.

5. Will the presents _____ been wrapped for the party?

   Yes, they _____ have.

6. Won't games have _____ organized for the _____?

   No, _____ won't _____.

7. _____ the guests have _____ invited for the party?

   Yes, _____ _____ have.

8. Won't the table _____ been _____ for the party?

   No, _____ _____ _____.

248

Section G Let's have fun

Birthday party!

Party List

balloons ✓	table ✗
candles ✗	candy ✗
games ✓	presents ✓
guests ✓	cake ✗
room ✓	drinks ✗

Answer the questions using the information above

1. Will the room have been decorated for the party?

_____

2. Will the table have been set for the party?

_____

3. Won't the candy have been put out for the party?

_____

4. Won't the balloons have been blown up for the party?

_____

1. The presents will have been wrapped. **True** ☐ **False** ☐

2. The drinks will have been poured. **True** ☐ **False** ☐

3. The cake won't have been baked. **True** ☐ **False** ☐

4. The candles won't have been lit. **True** ☐ **False** ☐

Lesson 54: At the park

在公园

When you were at the park, what did you see?
When I was at the park, I saw a yellow kite.

Section A — Words

1. **a new slide**
   一座新的溜滑梯
2. **(my) best friend**
   我最好的朋友
3. **a yellow kite**
   一只黄色的风筝
4. **a big dog**
   一条大狗
5. **high monkey bars**
   高高的单杠
6. **an old picnic table**
   一张旧的野餐桌
7. **some ducks**
   一些鸭子
8. **some big trees**
   一些大树
9. **a running track**
   一条跑道
10. **a basketball court**
    一个篮球场

Section B — Make a sentence

When you were at the park, what did you see?

When I was at the park, I saw <u>a new slide</u>.

When she was at the park, what did she see?

When she was at the park, she saw <u>some ducks</u>.

Learn: my, his, her, their, our

Section C — Make a question

Did you see <u>a running track</u> when you were at the park?
Yes, I did. / No, I didn't. I saw <u>a basketball court</u>.

Didn't he see <u>a new slide</u> when he was at the park?
Yes, he did. / No, he didn't. He saw <u>an old picnic table</u>.

Section D — Learn a verb

keep – keeping – kept – kept 保持

He **keeps** a spare tire in the back of his car.

Keeping the house warm in winter can be difficult in Canada.

I **kept** forgetting to bring my kite to the park.

My grandmother has **kept** this picture for over fifty years.

Section E — Learn an idiom

A walk in the park

Meaning: Something that is very easy to accomplish.

"Passing that English test was *a walk in the park*."

| Section F | Write |

Trace and fill in the words

1. When you _____ at the park, what did you see?

When I _____ at the park, I saw a _____ court.

2. When she was at _____ park, what did she _____?

When she _____ at the park, she saw high _____ bars.

3. When _____ were at the park, _____ did you see?

When I _____ at the park, I saw an old picnic _____.

4. _____ he was at the park, what _____ he _____?

When he was at the _____, he saw _____ ducks.

5. Did you see a new slide _____ you were at the park?

Yes, I _____.

6. Did he see a yellow kite when he _____ at the _____?

No, he _____. He saw _____ big dog.

7. _____ she see a _____ track when she was at the park?

Yes, _____ _____.

8. Did you _____ some big trees _____ you were at the park?

No, _____ _____. I _____ my best friend

Section G — Let's have fun

At the park!

Write the sentences

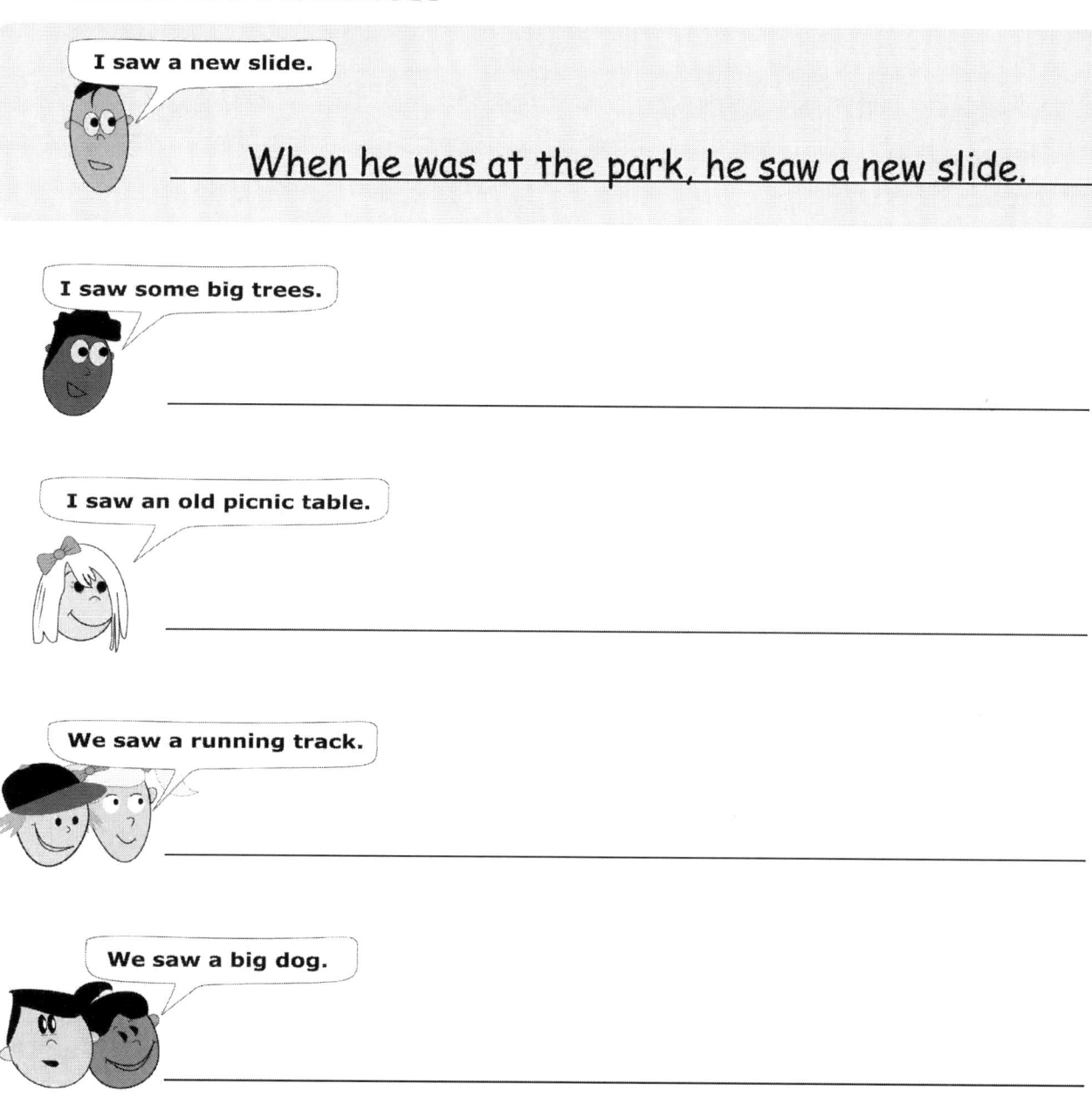

"I saw a new slide."

When he was at the park, he saw a new slide.

"I saw some big trees."

_____

"I saw an old picnic table."

_____

"We saw a running track."

_____

"We saw a big dog."

_____

When you were at the park, what did you see?

_____

Lesson 55: On the street

在街上

When you were walking to school, what did you see?
When I was walking to school, I saw some shops.

Section A Words

1. a police car
   一辆警车
2. a bus
   一辆巴士
3. an ambulance
   一辆救护车
4. a truck
   一辆卡车
5. a fire engine
   一辆消防车
6. some traffic lights
   一些红绿灯
7. a fire hydrant
   一个消防栓
8. a trash can
   一个垃圾桶
9. a stop sign
   一个停车标志
10. some shops
    一些商店

Section B Make a sentence

When <u>you</u> were walking to school this morning, what did you see?

When I was walking to school this morning, I saw <u>an ambulance</u>.

When <u>he</u> was walking to school this morning, what did he see?

When he was walking to school this morning, he saw <u>a fire hydrant</u>.

| Section C | Make a question |

Did you see <u>a police car</u> driving on the street this morning?
Yes, I did. / No, I didn't.

Did he see <u>a stop sign</u> on the street this morning?
Yes, he did. / No, he didn't.

| Section D | Learn a verb |

drive – driving – drove – driven 驾驶/开车

My dad **drives** a big truck.
She is **driving** behind an ambulance.
A police officer **drove** his police car really fast on our street.
I have never **driven** my car through a stop sign.

| Section E | Learn an idiom |

Hit the streets

Meaning: To start walking somewhere with a purpose.

"We *hit the streets* and looked everywhere for my lost dog."

| Section F | Write |

Trace and fill in the words

1. When she was _____ to school this morning, what did she _____?

When she was walking to _____ this morning, she _____ a police car.

2. When he _____ walking to school this morning, _____ did _____ see?

When _____ was walking to school _____ morning, he saw _____ fire engine.

3. When you _____ walking _____ school this morning, _____ did you _____?

When I _____ walking to school this morning, I _____ a stop sign.

4. Did he _____ a bus driving on the street this morning?

Yes, he _____.

5. Did she see a truck _____ on the _____ this morning?

No, she _____.

6. _____ you see a trash can on the street this _____?

Yes, _____ _____.

256

Section G Let's have fun

On the street!

1. When you were walking to school this morning, what did you see?

When I was walking to school this morning, _____

2. When she was walking to school this morning, what did she see?

_____

3. When he was walking to school this morning, what did he see?

_____

4. When they were walking to school this morning, what did they see?

_____

Lesson 56: Seasons

季节

What do you like to do in autumn?
I really like to hike in autumn.

Section A | Words

1. ski/skiing
   滑雪
2. run/running
   跑步
3. surf/surfing
   冲浪
4. hike/hiking
   远足
5. swim/swimming
   游泳
6. exciting
   振奋人心的
7. healthy
   健康的
8. great
   极好的
9. fun
   好玩的
10. relaxing
    放松的

Section B | Make a sentence

What do you like to do in winter?

I really like to ski in winter.

Why do you like to ski?

I like skiing because it is exciting.

Learn: spring, summer, autumn, winter

Section C — Make a question

Do you like to <u>surf</u> in <u>summer</u>?
Yes, I really like to surf in summer. / No, I don't like to.

Does he like to <u>run</u> in <u>spring</u>?
Yes, he really likes to run in spring. / No, he doesn't like to.

Section D — Learn a verb

hike – hiking – hiked – hiked 远足

I love to **hike** in spring when the flowers are in bloom.
She'll be **hiking** the exciting trail with me this weekend.
It was relaxing when we **hiked** in autumn last year.
Have you **hiked** that great mountain in winter?

Section E — Learn an idiom

In season

Meaning: When fruits or vegetables are ready for eating.

"Those apples aren't *in season* until autumn."

| Section F | Write |

Trace and fill in the words

1. What _____ you like to do in summer?

I really _____ to surf in summer.

2. Why do you like to surf?

I like surfing because it _____ exciting.

3. What does he like _____ do _____ autumn?

He _____ likes _____ run in autumn.

4. Why _____ he _____ to run?

He likes _____ because _____ is healthy.

5. Do you _____ to ski in winter?

Yes, I really like to _____ in winter.

6. Does _____ like to hike in spring?

No, she _____ like _____.

7. Do _____ like to swim _____ summer?

Yes, they _____ like to swim in _____.

8. _____ he _____ to surf in autumn?

No, he _____ _____ _____.

Section G | Let's have fun

Seasons!

Unscramble the sentences

really / I / to / in / like / summer / swim

1. _____.

in / likes / winter / She / ski / to / really

2. _____.

in / hike / to / spring / like / really / They

3. _____.

is / running / it / He / because / likes / healthy

4. _____.

fun / it / because / is / They / swimming / like

5. _____.

is / surfing / it / I / because / like / exciting

6. _____.

Test 14   Lesson 53 - 56

Write the answer next to the letter "A"

A: ___ **1.** The room will ___ decorated.

a. had been   b. has been   c. been   d. have been

A: ___ **2.** Won't the candles have been lit for the party? Yes, ___.

a. they will   b. it will   c. they will have   d. it will have

A: ___ **3.** My coworker often ___ my reports.

a. copy   b. copies   c. copied   d. copying

A: ___ **4.** "My father is really funny. He is always the life ___ the party."

a. of   b. for   c. in   d. at

A: ___ **5.** When I was ___ on the street this morning, I ___ a truck.

a. walking, saw   b. walk, saw   c. walking, see   d. walked, seeing

A: ___ **6.** ___ he see a bus on the street this morning? No, he ___.

a. Did, don't   b. Does, didn't   c. Did, doesn't   d. Did, didn't

A: ___ **7.** It's going to rain, so she will be ___ to work tomorrow.

a. have driven   b. driving   c. drives   d. drove

A: ___ **8.** "To find more customers, you'll need to ___ the streets."

a. walk   b. hit   c. run   d. kick

A: ___ **9.** Why do you like ___? I like ___ because it's healthy.

a. run, running   b. did, went   c. to run, running   d. to run, run

A: ___ **10.** ___ you like to swim in summer? Yes, I ___ like to swim in summer.

a. Do, really   b. Does, real   c. Did, really   d. Are, very

A: ___ **11.** I'm really excited because we'll be ___ a beautiful mountain.

a. have hiked   b. hike   c. hiked   d. hiking

A: ___ **12.** "We can't buy any peaches because they aren't ___ season."

a. in   b. of   c. at   d. on

A: ___ **13.** When he ___ at the park, he ___ his best friend.

a. is, see   b. was, saw   c. were, saw   d. was, sees

A: ___ **14.** Did you ___ some big trees when you ___ at the park?

a. saw, were   b. see, was   c. seen, are   d. see, were

A: ___ **15.** The red kite ___ falling to the ground at the park yesterday.

a. kept   b. keep   c. keeps   d. is

A: ___ **16.** "Don't worry. This essay will be a ___ in the park."

a. run   b. fun   c. walk   d. sleep

Answers on page 463

Lesson 57: Outdoor activities

户外运动

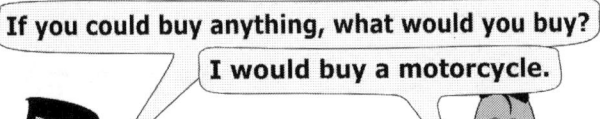

If you could buy anything, what would you buy?
I would buy a motorcycle.

Section A — Words

1. **kayaking**
   皮艇运动
2. **skydiving**
   跳伞
3. **diving**
   潜水
4. **camping**
   露营
5. **snowboarding**
   滑雪板
6. **motorcycle**
   摩托车
7. **boat**
   船
8. **horse**
   马
9. **bike**
   自行车
10. **kayak**
    皮艇

Section B — Make a sentence

If you could do anything, what would you do?
I would go **kayaking**.

If you could buy anything, what would you buy?
I would buy a **boat**.

Note: Use words 1 – 5 for the first sentence. Use words 6 - 10 for the second sentence.

Section C — Make a question

If you could <u>go camping</u>, would you?
Yes, I would. / No, I wouldn't.

If you could buy a <u>horse</u>, would you?
Yes, I would. / No, I wouldn't.

Section D — Learn a verb

bring – bringing – brought – brought 带

Please **bring** the two kayaks to the lake.

We'll be **bringing** our bikes when we go camping.

I **brought** my snowboard, so I could go snowboarding.

I haven't **brought** any equipment to go diving.

Section E — Learn an idiom

The great outdoors

Meaning: Areas of nature that are away from the city.

"He likes to get away from the city and go to *the great outdoors*."

Section F   Write

Trace and fill in the words

1. If you _____ do anything, what would you do?

I _____ go skydiving.

2. If you could buy _____, what _____ you buy?

I would _____ a motorcycle.

3. If you _____ do anything, _____ would you _____?

I _____ _____ snowboarding.

4. _____ you could buy _____, what _____ you buy?

I _____ _____ _____ horse.

5. If you could _____ kayaking, would you?

Yes, _____ would.

6. If you _____ buy a boat, _____ you?

No, _____ wouldn't.

7. If _____ could _____ diving, would _____?

Yes, I _____.

8. _____ you could _____ a bike, _____ you?

No, _____ _____.

266

Section G | Let's have fun

Outdoor activities!

Write the words in the right place!

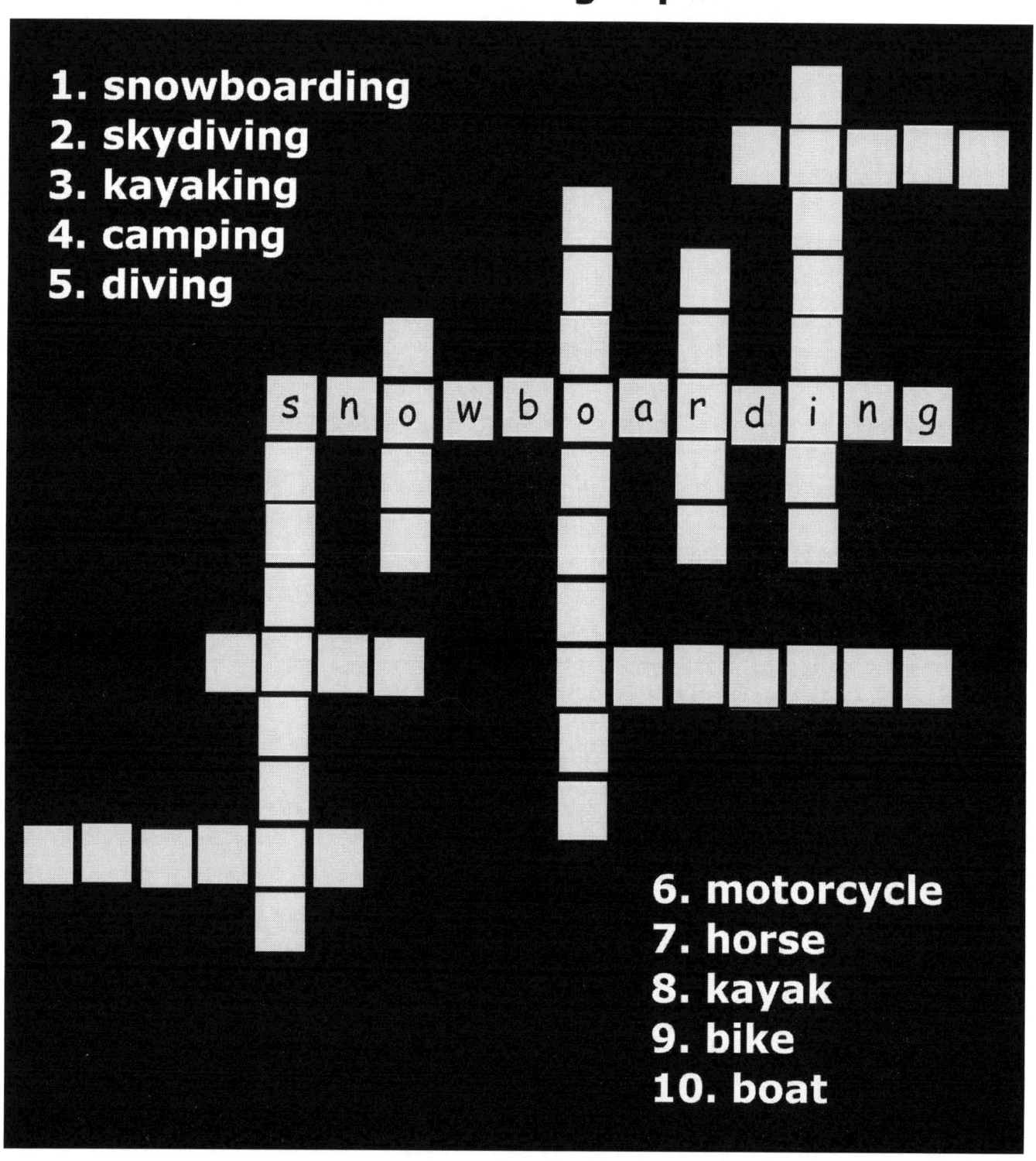

1. snowboarding
2. skydiving
3. kayaking
4. camping
5. diving

s n o w b o a r d i n g

6. motorcycle
7. horse
8. kayak
9. bike
10. boat

Lesson 58: Skills

技能

How old were you when you learned how to ski?
I was six years old when I learned how to ski.

Section A — Words

1. ride a bike
   骑自行车
2. play the piano
   弹钢琴
3. speak French
   说法语
4. swim
   游泳
5. fly a kite
   放风筝
6. ski
   滑雪
7. skateboard
   滑板
8. ride a horse
   骑马
9. use a computer
   用电脑
10. paint pictures
    画画

Section B — Make a sentence

How old were you when you learned how to <u>ride a horse</u>?

I was <u>ten</u> years old when I learned how to ride a horse.

How old was she when she learned how to <u>fly a kite</u>?

She was <u>eight</u> years old when she learned how to <u>fly a kite</u>.

Section C — Make a question

Were you <u>five</u> years old when you learned how to <u>ride a bike</u>?
Yes, I was. / No, I wasn't. I was <u>six</u> years old.

Was he <u>ten</u> years old when he learned how to <u>swim</u>?
Yes, he was. / No, he wasn't. He was <u>eight</u> years old.

Section D — Learn a verb

sing – singing – sang – sung 唱歌

My brother likes to **sing** in the shower.
She is **singing** a traditional Chinese song.
My father **sang** to me every night when I was a baby.
He hasn't **sung** my favorite song in concert for over a year.

Section E — Learn an idiom

Learn the hard way

Meaning: To learn something in an unpleasant or difficult way.

"He *learned the hard way* that skateboarding isn't easy."

| Section F | Write |

Trace and fill in the words

1. How old were you _____ you learned how to play the piano?

I _____ eight years old when I _____ how to play the piano.

2. How old _____ she when she learned _____ to use a computer?

She was nine years old _____ she learned how to _____ a computer.

3. How old _____ you when you _____ how to ride a bike?

I was four _____ old when I learned _____ to ride a _____.

4. Were you ten years old _____ you learned how _____ speak French?

Yes, I _____.

5. Were you six years old when you _____ how to skateboard?

No, I _____. I was seven _____ old.

6. Was he thirteen _____ old when he _____ how to ski?

No, _____ _____. He was twelve years _____.

| Section G | Let's have fun |

Skills!

Write the sentences

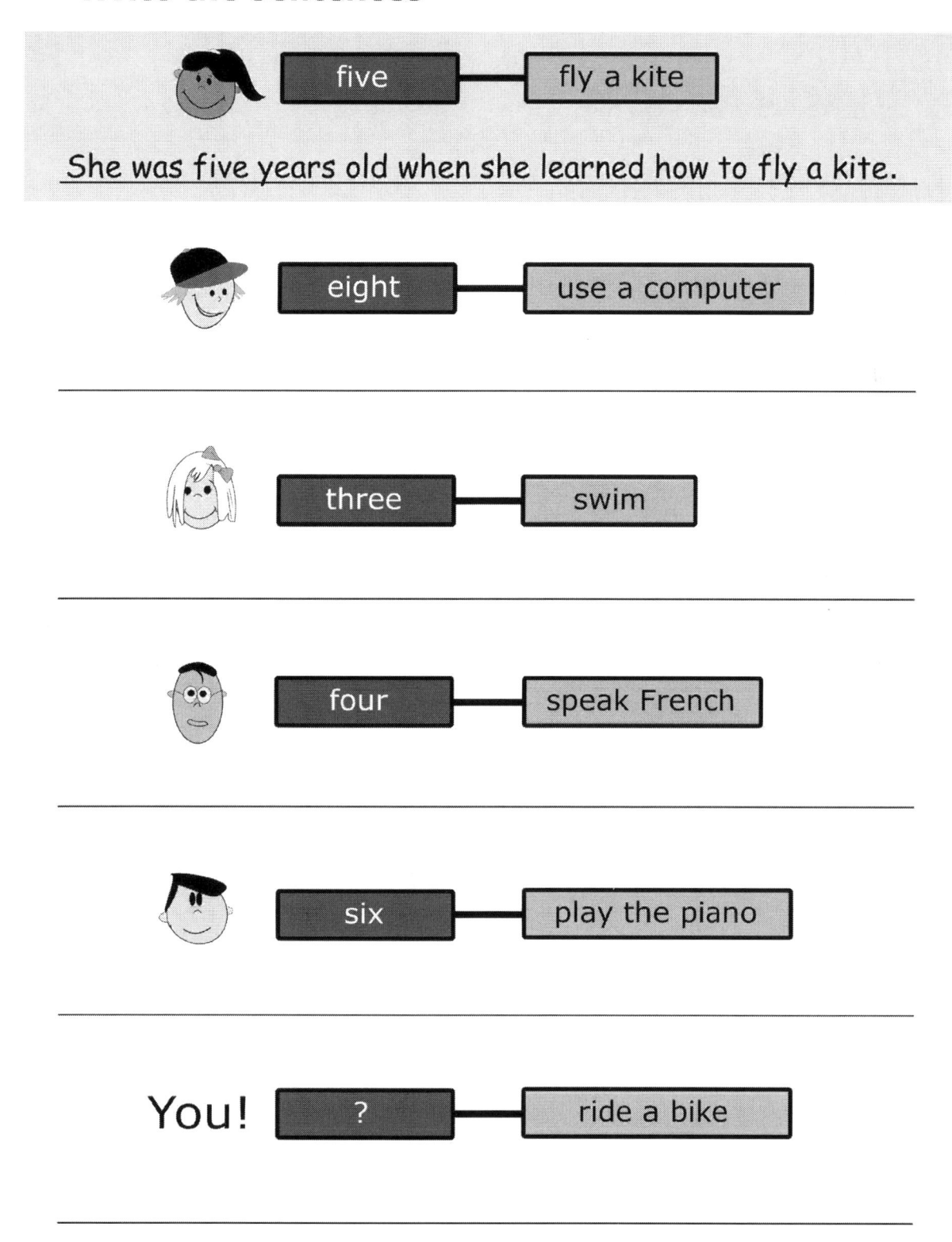

[five] — [fly a kite]

She was five years old when she learned how to fly a kite.

[eight] — [use a computer]

_____

[three] — [swim]

_____

[four] — [speak French]

_____

[six] — [play the piano]

_____

You! [?] — [ride a bike]

_____

Lesson 59: Capital cities

首都城市

> Is Beijing the capital city of Thailand?
> No, it isn't. Beijing is the capital city of China.

Section A — Words

1. **Washington, D.C./USA**
   华盛顿特区/美国
2. **London/England**
   伦敦/英国
3. **Paris/France**
   巴黎/法国
4. **Madrid/Spain**
   马德里/西班牙
5. **Bangkok/Thailand**
   曼谷/泰国
6. **Beijing/China**
   北京/中国
7. **Cape Town/South Africa**
   开普敦/南非
8. **Canberra/Australia**
   坎培拉/澳大利亚
9. **Wellington/New Zealand**
   威灵顿/纽西兰
10. **Ottawa/Canada**
    渥太华/加拿大

Section B — Make a sentence

Where would you like to travel to in the future?

I would like to travel to <u>Paris</u>.

I think <u>Paris</u> would be a <u>beautiful</u> city to visit.

<u>Paris</u> is the capital city of <u>France</u>.

Learn: beautiful, wonderful, great, fun

Section C — Make a question

Is <u>Paris</u> the capital city of <u>France</u>?
Yes, it is.

Is <u>Bangkok</u> the capital city of <u>China</u>?
No, it isn't. Bangkok is the capital city of Thailand.

Section D — Learn a verb

wait – waiting – waited – waited 等

I will **wait** to go to Australia to try meat pies.
They are **waiting** at the main train station in London.
He **waited** to see a doctor for one hour.
I have **waited** a long time to go to Canada.

Section E — Learn an idiom

Travel light

Meaning: To travel without bringing too many things.

"She always *travels light* when she goes to Europe."

Section F   Write

Trace and fill in the words

1. Where _____ you like to travel to _____ the future?

   I would _____ to travel _____ Madrid.

   I _____ Madrid would _____ a great place to visit.

   Madrid is _____ capital _____ of Spain.

2. Where would you _____ to _____ to in the future?

   I would _____ _____ travel to Bangkok.

   I think _____ would be a fun _____ to _____.

   Bangkok _____ the _____ city _____ Thailand.

3. Is Canberra _____ capital city _____ Australia?

   Yes, it _____.

4. Is Wellington the _____ _____ of Canada?

   No, it _____. Wellington is the _____ city of New Zealand.

5. Is _____ the _____ city _____ England?

   Yes, _____ _____.

6. _____ Paris _____ capital _____ of China?

   No, it _____. Paris is the _____ city of _____.

Section G   Let's have fun

Capital cities!

CROSSWORD PUZZLE

Across
1. Wellington is the capital city of _____.
2. Bangkok is the capital city of _____.
3. _____ is the capital city of Australia.

Down
4. _____ is the capital city of Canada.
5. Beijing is the capital city of _____.
6. Cape Town is the capital city of _____.
7. _____ is the capital city of England.
8. _____ is the capital city of Spain.

The capital city of the USA is _____.

The capital city of France is _____.

Lesson 60: Personalities

性格

> What is he like?
> He is a really interesting person. He isn't lazy.

Section A — Words

1. outgoing
   外向的
2. shy
   害羞的
3. generous
   慷慨的
4. studious
   好学的
5. lazy
   懒惰的
6. funny
   滑稽的
7. interesting
   有趣的
8. smart
   聪明的
9. easygoing
   随和的
10. serious
    严肃的

Section B — Make a sentence

What is <u>he</u> like?

He's a really <u>outgoing</u> person.

He isn't <u>shy</u>.

What are <u>they</u> like?

They're really <u>serious</u> people.

They aren't <u>funny</u>.

Section C — Make a question

Is she a <u>studious</u> person?
Yes, she is. / No, she isn't. She's a really <u>fun</u> person.

Are they <u>easygoing</u> people?
Yes, they are. / No, they aren't. They're really <u>serious</u> people.

Section D — Learn a verb

pay – paying – paid – paid 支付

My parents want to **pay** for dinner.
I'll be **paying** for the groceries this week.
I think you **paid** too much for this car!
I will have **paid** off my loan by next year.

Section E — Learn an idiom

(Not) be in the mood

Meaning: To (not) feel like doing something.

"We invited him to the movie, but he *wasn't in the mood*."

| Section F | Write |

Trace and fill in the words

1. What _____ he like?

He's a _____ funny person.

_____ isn't serious.

2. What is she like?

She's _____ really studious _____.

She _____ lazy.

3. Are you _____ outgoing person?

Yes, I _____.

4. Is he a smart _____?

No, _____ isn't. He's a _____ generous person.

5. Is she an easygoing _____?

Yes, _____ _____.

6. Are they outgoing _____?

No, they _____. They're _____ studious people.

7. Is he a shy person?

No _____ isn't. He is _____ outgoing _____.

8. Are they serious people?

Yes, _____ _____.

Section G | Let's have fun

Personalities!

Find the words!

```
J G E B W W B Q T L I B O O L D X I
X O T W K M T C X S M M L O T B H N
V U L E F N G K F O A O L S B S A T
R T O S A U S G A C P S P T U H I E
Y G Z E K S N S R P P M I U B Y W R
C O J H B W Y N T L U A P D L F L E
W I N E M H C G Y O N R J I B Y A S
K N P Q U I M J O D U T H O J Q Z T
X G W H Q O S E R I O U S U J Q Y I
G G E N E R O U S S N P W S X D S N
M N U N J G N C I I N G E T L P W G
D P K U Y Z Y Q Z P H N U W K H F G
```

o_tgo_n_
stu_iou_
s_y
la_y
s_a_t

f_n_y
ea_ygoi_g
g_ne_ou_
se_io_s
i_te_est_ng

Test 15   Lesson 57 - 60

Write the answer next to the letter "A"

A: ___ **1.** If you ___ do anything, what ___ you do?

a. can, will   b. could, will   c. would, could   d. could, would

A: ___ **2.** If you could buy a boat, ___ you? Yes, I ___.

a. will, would   b. would, would   c. would, will   d. will, will

A: ___ **3.** I ___ some cupcakes for the party, but nobody ate them.

a. brought   b. didn't bring   c. bring   d. bringing

A: ___ **4.** "My father and I love the ___ outdoors."

a. healthy   b. exciting   c. amazing   d. great

A: ___ **5.** I ___ five years old when I ___ how to ride a bike.

a. was, learned   b. am, learn   c. were, learning   d. is, learned

A: ___ **6.** Was he seven years old when he learned how to ski?

a. Yes, he were.   b. Yes, he was.   c. Yes, he would.   d. Yes, he, did.

A: ___ **7.** My grandmother ___ beautifully.

a. sing   b. singing   c. sings   d. were singing

A: ___ **8.** "He learned the ___ way when he rode without a helmet."

a. easy   b. difficult   c. terrible   d. hard

280

A: ___ **9.** I ___ Wellington would be a great place ___ visit.

a. feel, go   b. think, to   c. see, and   d. thought, do

A: ___ **10.** Is Madrid the capital city of Spain?

a. Yes, it was.   b. Yes it is.   c. Yes, is.   d. Yes, it is.

A: ___ **11.** I have been ___ for the bus for over 30 minutes.

a. waiting   b. waited   c. wait   d. be waiting

A: ___ **12.** "You should travel ___ when you go backpacking in Europe."

a. safe   b. slow   c. light   d. heavy

A: ___ **13.** He's ___ generous person.

a. a real   b. the really   c. really   d. a really

A: ___ **14.** I ___ too much for food when I was in Paris.

a. paying   b. paid   c. will pay   d. has paid

A: ___ **15.** Are ___ funny people? No, they aren't. ___ really shy people.

a. they, They   b. them, They're   c. they, They're   d. they, Their

A: ___ **16.** "I'm ___ mood for pizza."

a. in a   b. in the   c. on the   d. in this

Answers on page 463

Lesson 61: The body

身体

What happened to your finger?
I hurt my finger while playing volleyball.

Section A — Words

1. head
   头
2. shoulder
   肩膀
3. neck
   脖子
4. stomach
   胃
5. arm
   手臂
6. hand
   手
7. finger
   手指
8. leg
   腿
9. foot
   脚
10. toe
    脚趾

Section B — Make a sentence

What happened to your <u>shoulder</u>?

I hurt my shoulder while playing <u>baseball</u>.

What happened to his <u>leg</u>?

He hurt his leg while playing <u>soccer</u>.

Section C — Make a question

Did you hear about what happened to <u>Matthew</u>'s <u>hand</u>?
Yes, I did. / No, I didn't.

Did he hear about what happened to <u>Jessica</u>'s <u>finger</u>?
Yes, he did. / No, he didn't.

Section D — Learn a verb

hurt – hurting – hurt – hurt 伤害

Be careful not to **hurt** your toe on the step.

This pillow is **hurting** my neck.

Yesterday, I **hurt** my arm while skateboarding.

She had **hurt** her stomach, so she couldn't play volleyball.

Section E — Learn an idiom

Cost an arm and a leg

Meaning: When something is very expensive.

"Her vacation to Canberra *cost an arm and a leg*."

| Section F | Write |

Trace and fill in the words

1. What _____ to your neck?

   I hurt my _____ while playing _____.

2. What happened to _____ finger?

   She hurt her _____ while _____ golf.

3. _____ happened to their _____?

   They hurt _____ arms _____ playing volleyball.

4. What _____ _____ your _____?

   I _____ _____ hand while _____ cricket.

5. Did you hear about what happened to _____ stomach?

   Yes, _____ _____.

6. _____ he hear about _____ happened to Amy's neck?

   No, _____ _____.

7. Did _____ hear _____ what _____ to Kevin's shoulder?

   _____ they _____.

8. _____ she _____ about what _____ to John's leg?

   _____, _____ _____.

| Section G | Let's have fun |

The body!

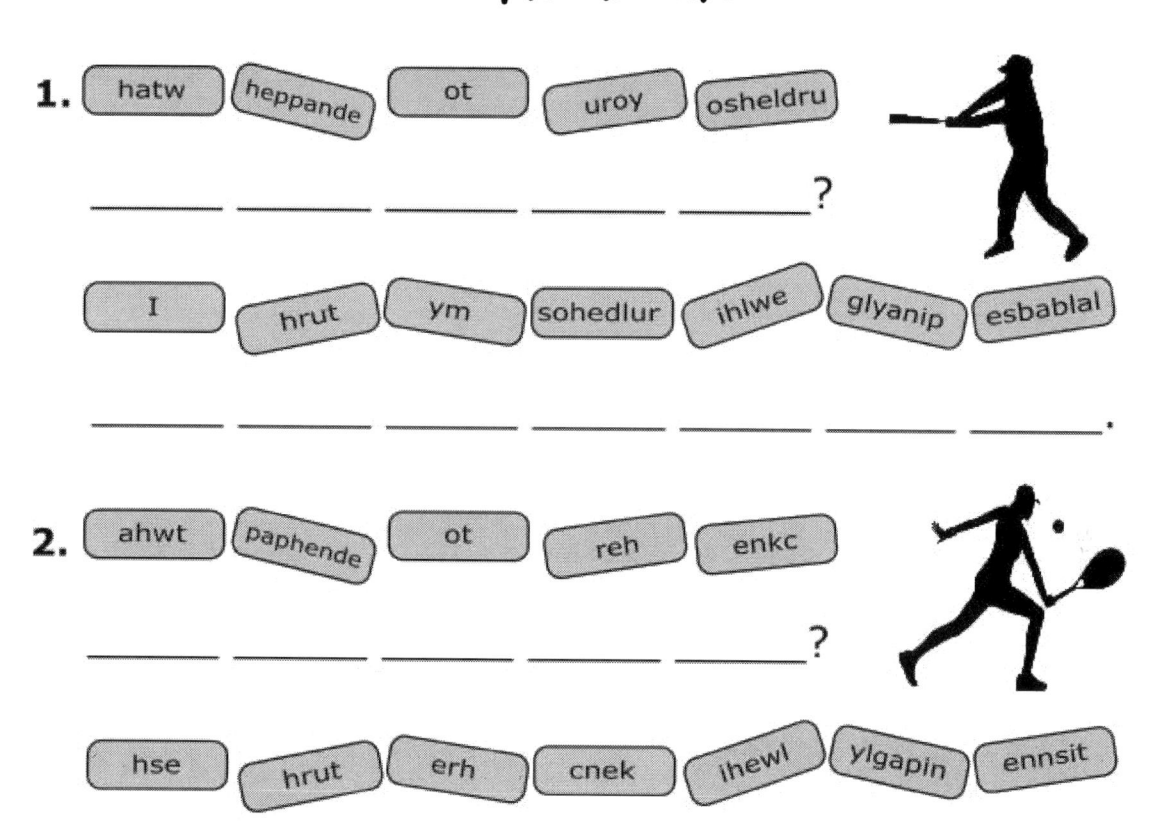

1. hatw | heppande | ot | uroy | osheldru

___ ___ ___ ___ ___?

I | hrut | ym | sohedlur | ihlwe | glyanip | esbablal

___ ___ ___ ___ ___ ___ ___.

2. ahwt | paphende | ot | reh | enkc

___ ___ ___ ___ ___?

hse | hrut | erh | cnek | ihewl | ylgapin | ennsit

___ ___ ___ ___ ___ ___ ___.

Complete the words

h__a__   st__m __ __h

h__n__   f__ __t

s__ou__d__r   __r__

l__ __   __ __e

f__n__e__   n__ __k

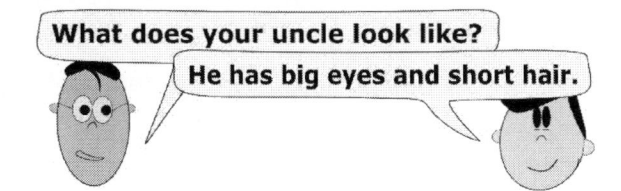

Lesson 62: The face

脸

What does your uncle look like?
He has big eyes and short hair.

Section A   Words

1. **eye**
   眼睛
2. **eyebrow**
   眉毛
3. **eyelash**
   眼睫毛
4. **nose**
   鼻子
5. **chin**
   下巴
6. **cheek**
   脸颊
7. **mouth**
   嘴巴
8. **lip**
   嘴唇
9. **hair**
   头发
10. **ear**
    耳朵

Section B   Make a sentence

What does your <u>sister</u> look like?
She has <u>blue</u> <u>eyes</u> and <u>curly</u> <u>hair</u>.

What does your <u>brother</u> look like?
He has a <u>pointy</u> chin and a <u>long</u> <u>nose</u>.

Learn: curly, straight, short, long, pointy, big, small

Section C — Make a question

Does your <u>father</u> have a <u>big</u> <u>mouth</u>?
Yes, he does. / No, he doesn't. It's <u>small</u>.

Does your <u>mother</u> have <u>small</u> <u>lips</u>?
Yes, she does. / No, she doesn't. They're <u>big</u>.

Section D — Learn a verb

face – facing – faced – faced 面对

I need to **face** my boss on Monday morning.
We have been **facing** many problems recently.
I was **faced** with a challenge at work today.
She hasn't **faced** the teacher yet.

Section E — Learn an idiom

Face to face

Meaning: To be in the same place when you meet someone.

"It was very important, so I met my friend *face to face*."

| Section F | Write |

Trace and fill in the words

1. What _____ your aunt _____ like?

   She _____ a big mouth _____ small ears.

2. _____ does your cousin look _____?

   He has _____ cheeks and _____ hair.

3. _____ _____ your grandfather _____ _____?

   _____ has brown _____ and _____ lips.

4. _____ _____ your uncle _____ _____?

   _____ has _____ _____ and _____ eyelashes.

5. _____ your father _____ a pointy chin?

   Yes, he _____.

6. Does _____ mother have _____ eyebrows?

   No, _____ _____.

7. Does _____ grandmother have a _____ nose?

   Yes, _____ _____.

8. _____ your _____ have _____ hair?

   _____, _____ _____.

Section G | Let's have fun

The face!

Unscramble the words and connect them to the face

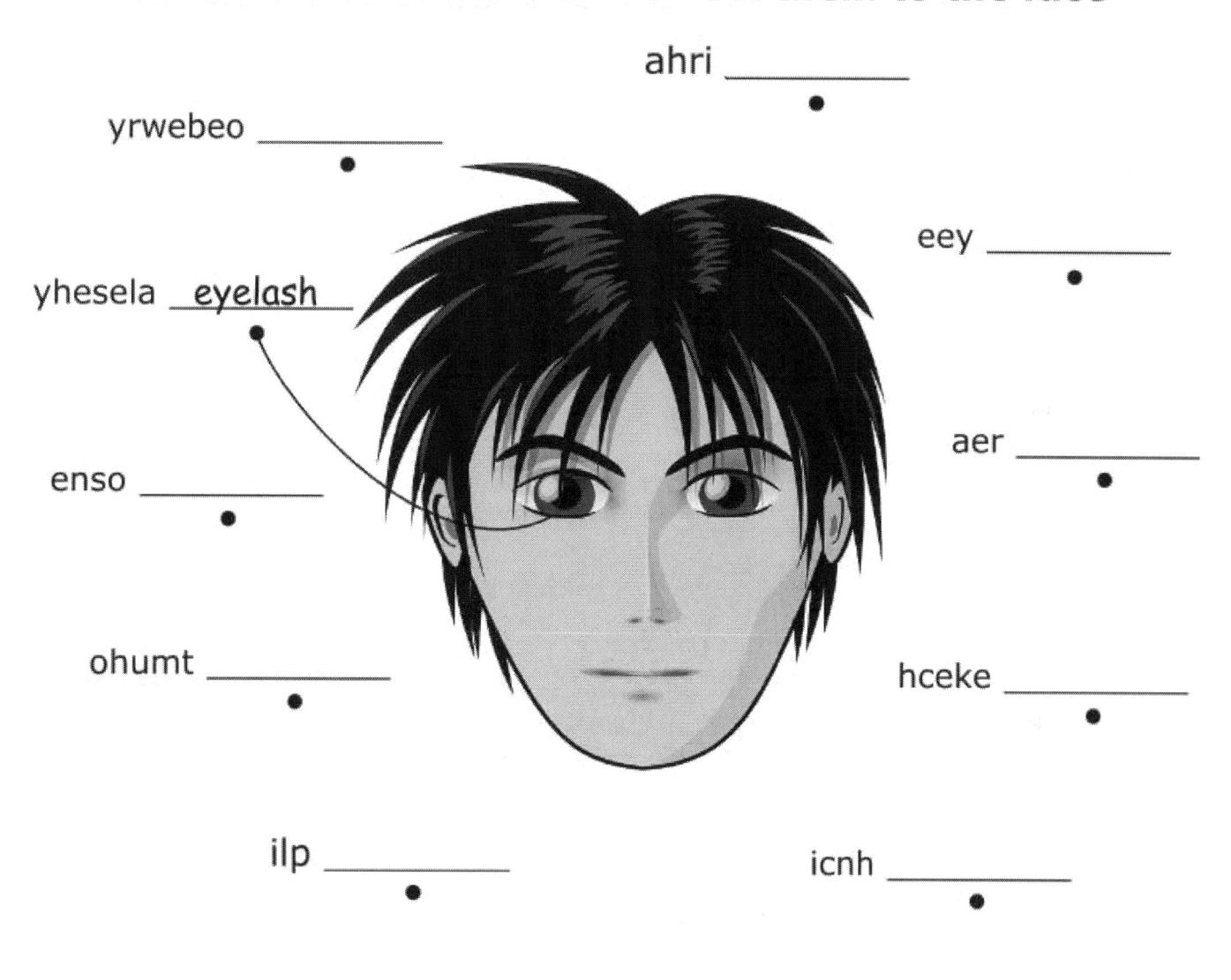

ahri _____

yrwebeo _____

eey _____

yhesela _eyelash_

aer _____

enso _____

ohumt _____

hceke _____

ilp _____

icnh _____

What does your friend look like?

_____

Does your friend have brown hair?

_____

Lesson 63: Actions

动作

Which river were you running by?
I was running by the river that I found last week.

Section A — Words

1. walk
   走路
2. run
   跑步
3. swim
   游泳
4. jump
   跳
5. sleep
   睡觉
6. sit
   坐
7. stand
   站
8. fall
   跌倒
9. kneel
   跪
10. crawl
    爬

Section B — Make a sentence

Which <u>bridge</u> was he <u>walking</u> <u>under</u>?

He was walking under the <u>brown</u> bridge that he <u>found</u> <u>yesterday</u>.

Which <u>tent</u> were they <u>sleeping</u> <u>in</u>?

They were sleeping in the <u>pink</u> tent that they <u>bought</u> <u>last month</u>.

Learn: on, over, under, by, in, at

| Section C | Make a question |

Were you <u>jumping</u> <u>over</u> the <u>fence</u> that you fixed <u>two weeks ago</u>?
Yes, I was. / No, I wasn't.

Was she <u>swimming</u> <u>in</u> the <u>lake</u> that she found <u>last year</u>?
Yes, she was. / No, she wasn't.

| Section D | Learn a verb |

realize – realizing – realized – realized 明白

You will **realize** walking over the bridge is not easy.
I'm now **realizing** that I shouldn't have gone running.
He **realized** that there was nobody swimming at the beach.
I hadn't **realized** that you had fallen down.

| Section E | Learn an idiom |

All talk and no action

Meaning: Someone who talks a lot, but doesn't do anything.

"He said he did many things, but he was *all talk and no action*."

Section F Write

Trace and fill in the words

1. Which house was _____ standing by?

   He _____ standing by the white _____ that he painted _____ July.

2. _____ pool was she _____ in?

   _____ was swimming _____ the green _____ that she _____ last week.

3. _____ chair were _____ _____ on?

   I _____ _____ on the blue _____ that _____ _____ last _____.

4. _____ you kneeling _____ the mailbox that you fixed three days ago?

   Yes, _____ _____.

5. _____ he running _____ the park that he _____ last _____?

   No, _____ _____.

6. Were _____ crawling _____ the table that _____ bought _____ _____?

   No, _____ _____.

292

Section G — Let's have fun

Actions!

Make sentences with the words

brother + sleep + in + bedroom + cleaned + yesterday

My brother was sleeping in the bedroom that he cleaned yesterday.

sister + walk + over + bridge + found + last month

_____

friend + run + by + river + discovered + two weeks ago

_____

dog + crawl + under + fence + broke + last night

_____

teacher + swim + at + beach + talked about + last year

_____

father + sit + on + chair + made + ten years ago

_____

uncle + stand + in + tent + fixed + this morning

_____

aunt + kneel + on + rug + bought + last week

_____

Lesson 64: Time

时间

Which time are you going to arrive?
I'm going to arrive at nine o'clock.

Section A — Words

1. **half past**
   三十分
2. **a quarter to**
   四十五分
3. **a quarter past**
   十五分
4. **ten minutes past**
   十分
5. **ten minutes to**
   五十分
6. **o'clock**
   点
7. **second**
   秒
8. **minute**
   分钟
9. **hour**
   小时
10. **midnight**
    半夜

Section B — Make a sentence

What time are you going to arrive?

I'm going to arrive at a quarter to three.

How long are you going to stay?

I'm probably going to stay for 30 minutes.

Learn: probably, arrive, leave, stay, for

Section C — Make a question

Do you know what time he's going to <u>arrive</u>?
Yes, I do. He's probably going to arrive at <u>half past</u> <u>ten</u>.
/ No, I don't. He didn't tell me.

Do you know what time they're going to <u>leave</u>?
Yes, I do. They're probably going to leave at <u>midnight</u>.
/ No, I don't. They didn't tell me.

Section D — Learn a verb

arrive – arriving – arrived – arrived 到达

The manager always **arrives** five minutes early.

She'll be **arriving** in twenty minutes.

We **arrived** at the cinema at a quarter past seven.

I will have **arrived** at the office by nine o'clock.

Section E — Learn an idiom

Have a hard time

Meaning: When something is very difficult for you.

"He was *having a hard time* with math, so he had to study more."

Section F — Write

Trace and fill in the words

1. What _____ are you going to _____?

I'm _____ to arrive at a _____ to four.

2. _____ time is he _____ to arrive?

He's going to _____ at _____ past eight.

3. _____ long _____ he going to _____?

_____ probably _____ to stay for one _____.

4. How _____ are _____ _____ to stay?

They're _____ going to _____ for two _____.

5. Do you know what _____ you're _____ to leave?

Yes, I do. I'm _____ going to _____ at two _____.

6. Do you _____ what time they're _____ to _____?

No, I _____. _____ didn't tell _____.

7. _____ you know _____ time we're going to _____?

Yes, I _____. _____ probably _____ to arrive at _____ _____.

8. Do you know what _____ he's _____ to _____?

No, _____ _____. _____ didn't tell _____.

Section G Let's have fun

Time!

Connect the times

3:45	• seven o'clock
5:15	• half past eight
7:00	• a quarter past five
8:30	• a quarter to four
9:10	• ten minutes to two
1:50	• ten minutes past nine

Write the times

7:45 _____

2:15 _____

11:00 _____

1:30 _____

9:50 _____

6:10 _____

Answer the questions

What time are you going to arrive?

_____

How long are you going to stay?

_____

Test 16   Lesson 61 - 64

Write the answer next to the letter "A"

A: ___ **1.** She hurt her ___ while playing ___.

a. arm, game   b. hand, out   c. foot, hockey   d. cost, legs

A: ___ **2.** Did you ___ about what ___ to Tom's finger?

a. hear, happen   b. heard, happen   c. hear, happened   d. hears, had

A: ___ **3.** Be careful not to ___ your head on the door.

a. hurt   b. hurts   c. hurting   d. hurtful

A: ___ **4.** "His expensive new car cost him an ___ and a ___."

a. ear, mouth   b. arm, leg   c. eye, foot   d. arm, hand

A: ___ **5.** What ___ your father ___ like?

a. is, look   b. can, looks   c. were, looking   d. does, look

A: ___ **6.** She has a ___ chin and a ___ nose.

a. long, small   b. big, curly   c. lip, straight   d. best, no

A: ___ **7.** ___ your sister ___ straight hair?

a. Do, is   b. Does, have   c. Do, has   d. Does, is

A: ___ **8.** "It was big news, so I told her ___ to ___."

a. met, her   b. face, face   c. straight, face   d. face, her

A: ___ **9.** He was ___ by the ___ road that he found last year.

a. over, fall　　b. walks, black　　c. jump, green　　d. walking, old

A: ___ **10.** ___ you sleeping by the tree that you ___ last week?

a. Was, found　　b. Is, find　　c. Were, found　　d. Did, finding

A: ___ **11.** They ___ it was the same bridge as before.

a. realized　　b. realizes　　c. realizing　　d. were realized

A: ___ **12.** "I didn't think he'd do it, because he's all ___ and no ___."

a. talk, action　　b. say, doing　　c. speak, done　　d. talks, actions

A: ___ **13.** He's going to ___ at a quarter ___ nine.

a. arriving, to　　b. arrives, past　　c. arrival, half　　d. arrive, to

A: ___ **14.** I'm probably going to ___ for 12 ___.

a. arrive, hour　　b. stay, minutes　　c. staying, midnight　　d. stays, hours

A: ___ **15.** The boss always ___ 20 minutes early.

a. arrive　　b. arriving　　c. arrives　　d. arrival

A: ___ **16.** "He had a very ___ time on the science test."

a. soft　　b. late　　c. arrival　　d. hard

Answers on page 463

Lesson 65: Tastes

味觉

> How do the hot dogs taste at that place?
> They taste really delicious, so I recommend them.

Section A — Words

1. **sweet**
   甜的
2. **sour**
   酸的
3. **bitter**
   苦的
4. **salty**
   咸的
5. **spicy**
   辣的
6. **delicious**
   美味的
7. **yummy**
   好吃的
8. **oily**
   油腻的
9. **yucky**
   不好吃的
10. **disgusting**
    恶心的

Section B — Make a sentence

How does the <u>chicken</u> taste at that place?

Unfortunately, it tastes <u>oily</u>, so I don't recommend it.

How do the <u>noodles</u> taste at that place?

They taste really <u>spicy</u>, so I recommend them.

Learn: so, really, unfortunately, definitely

Section C — Make a question

Do you recommend the <u>ice cream</u>?
Yes, I definitely do. / No, I don't. It's too <u>sweet</u>.

Do you recommend the <u>tacos</u>?
Yes, I definitely do. / No, I don't. They're too <u>salty</u>.

Section D — Learn a verb

recommend – recommending – recommended – recommended 推荐

He **recommends** that tea house near his school.

I've been **recommending** that restaurant for years.

She **recommended** eating the delicious pie to me.

The coffee at that café had been **recommended** many times.

Section E — Learn an idiom

Leave a bad taste in <u>one's</u> mouth

Meaning: To have a bad memory about something.

"His unhappy birthday party *left a bad taste in* his *mouth*."

Section F   Write

Trace and fill in the words

1. How _____ the juice taste at that _____?

Unfortunately, it _____ sour, so I don't _____ it.

2. _____ do the french fries _____ at _____ place?

_____, _____ taste _____, so I don't recommend _____.

3. How _____ the coffee _____ at that _____?

It _____ really _____, so I _____ _____.

4. _____ _____ the salad taste at _____ _____?

_____ _____ really yummy, so I _____ _____.

5. _____ you recommend the bananas?

No, I _____. _____ too bitter.

6. Do you _____ the sausage?

No, _____ _____. _____ too _____.

7. Does _____ _____ _____ soup?

Yes, he definitely _____.

8. Do _____ _____ the _____?

Yes, _____ _____ _____.

Section G   Let's have fun

Tastes!

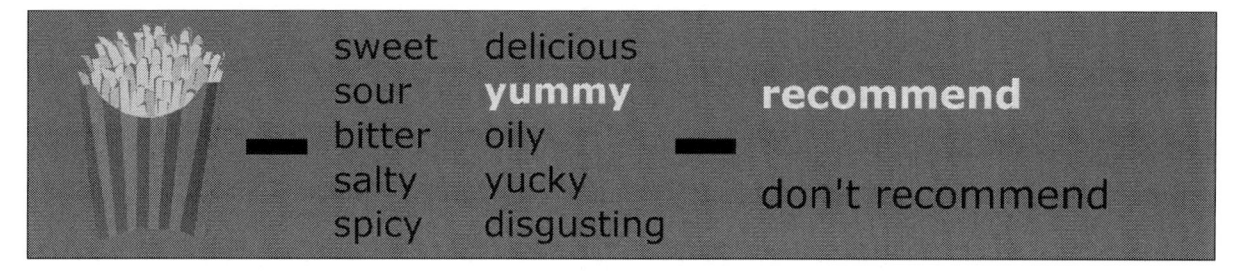

sweet	delicious	
sour	**yummy**	**recommend**
bitter	oily	
salty	yucky	don't recommend
spicy	disgusting	

How do the french fries taste at that place?
They taste really yummy, so I recommend them.

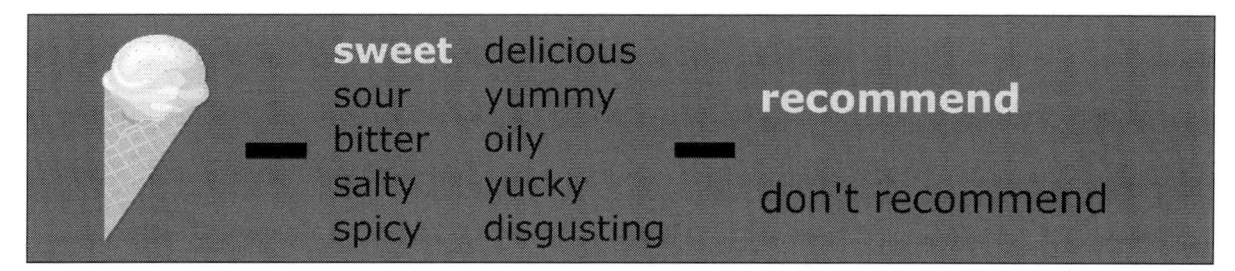

sweet	delicious	
sour	yummy	**recommend**
bitter	oily	
salty	yucky	don't recommend
spicy	disgusting	

How does the ice cream taste at that place?
_____

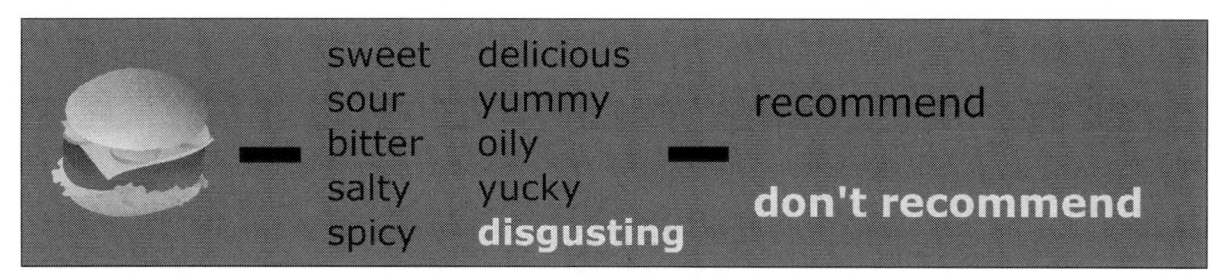

sweet	delicious	
sour	yummy	recommend
bitter	oily	
salty	yucky	**don't recommend**
spicy	**disgusting**	

How do the hamburgers taste at that place?
_____

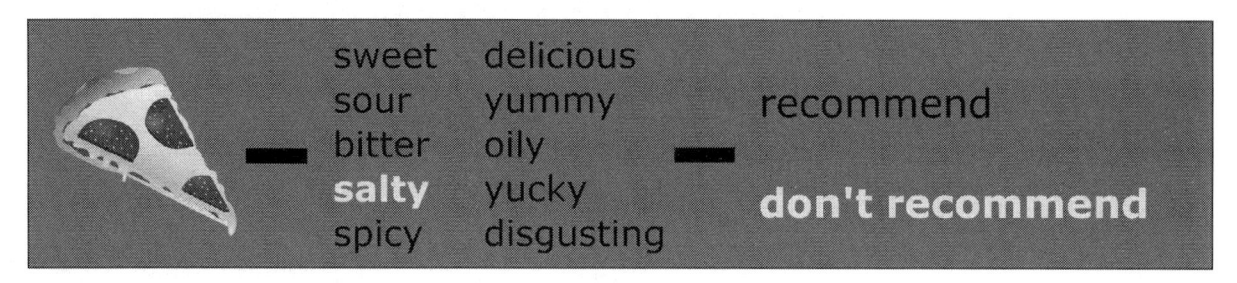

sweet	delicious	
sour	yummy	recommend
bitter	oily	
salty	yucky	**don't recommend**
spicy	disgusting	

How does the pizza taste at that place?
_____

Lesson 66: Condiments

调味料

What do you like to add to your sandwich? I like to add some salt and mayonnaise to my sandwich.

Section A — Words

1. ketchup
   番茄酱
2. mustard
   芥末
3. soy sauce
   酱油
4. vinegar
   醋
5. sugar
   糖
6. salt
   盐巴
7. pepper
   胡椒
8. chili sauce
   辣椒酱
9. mayonnaise
   美乃滋酱
10. barbecue sauce
    沙茶酱

Section B — Make a sentence

What do you like to add to your <u>steak</u>?

I like to add some <u>salt</u> and <u>pepper</u> to my steak.

What does he like to add to his <u>hamburger</u>?

He likes to add some <u>ketchup</u> and <u>mustard</u> to his hamburger.

Learn: add

Section C | Make a question

Do you like to add <u>soy sauce</u> to your <u>rice</u>?
Yes, I really like to add soy sauce.

Doesn't he like to add <u>vinegar</u> to his <u>salad</u>?
No, he doesn't like to add vinegar.

Section D | Learn a verb

add – adding – added – added 加

I always **add** a little sugar to my coffee.
She is **adding** a new photo to her website.
David **added** some chili sauce to his hot dog.
He hasn't **added** any condiments to the table yet.

Section E | Learn an idiom

Spice <u>something</u> up

Meaning: To make something more interesting.

"The teacher *spiced* the class *up* by telling some jokes."

| Section F | Write |

Trace and fill in the words

1. What do you like to _____ to your vegetables?

I like to add _____ salt and chili sauce to my _____.

2. What _____ he like to add to _____ burritos?

He _____ to _____ some pepper and _____ to his burritos.

3. _____ do _____ like to add to their _____?

_____ like to add _____ and _____ to their tacos.

4. What _____ she _____ to add to _____ hot dogs?

She _____ to add sugar and _____ to her _____.

5. Do you _____ to add _____ to your onion rings?

Yes, I _____ like to _____ ketchup.

6. _____ she like to _____ _____ to her pancake?

No, _____ _____ like to _____ soy sauce.

7. _____ you like to _____ vinegar to your _____?

No, I don't _____ _____ add _____.

8. Do they _____ to add mustard to _____ _____?

Yes, _____ _____ like to _____ _____.

Section G — Let's have fun

Condiments!

1.
- What do you like to add to your hamburger?
- I like to add ketchup and mustard to my hamburger.

2.
- What do you like to add to your hot dog?
- It like to add chili sauce to my hot dog.

3.
- What do you like to add to your steak?
- I like to add salt and pepper to my steak.

4.
- What do you like to add to your salad?
- I like to add soy sauce and vinegar to my salad.

True of False? Circle the answer

1. She likes to add ketchup and mustard to her hamburger.   **True   False**

2. She likes to add barbecue sauce to her hot dog.   **True   False**

3. He likes to add salt and mayonnaise to his steak.   **True   False**

4. He likes to add soy sauce and vinegar to his salad.   **True   False**

Circle Yes or No

1. Does she like to add ketchup and soy sauce to her hamburger?   **Yes   No**

2. Does she like to add chili sauce to her hot dog?   **Yes   No**

3. Does he like to add salt and pepper to his steak?   **Yes   No**

4. Does he like to add soy sauce and vinegar to his salad?   **Yes   No**

Lesson 67: At a restaurant

在餐厅

> What was your opinion of the restaurant last night?
> I thought the chef was excellent, but the servers were rude.

Section A — Words

1. menu
   菜单
2. server
   服务员
3. chef
   厨师
4. takeout
   外带
5. beverage
   饮料
6. napkin
   餐巾
7. buffet
   自助餐
8. main meal
   主餐
9. dessert
   点心
10. bill
    帐单

Section B — Make a sentence

What was your opinion of the restaurant last night?
I thought the <u>beverages</u> were <u>delicious</u>, but the <u>main meal</u> was <u>disgusting</u>.

What was your opinion of the restaurant last night?
I thought the <u>servers</u> were <u>friendly</u>, but the <u>menu</u> was <u>expensive</u>.

Learn: opinion

Section C | Make a question

Was the <u>chef</u> <u>good</u> last night?
Yes, he was very good, but I didn't like the <u>dessert</u>.

Wasn't the <u>buffet</u> <u>yummy</u> last night?
Yes, it was very yummy, but I didn't like the <u>beverages</u>.

Section D | Learn a verb

order – ordering – ordered – ordered 订购

I will **order** takeout for tonight's dinner.
He was **ordering** pizza when we got home.
She **ordered** three cakes for dessert.
We haven't **ordered** dinner yet.

Section E | Learn an idiom

Dine out

Meaning: To go out to eat at a restaurant, not at home.

"Their anniversary was a special day, so they decided to *dine out*."

Section F | **Write**

Trace and fill in the words

1. What _____ your opinion of the _____ last night?

I thought the _____ were _____, but the buffet was yummy.

2. _____ was your _____ of the restaurant last night?

I _____ the main meals _____ yummy, but the _____ was _____.

3. _____ _____ your opinion of the _____ _____ night?

I _____ the _____ were _____, but the _____ was _____.

4. Wasn't the server good last _____?

Yes, _____ was very _____, but I didn't like the _____.

5. Was the main meal _____ _____ night?

Yes, it _____ very _____, but I _____ like the _____.

6. Was the takeout _____ _____ _____?

Yes, it was very _____, but I didn't like the _____.

Section G Let's have fun

At a restaurant!

Find the words!

```
q a j j i n p y d e s s e r t p x v
j w q j s k g t q q i i p b y r m n
s t t q g e h k i b m b v e r l d z
b u a w b m r m k c e u z v o z s m
v t r k t c a v h j n f n e t x i r
e e w t e i h i e k u f o r b c z o
z u k z o o w e n r m e b a l d i c
p p t e g b u r f m c t i g t c q p
q w b d g q k t e v e x l e x l g j
f s h s v s h x d b u a l r a x a z
f m f p a t n a p k i n l c o t m m
w b f f m q g r t f r s c y y v p k
```

b_v_r_ge   m_in m_ _l
b_l_   m_n_
b_f_e_   n_pk_n
c_e_   se_v_r
d_ss_r_   t_ke_u_

Lesson 68: Tableware

餐具

> I'd like to set the table. Where are the bowls kept?
> I think the bowls are kept in the top cupboard. I saw Mom put them there this morning.

Section A — Words

1. **knife**
   刀子
2. **fork**
   叉子
3. **spoon**
   汤匙
4. **chopsticks**
   筷子
5. **plate**
   盘子
6. **bowl**
   碗
7. **glass**
   玻璃杯
8. **placemat**
   餐垫
9. **toothpick**
   牙签
10. **tablecloth**
    桌布

Section B — Make a sentence

I'd like to set the table. Where are the <u>spoons</u> kept? I think the spoons are kept in the <u>top</u> cupboard. I saw <u>Mom</u> put them there last week.

I'd like to set the table. Where is the <u>tablecloth</u> kept? I think the tablecloth is kept in the <u>bottom</u> cupboard. I saw <u>Dad</u> put it there last week.

Learn: top, bottom, set the table

Section C — Make a question

Do you know where the <u>placemats</u> are?
Yes, I think they're in the <u>top</u> cupboard. / No, I don't.

Do you know where the <u>knife</u> is?
Yes, I think it's in the <u>bottom</u> cupboard. / No, I don't.

Section D — Learn a verb

misplace – misplacing – misplaced – misplaced 错置

Don't **misplace** your napkin.

He's always **misplacing** the placemats.

I **misplaced** my favorite bowl again.

She has **misplaced** all of the chopsticks.

Section E — Learn an idiom

Like a hot knife through butter

Meaning: Something that is quick and easy to do.

"The test was easy because he studied hard, so he went through it *like a hot knife through butter*."

Section F   Write

Trace and fill in the words

1. I'd like to set the _____. Where are the _____ kept?

   I _____ the plates are kept in the top _____. I saw

   Dad put them _____ last week.

2. _____ like to _____ the table. Where are the glasses

   _____?

   I think the _____ are kept in the bottom cupboard. I

   _____ Sarah put _____ there last _____.

3. I'd _____ to set _____ table. Where _____ the

   bowls _____?

   I think the _____ are kept in the _____ cupboard. I

   saw Michelle _____ them there _____ week.

4. Do _____ know where the placemats _____?

   Yes, I _____ they're _____ the top cupboard.

5. _____ you _____ where _____ knife is?

   No, _____ _____.

6. Do you know _____ the toothpicks _____?

   Yes, I _____ _____ in the bottom _____.

314

Section G Let's have fun

Tableware!

Answer the questions

[bowl] — [bottom] — [Dad] — [last Friday]

1. I'd like to set the table. Where is the bowl kept?
   <u>I think the bowl is kept in the bottom cupboard.</u>
   <u>I saw dad put it there last Monday.</u>

[plates] — [top] — [Mom] — [last night]

2. I'd like to set the table. Where are the plates kept?

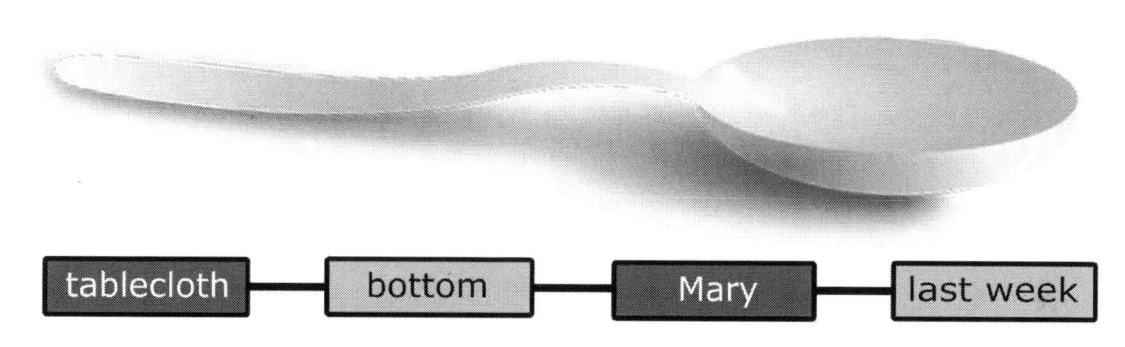

_____

[tablecloth] — [bottom] — [Mary] — [last week]

3. I'd like to set the table. Where is the tablecloth kept?

_____

[forks] — [top] — [John] — [yesterday]

4. I'd like to set the table. Where are the forks kept?

_____

[spoon] — [bottom] — [Susan] — [last Monday]

5. I'd like to set the table. Where is the spoon kept?

_____

Test 17　　Lesson 65 - 68

Write the answer next to the letter "A"

A: ___ 1. They ___ really ___, so I recommend them.

a. taste, yummy　　b. tastes, spicy　　c. tasted, yucky　　d. tasting, sour

A: ___ 2. Do you recommend ___? Yes, I ___.

a. pancake, do　b. the pancakes, do　c. pancakes, can　d. pancake, will

A: ___ 3. He ___ the cake to me at the party last week.

a. recommends　　b. recommended　　c. recommending　　d. recommend

A: ___ 4. "The terrible vacation left a bad ___ in his mouth."

a. tasting　　　　b. tastes　　　　c. taste　　　　d. tasteful

A: ___ 5. She likes to ___ vinegar and chili sauce ___ her rice.

a. adding, on　　b. adds, to　　c. added, on　　d. add, to

A: ___ 6. ___ he like to ___ mayonnaise to his sandwich?

a. Doesn't, add　　b. Don't, add　　c. Do, add　　d. Does, adding

A: ___ 7. He was ___ videos to his website.

a. add　　　　b. adds　　　　c. adding　　　　d. added

A: ___ 8. "She ___ her weekends by taking dance lessons."

a. spiced up　　　b. spiced on　　　c. spiced in　　　d. spicing up

316

A: ___ **9.** I thought the chef was ___, but the bill was ___.

a. cooking, food   b. nice, nice   c. great, expensive   d. off, on

A: ___ **10.** It was very ___, but I didn't like the ___.

a. buffet, food   b. takeout, chef   c. server, napkin   d. yummy, dessert

A: ___ **11.** They have ___ from that restaurant many times.

a. order   b. ordered   c. orders   d. ordering

A: ___ **12.** "Because it was a special birthday, they decided to ___."

a. dine up   b. dine out   c. dine over   d. dine by

A: ___ **13.** He'd like to ___ the table. Where are the spoons ___?

a. sets, kept   b. setting, at   c. set, kept   d. set, keep

A: ___ **14.** Do you know where the ___?

a. glass are   b. glasses are   c. glasses kept   d. glass kept

A: ___ **15.** She is always ___ the chopsticks.

a. misplacing   b. misplaced   c. misplaces   d. misplace

A: ___ **16.** "She completed the easy test like a hot ___ through ___."

a. knives, water   b. spoon, bother   c. knife, butter   d. fork, cutter

Answers on page 463

Lesson 69: Kitchenware

厨房用品

> What do you want me to do with the whisk when I'm finished?
> You can leave it in the sink.

Section A — Words

1. **spatula**
   锅铲
2. **can opener**
   开罐器
3. **whisk**
   打蛋器
4. **peeler**
   削皮刀
5. **rolling pin**
   擀面杖
6. **plastic wrap**
   保鲜膜
7. **oven mitt**
   隔热手套
8. **tongs**
   夹子
9. **dishcloth**
   抹布
10. **dish soap**
    洗碗精

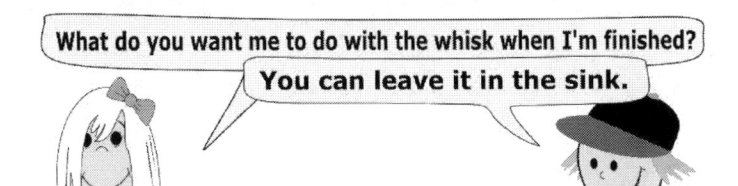

Section B — Make a sentence

What do you want me to do with the <u>spatula</u> when I'm finished?
You can leave it <u>in</u> the <u>sink</u>.

What do you want her to do with the <u>dish soap</u> when she's finished?
She can leave it <u>by</u> the <u>microwave oven</u>.

Section C — Make a question

Have you finished with the <u>rolling pin</u> yet?
Yes, I have. I put it <u>in</u> the <u>rice cooker</u>. / No, I haven't.

Has he finished with the <u>oven mitts</u> yet?
Yes, he has. He put them <u>on</u> the <u>oven</u>. / No, he hasn't.

Section D — Learn a verb

fry – frying – fried – fried 炒

Use the spatula to **fry** some eggs.

Mom is **frying** some hash browns for breakfast.

I **fried** some fish with the tongs.

The sausages can be **fried** in the frying pan.

Section E — Learn an idiom

Whisk <u>someone</u> / <u>something</u> away

Meaning: To move someone or something away quickly.

"The firemen came and *whisked* her *away* from the fire."

Section F Write

Trace and fill in the words

1. What do you _____ me to do with _____ dish soap

   when I'm _____?

   You can _____ _____ by the oven.

2. What do _____ want _____ to do with the rolling pin

   when he's _____?

   _____ can leave _____ in the _____.

3. _____ do you _____ her to do _____ the peeler

   _____ _____ done with _____?

   She can _____ it _____ the microwave oven.

4. Have you _____ with the tongs yet?

   Yes, _____ have. I _____ them by the stove.

5. _____ she finished _____ the spatulas yet?

   Yes, _____ has. She put _____ in the rice cooker.

6. Has _____ finished with _____ plastic wrap yet?

   Yes, _____ _____. He put _____ by the oven.

7. Has he _____ with _____ dish soap _____?

   No, _____ _____.

Section G   Let's have fun

Kitchenware!

Answer the questions using the information in the picture

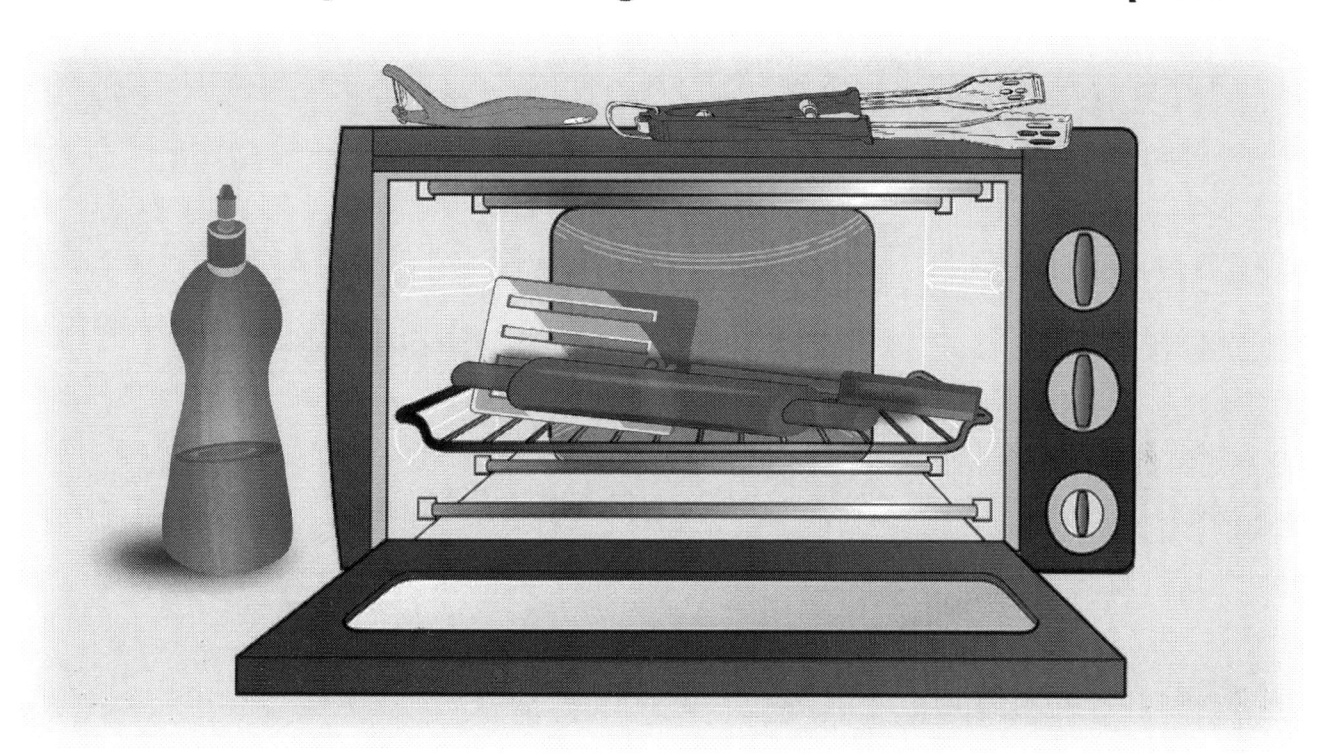

1. What do you want me to do with the rolling pin when I'm finished?
   You can _____ it _____ the oven.

2. What do you want him to do with the dish soap when he's finished?
   _____

3. What do you want her to do with the spatula when she's finished?
   _____

4. What do you want them to do with the peeler when they're finished?
   _____

5. What do you want Kevin to do with the tongs when he's finished?
   _____

Lesson 70: Home appliances

家电

What did you end up getting at the electronics store?
I got the heater instead of the kettle.

Section A — Words

1. **air conditioner**
   冷气机
2. **dishwasher**
   洗碗机
3. **electric fan**
   电风扇
4. **heater**
   暖气机
5. **telephone**
   电话
6. **stereo**
   音响
7. **iron**
   熨斗
8. **vacuum cleaner**
   吸尘器
9. **kettle**
   水壶
10. **blow dryer**
    吹风机

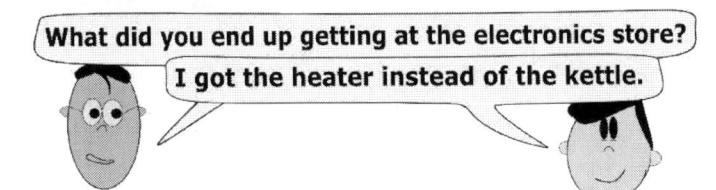

Section B — Make a sentence

What did he end up getting at the electronics store?

He got the <u>air conditioner</u> instead of the <u>electric fan</u>.

What will he end up getting at the electronics store?

He will get the <u>kettle</u> instead of the <u>blow dryer</u>.

Learn: end up, instead of

Section C — Make a question

Did you end up getting the <u>vacuum cleaner</u>?
Yes, I did. / No, I got the <u>heater</u> instead.

Will you end up getting the <u>iron</u>?
Yes, I will. / No, I'll get the <u>telephone</u> instead.

Section D — Learn a verb

repair – repairing – repaired – repaired 修理

My brother is going to **repair** the broken stereo.

He will be **repairing** the dishwasher tomorrow.

He **repaired** the old heater before winter.

I will have **repaired** the telephone by Sunday.

Section E — Learn an idiom

Iron out

Meaning: To fix some problems or difficulties.

"My presentation is almost finished. I just have to *iron out* a few small things."

| Section F | Write |

Trace and fill in the words

1. What _____ you end up getting at the _____ store?

   I got the _____ instead of _____ stereo.

2. _____ will she end up _____ at the electronics store?

   She _____ get the heater _____ of the _____.

3. What will he end up _____ at the _____ _____?

   _____ will get the _____ _____ of the _____.

4. What did he _____ up _____ at the electronics store?

   _____ _____ the _____ _____ of the iron.

5. Did he end up getting the _____?

   Yes, _____ _____.

6. _____ he end up _____ the telephone?

   No, _____ get the _____ instead.

7. Will _____ end _____ getting _____ stereo?

   _____, we'll _____ the electric fan _____.

8. Did _____ _____ up _____ the _____?

   No, they _____ _____ dishwasher instead.

Section G   Let's have fun

Home appliances!

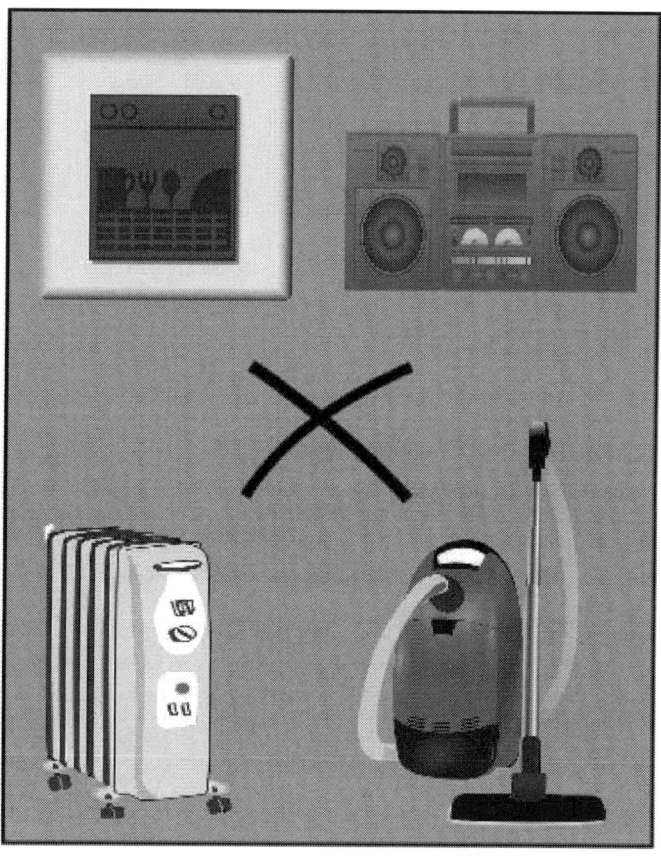

What did he end up getting at the electronics store?

He got the:

- _____ instead of the _____
- _____ instead of the _____
- _____ instead of the _____
- _____ instead of the _____

Lesson 71: Stationery

文具

> What supplies to we need for the office? We've run out of pens. The thumbtacks have also run out. However, we still have enough paper clips.

Section A — Words

1. **paper clip**
   回纹针
2. **thumbtack**
   图钉
3. **scissors**
   剪刀
4. **stapler**
   钉书机
5. **ballpoint pen**
   原子笔
6. **calculator**
   计算机
7. **mechanical pencil**
   自动笔
8. **pencil lead**
   笔芯
9. **binder paper**
   活页纸
10. **folder**
    文件夹

Section B — Make a sentence

What supplies do we need for the office?

We've run out of <u>paper clips</u>.

The <u>pencil leads</u> have also run out.

However, we still have enough <u>binder paper</u>.

Learn: supplies, run out of, however

Note: The word, *supplies*, in this sentence is a noun

Section C — Make a question

Will we have run out of <u>ballpoint pens</u> by <u>Friday</u>?
Yes, I think so. / No, I don't think so.

Will <u>John</u> have run out of <u>thumbtacks</u> by <u>Monday</u>?
Yes, he thinks so. / No, he doesn't think so.

Section D — Learn a verb

supply – supplying – supplied – supplied 供应

This shop **supplies** Japanese stationery.

His company has been **supplying** mechanical pencils to us.

They **supplied** rulers to the students last year.

Folders are **supplied** by the Chinese company.

Section E — Learn an idiom

Be as sharp as a tack

Meaning: To be intelligent.

"He solved the problem quickly because he*'s as sharp as a tack*."

Section F — Write

Trace and fill in the words

1. What supplies do we need _____ the office?

   We've run _____ of thumbtacks.

   The _____ have also _____ out.

   _____, we still have _____ folders.

2. What _____ do they _____ for the _____?

   They've _____ out of calculators.

   The ballpoint pens _____ also run _____.

   However, _____ still have enough _____.

3. Will we _____ run out of ballpoint pens by _____?

   No, I _____ think _____.

4. _____ Peter have run out of _____ by Tuesday?

   Yes, he _____ _____.

5. Will _____ have run out of ballpoint pens by _____?

   _____, they _____ _____.

6. Will Amy have _____ _____ of _____ by Sunday?

   No, she _____ think _____.

Section G Let's have fun

Stationery!

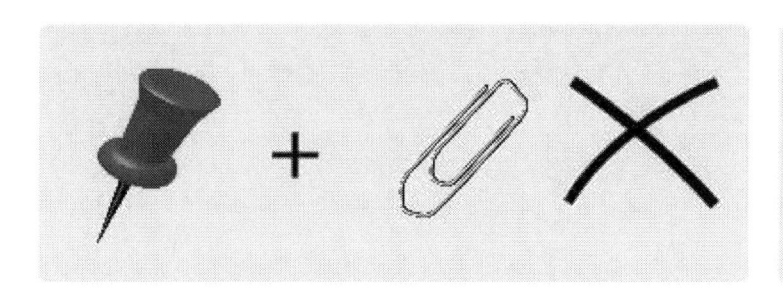

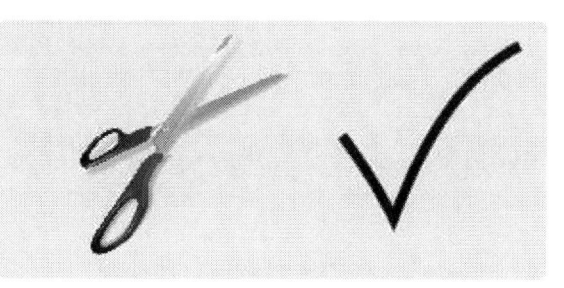

We've run out of thumbtacks.

We've also

However, we still have enough

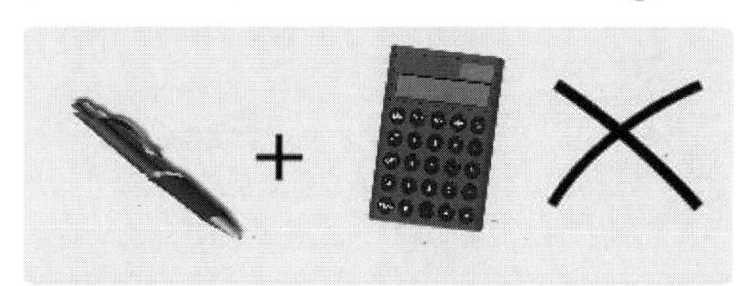

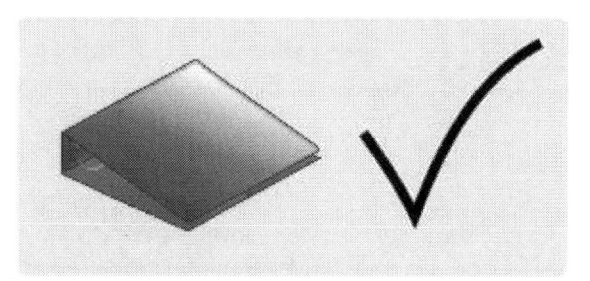

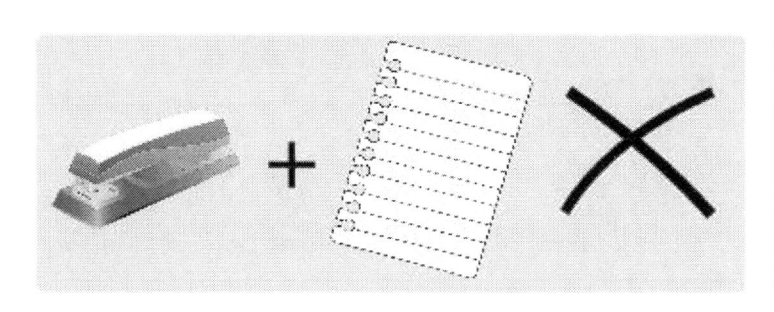

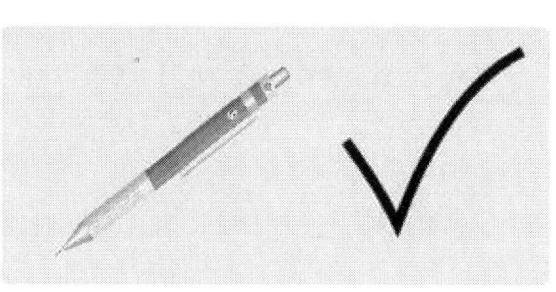

Lesson 72: Computers

电脑

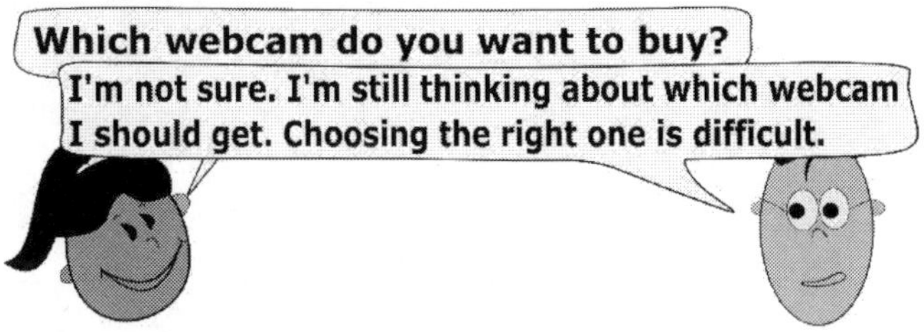

> Which webcam do you want to buy?
> I'm not sure. I'm still thinking about which webcam I should get. Choosing the right one is difficult.

Section A | Words

1. **desktop computer**
   桌上型电脑
2. **laptop computer**
   笔记型电脑
3. **keyboard**
   键盘
4. **mouse**
   滑鼠
5. **mouse pad**
   滑鼠垫
6. **tablet**
   平板电脑
7. **flash drive**
   随身碟
8. **printer**
   影印机
9. **speaker**
   喇叭
10. **webcam**
    网路摄影机

Section B | Make a sentence

Which <u>printer</u> do you want to buy?

I'm not sure.

I'm still thinking about which <u>printer</u> I should get.

Choosing the right one is <u>important</u>.

Learn: important, confusing, difficult, frustrating, about

Section C — Make a question

Are you still thinking about which <u>tablet</u> to buy?
Yes, I am. / No, I'm not.

Is he still thinking about which <u>webcam</u> to buy?
Yes, he is. / No, he isn't.

Section D — Learn a verb

download – downloading – downloaded – downloaded 下载

You can **download** the file from this website.

I'm currently **downloading** the movie.

She **downloaded** some music yesterday for our road trip.

All the files have been **downloaded**.

Section E — Learn an idiom

Pull the plug

Meaning: To suddenly end something.

"She *pulled the plug* on their dinner plans, and ate alone instead."

| Section F | Write |

Trace and fill in the words

1. Which webcam _____ you _____ to buy?

   I'm _____ sure.

   I'm _____ thinking about which _____ I should get.

   _____ the right _____ is confusing.

2. _____ keyboard does _____ want to _____?

   _____ not _____.

   He's still _____ about which _____ he should get.

   Choosing the _____ one _____ _____.

3. _____ you still thinking about which _____ to buy?

   Yes, _____ _____.

4. Is he still _____ _____ which _____ to buy?

   No, _____ _____.

5. _____ she _____ thinking about which mouse to buy?

   _____, _____ is.

6. Are _____ still _____ about which _____ to buy?

   _____, they're _____.

Section G   Let's have fun

Computers!

Draw the pictures! Write the words!

flash drive

printer

laptop computer

mouse pad

tablet

Test 18   Lesson 69 - 72

Write the answer next to the letter "A"

A: ___ 1. When he's ___ with the tongs, he can leave ___ in the sink.

a. finish, them   b. finish, it   c. finished, them   d. finished, it

A: ___ 2. ___ you ___ with the oven mitts yet? No, I haven't.

a. Have, finished   b. Have, finishing   c. Has, finished   d. Had, finish

A: ___ 3. He was using the spatula when he was ___ some bacon.

a. fry   b. fried   c. frying   d. fries

A: ___ 4. "The police officer came to ___ him away from danger."

a. peeler   b. whisk   c. spatula   d. tongs

A: ___ 5. She ___ the stereo ___ of the dishwasher.

a. got, instead   b. gets, instead   c. getting, not   d. got, not

A: ___ 6. Did you end ___ getting the iron? No, I got the heater ___.

a. on, instead   b. by, rather   c. it, instead   d. up, instead

A: ___ 7. He will have ___ the dishwasher by Monday.

a. repair   b. repaired   c. repairs   d. repairing

A: ___ 8. "She had to ___ some things in her homework."

a. iron in   b. iron over   c. iron by   d. iron out

A: ___ **9.** The mechanical pencils ___ also run ___.

a. did, out   b. were, on   c. have, out   d. have, on

A: ___ **10.** ___ Kevin have run out of folders by ___?

a. Will, out   b. Will, Friday   c. Does, then   d. Yes, Monday

A: ___ **11.** They were ___ staplers to the workers.

a. supplies   b. supplying   c. supply   d. supplied

A: ___ **12.** "He got the highest score because he is as sharp as a ___."

a. scissors   b. knife   c. tack   d. pencil

A: ___ **13.** They're still ___ which tablet they should get.

a. think about   b. think on   c. thinks about   d. thinking about

A: ___ **14.** Are you still ___ about which mouse to buy? Yes, I ___.

a. sure, sure   b. thinking, am   c. think, think   d. thinking, do

A: ___ **15.** I haven't finished ___ that music yet.

a. download   b. downloading   c. downloaded   d. downloads

A: ___ **16.** "I didn't want to go, so I pulled the ___ on my vacation."

a. drive   b. mouse   c. plug   d. tablet

Answers on page 463

Lesson 73: Ocean life

海洋生物

> What hadn't you seen until you went swimming in the ocean?
> I had never seen a seal until I went swimming in the ocean. It was quite special.

Section A — Words

1. **octopus** 章鱼
2. **shark** 鲨鱼
3. **dolphin** 海豚
4. **whale** 鲸鱼
5. **seal** 海豹
6. **crab** 螃蟹
7. **squid** 乌贼
8. **jellyfish** 水母
9. **salmon** 鲑鱼
10. **tuna** 鲔鱼

Section B — Make a sentence

What hadn't you seen until you went swimming in the ocean?

I had never seen an <u>octopus</u> until I went swimming in the ocean.

It was quite <u>amazing</u>.

Learn: until, never, quite, special

Section C — Make a question

Had you seen a <u>dolphin</u> before you swam in the ocean?
Yes, I had. / No, I hadn't.

Had she seen a <u>squid</u> before she swam in the ocean?
Yes, she had. / No, she hadn't.

Section D — Learn a verb

swim – swimming – swam – swum 游泳

I love to **swim** in the ocean in summer.
The shark was **swimming** closely behind the seal.
They excitedly **swam** next to the humpback whale.
My co-worker hasn't **swum** in a long time.

Section E — Learn an idiom

Be like a fish out of water

Meaning: To be in an uncomfortable situation.

"It was her first time dancing, so she *was like a fish out of water*."

Section F — Write

Trace and fill in the words

1. What _____ you seen until you went _____ in the ocean?

   I had _____ seen a _____ until I went swimming in the _____.

   It was quite _____.

2. _____ hadn't you _____ _____ you went swimming in _____ ocean?

   I _____ never _____ a _____ _____ I went _____ in the ocean.

   It _____ quite _____.

3. Had you _____ a squid _____ you swam in the ocean?

   Yes, _____ had.

4. _____ she seen a _____ before _____ swam in the ocean?

   No, _____ _____.

5. Had _____ seen a _____ _____ they swam in the _____?

   No, _____ _____.

Section G | Let's have fun

Ocean life!

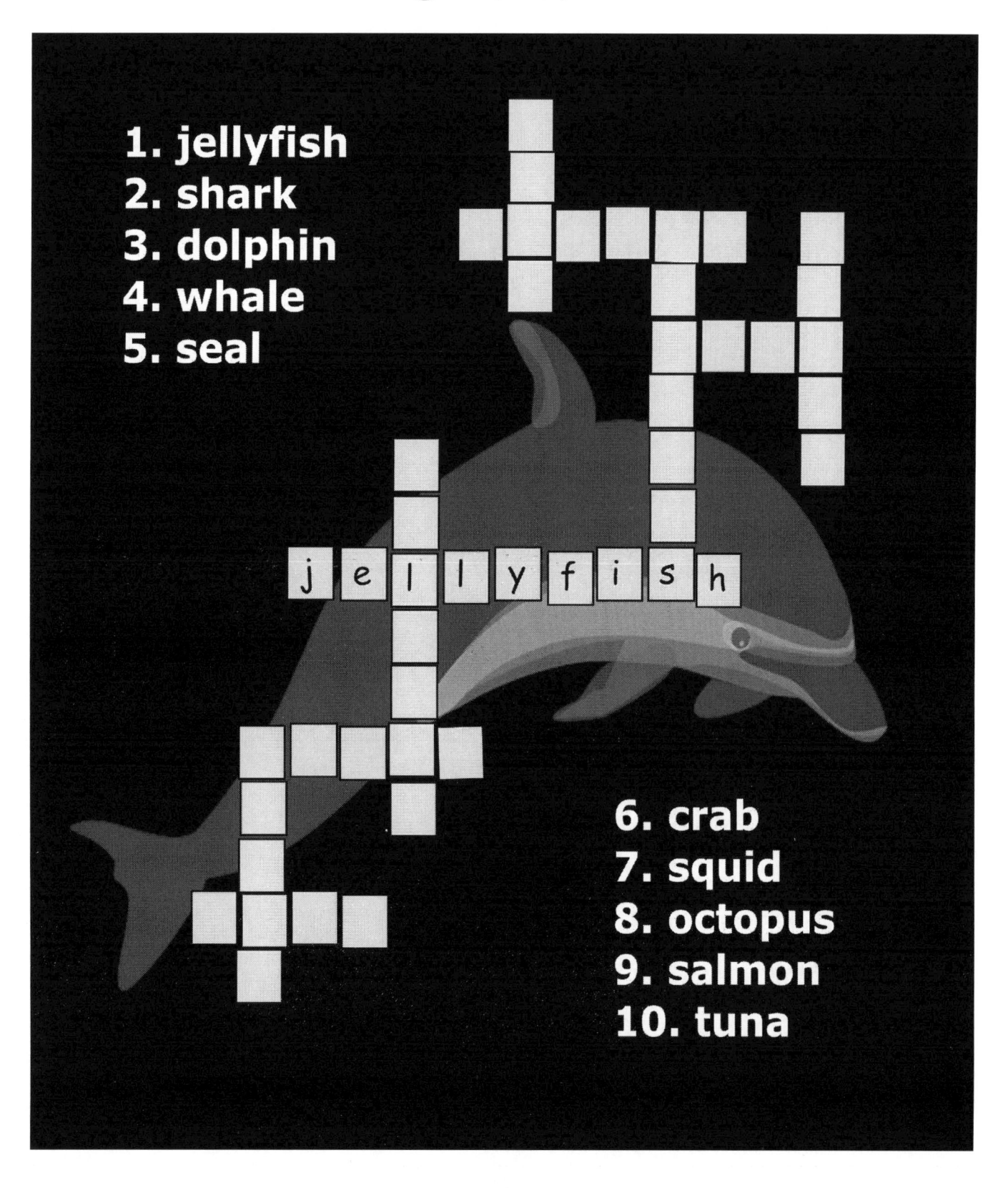

1. jellyfish
2. shark
3. dolphin
4. whale
5. seal

j e l l y f i s h

6. crab
7. squid
8. octopus
9. salmon
10. tuna

Lesson 74: Europe

欧洲

What is the best thing you have ever done?
I once took a road trip through Italy.
Italy is a very scenic country.
I hope to go back there one day.

Section A — Words

1. **Spain** 西班牙
2. **Romania** 罗马尼亚
3. **Poland** 波兰
4. **Germany** 德国
5. **Switzerland** 瑞士
6. **Russia** 俄国
7. **Croatia** 克罗埃西亚
8. **Sweden** 瑞典
9. **Greece** 希腊
10. **Italy** 义大利

Section B — Make a sentence

What is the best thing you have ever done?

I once took a road trip through <u>Germany</u>.

Germany is a very <u>beautiful</u> country.

I hope to go back there <u>one day</u>.

Learn: once, road trip, through, hope, one day, scenic

Section C — Make a question

Was your road trip through <u>Italy</u> <u>exciting</u>?
Yes, it was. / No, it wasn't.

Was their road trip through <u>Spain</u> <u>scenic</u>?
Yes, it was. / No, it wasn't.

Section D — Learn a verb

travel – traveling – traveled – traveled 旅行

Every December I **travel** to Greece with my family.
We are **traveling** through Poland for the first time.
She once **traveled** on a road trip through Switzerland.
He had **traveled** alone to Croatia when he was younger.

Section E — Learn an idiom

Down the road

Meaning: In the future.

"A few months *down the road*, they'll travel to Europe."

Section F — Write

Trace and fill in the words

1. What is the _____ thing you _____ ever done?

   I _____ took a road trip _____ _____.

   Poland is a very _____ country.

   I _____ to go _____ _____ one day.

2. What is the best _____ he _____ ever _____?

   _____ once took a _____ trip through Sweden.

   _____ is a _____ beautiful _____.

   He _____ to _____ back _____ one day.

3. _____ their road trip _____ Greece scenic?

   Yes, _____ was.

4. Was _____ road _____ through Croatia scary?

   No, it _____.

5. _____ her _____ trip through _____ exciting?

   _____, it _____.

6. Was his _____ _____ through Russia _____?

   _____, _____ _____.

Section G Let's have fun

Europe!

exciting / your / Was / through / Spain / road trip

1. _____?

a / Greece / took / once / road trip / I / through

2. _____.

a / beautiful / is / Switzerland / country / very

3. _____.

back / to / one / I / go / hope / day / there

4. _____.

scenic / Was / their / road trip / Poland / through

5. _____?

What is the best thing you have ever done?

_____

Lesson 75: At a hotel

在饭店

Which hotel will you be staying at in Paris tonight?
I'll be staying at the one near the river.
I chose it because I love the room service there.

Section A — Words

1. a lobby
   大厅
2. a reception
   柜台
3. an elevator
   电梯
4. a single room
   单人房
5. a double room
   双人房
6. room service
   客房服务
7. a fitness center
   健身中心
8. a swimming pool
   游泳池
9. a luggage room
   行李房
10. a luggage cart
    行李推车

Section B — Make a sentence

Which hotel will you be staying at in <u>Madrid</u> <u>next week</u>?

I'll be staying at the one near the <u>airport</u>.

Why did you choose that hotel?

I chose it because I love the <u>swimming pool</u> there.

Learn: near, stay

Section C — Make a question

Do you have <u>an elevator</u> at your hotel?
Yes, I do. / No, I don't.

Is there <u>a fitness center</u> at your hotel?
Yes, there is. / No, there isn't.

Section D — Learn a verb

stay – staying – stayed – stayed 停留

I want to **stay** at a hotel by the beach.
We're **staying** at a newly built hotel.
They **stayed** at an expensive hotel for two nights.
He had **stayed** at that hotel before.

Section E — Learn an idiom

Make room

Meaning: To make extra space for someone or something.

"He wanted to get in the car with us, so we had to *make room*."

Section F **Write**

Trace and fill in the words

1. Which _____ will you be _____ at in Paris next week?

   I'll _____ staying at the one near the _____.

2. Why _____ you choose that hotel?

   I _____ it _____ I love the _____ there.

3. _____ hotel will she be staying at in _____ next week?

   _____ be staying at the one _____ the _____.

4. Why did _____ choose that _____?

   She _____ it because she _____ the _____ there.

5. _____ you have a fitness center at _____ hotel?

   Yes, _____ _____.

6. _____ there room service _____ your hotel?

   No, _____ _____.

7. _____ you _____ a double room at your _____?

   _____, _____ don't.

8. _____ _____ a luggage cart _____ your hotel?

   _____, _____ _____.

346

Section G — Let's have fun

At a hotel!

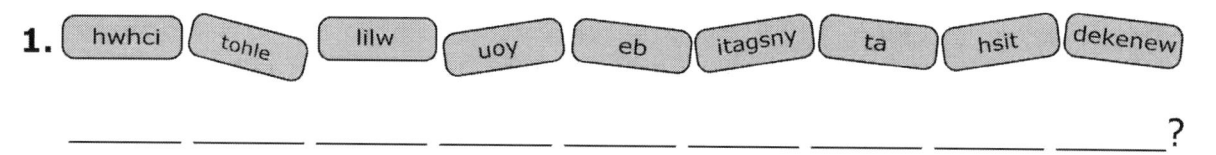

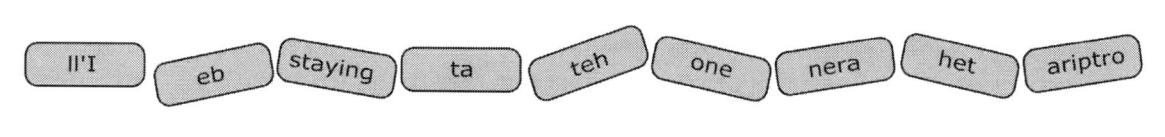

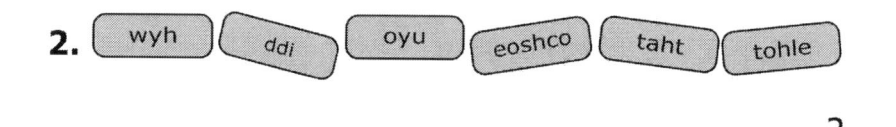

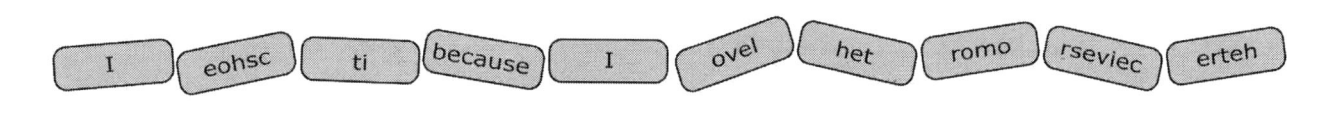

1. hwhci / tohle / lilw / uoy / eb / itagsny / ta / hsit / dekenew

_____ _____ _____ _____ _____ _____ _____ _____ _____?

ll'I / eb / staying / ta / teh / one / nera / het / ariptro

_____ _____ _____ _____ _____ _____ _____ _____ _____.

2. wyh / ddi / oyu / eoshco / taht / tohle

_____ _____ _____ _____ _____ _____?

I / eohsc / ti / because / I / ovel / het / romo / rseviec / erteh

_____ _____ _____ _____ _____ _____ _____ _____ _____ _____.

Complete the words

s _ i _ _ in _ po _ l   e _ ev _ to _

l _ b _ y   r _ c _ pti _ n

l _ gg _ _ e r _ o _   s _ ng _ e _ oo _

d _ _ bl _ r _ _ m   l _ g _ a _ ge c _ _ t

f _ tn _ s _ ce _ t _ r   r _ _ m se _ v _ c _

Which hotel will you be staying at?

_____.

Lesson 76: Furniture

家具

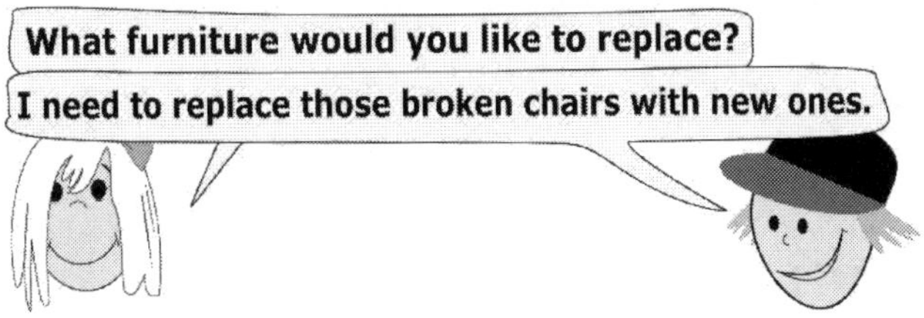

> What furniture would you like to replace?
> I need to replace those broken chairs with new ones.

Section A — Words

1. **broken chair**
   坏掉的椅子
2. **ugly dining table**
   不好看的餐桌
3. **glass coffee table**
   玻璃的茶几
4. **smelly sofa**
   臭的沙发
5. **awful armchair**
   可怕的扶手椅
6. **wooden desk**
   木头书桌
7. **plastic stool**
   塑胶凳子
8. **broken TV stand**
   坏掉的电视柜
9. **old chest of drawers**
   旧的抽屉柜
10. **dirty mattress**
    脏的床垫

Section B — Make a sentence

What furniture would you like to replace?

I need to replace that <u>dirty mattress</u> with a new one.

What furniture would you like to replace?

I need to replace those <u>plastic stools</u> with new ones.

Learn: broken, ugly, glass, smelly, awful, wooden, plastic, broken, old, dirty

Section C — Make a question

Would you like to replace any furniture?
Yes, I'd like to replace the <u>old chest of drawers</u>.
/ No, I'm very happy with the furniture.

Section D — Learn a verb

sit – sitting – sat – sat 坐

Every day, I **sit** on my sofa and watch TV.

He was **sitting** on the stool eating breakfast.

She **sat** on her armchair and fell asleep.

I haven't **sat** down for a long time.

Section E — Learn an idiom

Pull up a chair

Meaning: To sit together with someone.

"She was at the dining table and told me to *pull up a chair*."

Section F   Write

Trace and fill in the words

1. What _____ would you like to _____?

   I _____ to replace _____ broken chair with a new _____.

2. _____ furniture _____ you _____ to replace?

   _____ need to _____ those wooden _____ with new _____.

3. _____ _____ would _____ like to _____?

   I _____ to _____ _____ smelly sofa _____ a _____ one.

4. Would _____ like to _____ any furniture?

   Yes, _____ like _____ replace the broken _____.

5. _____ you _____ to replace any _____?

   No, _____ very _____ with _____ furniture.

6. _____ _____ like to replace any _____?

   _____, I'd _____ to _____ the dirty _____.

7. Would you _____ _____ replace any _____?

   Yes, _____ like to _____ the ugly _____.

Section G Let's have fun

Furniture!

that or those? - adjective? - one or ones?

I need to replace __that__ __dirty__ mattress with a new __one__.

I need to replace _____ _____ desks with new _____.

I need to replace _____ _____ chairs with new _____.

I need to replace _____ _____ dining table with a new _____.

I need to replace _____ _____ TV stand with a new _____.

I need to replace _____ _____ stools with new _____.

I need to replace _____ _____ armchair with a new _____.

I need to replace _____ _____ sofa with a new _____.

Write the number for the words

1   2   3   4   5   6

☐ desk   ☐ stool   ☐ chest of drawers
☐ chair   ☐ sofa   ☐ coffee table

Would you like to replace any furniture?

Yes, _____

No, _____

Test 19 — Lesson 73 - 76

Write the answer next to the letter "A"

A: ___ **1.** I had never ___ a crab until I went ___ in the ocean.

a. seen, swimming   b. saw, swam   c. see, swim   d. seeing, swum

A: ___ **2.** ___ you seen a tuna before you ___ in the ocean?

a. Have, swim   b. Have, swimming   c. Had, swam   d. Did, swimming

A: ___ **3.** Every morning, Simon ___ in the pool.

a. is swim   b. swimming   c. has swimming   d. swims

A: ___ **4.** "I felt like a ___ out of water at the new school."

a. whale   b. shark   c. squid   d. fish

A: ___ **5.** I ___ took a road ___ through Italy. It's a scenic country.

a. once, trip   b. one, trip   c. ever, travel   d. once, travel

A: ___ **6.** ___ their road trip through Spain ___? Yes, it was.

a. Was, beautiful   b. Has, good   c. Did, funny   d. Is, scenic

A: ___ **7.** They once ___ on a road trip through Europe.

a. travel   b. traveled   c. travels   d. traveling

A: ___ **8.** "We plan to travel to Poland ___ the ___."

a. down, road   b. later, trip   c. off, path   d. by, trip

A: ___ **9.** Which hotel ___ you be ___ at in Paris next month?

a. are, living   b. do, stay   c. will, staying   d. do, staying

A: ___ **10.** ___ a fitness center at your hotel?

a. Are there   b. There have   c. Is there   d. Do have

A: ___ **11.** We hadn't ___ in that nice hotel before.

a. stay   b. staying   c. stays   d. stayed

A: ___ **12.** "To put his luggage in the full car, he had to ___ room."

a. open   b. carry   c. make   d. stay

A: ___ **13.** I need to replace ___ smelly sofa with a new ___.

a. that, one   b. that, ones   c. those, ones   d. those, one

A: ___ **14.** They___ like to ___ the awful furniture.

a. 'll, replacing   b. 's, replaced   c. 're, replace   d. 'd, replace

A: ___ **15.** He was ___ the ugly sofa watching TV.

a. sit on   b. sitting on   c. sat over   d. sits on

A: ___ **16.** "She told me to ___ a chair and talk to her."

a. pull up   b. pull on   c. pull through   d. pull under

Answers on page 463

Lesson 77: Water activities

水上活动

What will you be doing on your summer vacation? I'll be going kiteboarding, unless it isn't windy.

Section A — Words

1. **water skiing**
   滑水
2. **windsurfing**
   风帆冲浪
3. **snorkeling**
   浮潜
4. **jet skiing**
   水上摩托车
5. **sailing**
   帆船
6. **kayaking**
   皮划艇
7. **diving**
   潜水
8. **surfing**
   冲浪
9. **fishing**
   钓鱼
10. **kiteboarding**
    风筝冲浪

Section B — Make a sentence

What will you be doing on your summer vacation?

We'll be going <u>snorkeling</u>, unless it's <u>rainy</u>.

What will you be doing on your summer vacation?

I'll be going <u>windsurfing</u>, unless it isn't <u>windy</u>.

Learn: unless, rainy, windy, sunny, cloudy

Section C — Make a question

Will you be <u>kiteboarding</u> on your summer vacation?
Yes, I plan to. / No, I don't plan to.

Will they be <u>jet skiing</u> on their summer vacation?
Yes, they plan to. / No, they don't plan to.

Section D — Learn a verb

plan – planning – planned – planned 计划

He **plans** to go diving on his summer vacation.

Susan is **planning** her winter vacation now.

My father **planned** to go sailing, but it started raining.

I haven't **planned** my weekend yet.

Section E — Learn an idiom

Swim in <u>something</u>

Meaning: To have a lot of something.

"He was *swimming in* money, so every year he bought a new car."

Section F | Write

Trace and fill in the words

1. _____ will he be doing on _____ summer vacation?

   He'll be going _____, unless it's _____.

2. What _____ _____ be doing on her summer vacation?

   _____ be _____ sailing, _____ it isn't windy.

3. What will they be doing on _____ summer _____?

   _____ be going _____, unless _____ _____.

4. What will we be doing on _____ _____ _____?

   We'll _____ _____ fishing, _____ it's _____.

5. _____ she be water skiing on _____ summer vacation?

   Yes, she _____ _____.

6. Will _____ be _____ on his summer _____?

   Yes, _____ _____ to.

7. Will they be _____ on _____ _____ vacation?

   _____, they _____ plan _____.

8. _____ _____ be _____ on her summer vacation?

   No, _____ _____ _____ _____.

Section G — Let's have fun

Water activities!

Make sentences with the information below

1. We	(snorkel)	is	(rainy)	
2. She	(kayak)	isn't	(sunny)	
3. They	(speedboat)	is	(cloudy)	
4. He	(sailboat)	isn't	(windy)	
5. We	(fishing rod)	is	(rainy)	
6. I	?	isn't	?	

1. <u>We'll be going snorkeling, unless it's rainy.</u>

2. _____

3. _____

4. _____

5. _____

6. _____

Lesson 78: Asia

亚洲

Which place are you looking forward to the most?
I'm looking forward to India the most.

Section A — Words

1. **China**
   中国
2. **Japan**
   日本
3. **Vietnam**
   越南
4. **India**
   印度
5. **Thailand**
   泰国
6. **Pakistan**
   巴基斯坦
7. **Philippines**
   菲律宾
8. **Indonesia**
   印度尼西亚
9. **Saudi Arabia**
   沙乌地阿拉伯
10. **Malaysia**
    马来西亚

Section B — Make a sentence

Which place are you looking forward to the most?

I'm looking forward to <u>Vietnam</u> the most.

Which place is he looking forward to the most?

He's looking forward to <u>China</u> the most.

Learn: look forward to, can't wait, not really

Section C — Make a question

Are you looking forward to <u>Indonesia</u>?
Yes, I can't wait! / No, not really.

Is she looking forward to <u>Japan</u>?
Yes, she can't wait! / No, not really.

Section D — Learn a verb

upload – uploading – uploaded – uploaded 上传

Can you help me **upload** this photo of me in India?

Uploading this selfie of us is taking a while.

Mary **uploaded** the file and emailed it to you.

I've already **uploaded** the photos we took in Indonesia.

Section E — Learn an idiom

Can't wait

Meaning: To be really excited for something that will happen.

"I *can't wait* to go traveling in Asia this spring!"

Section F   Write

Trace and fill in the words

1. _____ place is he _____ forward to the most?

   _____ looking _____ to _____ the most.

2. Which _____ are you looking _____ to the _____?

   _____ _____ forward to India _____ most.

3. Which place are _____ _____ forward to the most?

   They're _____ _____ to China the _____.

4. _____ place is _____ looking _____ to the most?

   She's looking _____ _____ Malaysia _____ most.

5. Is _____ looking _____ to Thailand?

   Yes, she _____ _____!

6. Are they _____ forward to _____?

   No, _____ really.

7. _____ you looking _____ _____ Indonesia?

   _____, we _____ _____!

8. Is he _____ _____ _____ Japan?

   _____, _____ _____.

360

Section G | Let's have fun

Asia!

We are = We're   She is = ____   He is = ____
They are = ____   I am = ____   It is = ____

Connect the sentences

Which place are you looking forward to the most? • — • I'm looking forward to Japan the most.

Are you looking forward to Thailand? •   • She's looking forward to Malaysia the most.

Which place is she looking forward to the most? •   • He's looking forward to India the most.

Is she looking forward to Vietnam? •   • Yes, she can't wait!

Which place is he looking forward to the most? •   • Yes, I can't wait!

Unscramble the sentences

to / He's / the / Saudi Arabia / looking / most / forward

1. _____.

forward / I'm / looking / to / most / the / Pakistan

2. _____.

looking / China / forward / They're / most / to / the

3. _____.

the / Indonesia / forward / We're / looking / most / to

4. _____.

Lesson 79: People

人们

Who is your friend?
He is from Japan. Japanese are pretty polite people.

Section A — Words

1. **American**
   美国人
2. **Chinese**
   中国人
3. **Spaniard**
   西班牙人
4. **German**
   德国人
5. **Canadian**
   加拿大人
6. **Australian**
   澳洲人
7. **Japanese**
   日本人
8. **Russian**
   俄国人
9. **South African**
   南非人
10. **Mexican**
    墨西哥人

Section B — Make a sentence

Who is your friend?

He is from <u>South Africa</u>. South Africans are pretty <u>friendly</u> people.

Who are your friends?

They are from <u>Mexico</u>. Mexicans are pretty <u>kind</u> people.

Learn: from, pretty, friendly, kind, interesting, polite, fun

Section C — Make a question

Is your friend a <u>Canadian</u>?
Yes, she is. / No, she's an <u>Australian</u>.

Are your friends <u>Chinese</u>?
Yes, they are. / No, they're <u>Japanese</u>.

Section D — Learn a verb

email – emailing – emailed – emailed 给电子邮件

I will **email** my Canadian friend tonight.
He's **emailing** you the document now.
My Chinese friend **emailed** me regarding the meeting we had.
Kevin will have **emailed** you the presentation by then.

Section E — Learn an idiom

A sea of people

Meaning: A large amount or crowd of people.

"There was *a sea of people* at the Beijing train station."

Section F — Write

Trace and fill in the words

1. Who are _____ friends?

   _____ are from _____. Germans are pretty _____ people.

2. Who _____ your friend?

   He is from Japan. _____ are _____ friendly people.

3. _____ is your _____?

   She _____ from _____. _____ are pretty _____ people.

4. _____ are _____ _____?

   _____ _____ from Australia. _____ are pretty _____ _____.

5. Are your _____ _____?

   No, _____ Canadian.

6. _____ your _____ a Spaniard?

   _____, she's _____ _____.

7. _____ _____ friend a _____?

   No, _____ _____ _____.

Section G — Let's have fun

People!

Connect the sentences - is or are? - adjective?

They ____ from Canada.   • Australians are pretty _____ people.

He ____ from Mexico.   • Canadians are pretty _____ people.

She ____ from Australia.   • Spaniards are pretty _____ people.

They ____ from Spain.   • Chinese are pretty _____ people.

He ____ from China.   • Mexicans are pretty _____ people.

They ____ from Russia.   • South Africans are pretty _____ people.

She ____ from Japan.   • Russians are pretty _____ people.

We ____ from South Africa.   • Americans are pretty _____ people.

They ____ from Germany.   • Japanese are pretty _____ people.

He ____ from the USA.   • Germans are pretty _____ people.

Where are you from?

Lesson 80: On an airplane

在飞机上

> How was the flight?
> Although first class was too expensive, the window seat was comfortable.

Section A — Words

1. **tray table**
   餐桌托盘
2. **aisle seat**
   靠走道座位
3. **window seat**
   靠窗座位
4. **overhead compartment**
   置物柜
5. **restroom**
   盥洗室
6. **flight attendant**
   空服员
7. **pilot**
   机长
8. **economy class**
   经济舱
9. **business class**
   商务舱
10. **first class**
    头等舱

Section B — Make a sentence

How was the flight?

Although the <u>overhead compartment</u> was too <u>small</u>, the <u>flight attendants</u> were <u>friendly</u>.

How was the flight?

Although <u>economy class</u> was too <u>crowded</u>, the <u>pilot</u> was <u>professional</u>.

Learn: although, too, turbulence

Section C — Make a question

Was the flight good?
Yes, it was. / No, it wasn't.

Was there any turbulence?
Yes, there was. / No, there wasn't.

Section D — Learn a verb

fly – flying – flew – flown

Sometimes she **flies** business class to Europe.

While **flying** to Asia, he watched several movies.

Helen **flew** to America in economy class.

I haven't **flown** with that airline before.

Section E — Learn an idiom

With flying colors

Meaning: To do something really well or successfully.

"She studied hard, so she passed the test *with flying colors*."

Section F — Write

Trace and fill in the words

1. How _____ the flight?

   Although the _____ seat was too _____, the pilot was professional.

2. _____ was the _____?

   Although the _____ was _____ dirty, the _____ seats were _____.

3. How _____ _____ _____?

   _____ the _____ class was too _____, the overhead _____ were _____.

4. _____ the flight _____?

   Yes, _____ was.

5. _____ there any _____?

   _____, _____ wasn't.

6. Was _____ any _____?

   No, _____ _____.

7. Was _____ _____ comfortable?

   Yes, _____ _____.

Section G Let's have fun

On an airplane!

Although the overhead compartment was too small, the tray table was big.

Although business class was too expensive, it was comfortable.

Although the flight attendants were too slow, they were friendly.

Although the pilot was good, there was turbulance.

1. What was too small?
   _____

2. Were the flight attendants friendly?
   _____

3. What was comfortable?
   _____

4. Was the pilot good?
   _____

5. How was business class?
   _____

Connect the words   **Write the words**

window•   •class

flight•   •seat

overhead•   •attendant

tray•   •compartment

first•   •table

Test 20   Lesson 77 - 80

Write the answer next to the letter "A"

A: ___ 1. We'll be ___ jet skiing, ___ it's windy.

a. trying, or   b. doing, only   c. going, but   d. going, unless

A: ___ 2. Will you be ___ on your summer vacation? Yes, I ___ to.

a. surf, plan   b. surfing, planning   c. surfed, planning   d. surfing, plan

A: ___ 3. She ___ to go kayaking on her summer vacation.

a. plan   b. plans   c. planning   d. planner

A: ___ 4. "She was ___ in homework, so she couldn't go on vacation."

a. swimming   b. surfing   c. diving   d. sailing

A: ___ 5. She ___ looking ___ to Malaysia the most.

a. 'd, foremost   b. 's, for   c. 's, forward   d. 'll, at

A: ___ 6. ___ you looking forward to India? Yes, I can't ___!

a. Do, want   b. Can't, win   c. Are, wait   d. Are, waist

A: ___ 7. ___ my photos from Pakistan took a long time.

a. Uploading   b. Upload   c. Uploads   d. Uploaded

A: ___ 8. "We can't ___ to take a vacation in Saudi Arabia."

a. maintain   b. stay   c. way   d. wait

A: ___ **9.** My friend is from Germany. ___ are pretty ___ people.

a. Germs, nice   b. Germans, kind   c. Germany, kinds   d. They, friend

A: ___ **10.** ___ your friends Russian? No, ___ American.

a. Were, he's   b. Is, she's   c. Are, they're   d. Does, we're

A: ___ **11.** I was ___ my friends late last night.

a. email   b. emailing   c. emails   d. emailed

A: ___ **12.** "There was a ___ of people at the park."

a. sea   b. band   c. beach   d. ball

A: ___ **13.** ___ the aisle seat was too small, ___ pilot was nice.

a. But, and   b. Also, but   c. Although, the   d. And, so

A: ___ **14.** ___ there any ___? Yes, there was.

a. Were, turbo   b. Was, turbulence   c. Did, flying   d. Has, turning

A: ___ **15.** Sometimes they ___ economy class to Africa.

a. flies   b. flying   c. flown   d. fly

A: ___ **16.** "He passed the job interview with ___ colors."

a. fly   b. flying   c. flies   d. flew

Answers on page 463

Lesson 81: At the post office

在邮局

Where is she right now?
She's at the post office buying a stamp.

Section A — Words

1. stamp
   邮票
2. envelope
   信封
3. letter
   信
4. package
   包裹
5. postcard
   明信片
6. zip code
   邮递区号
7. airmail
   航空信
8. express mail
   快递
9. postal worker
   邮政工人
10. mail carrier
    邮差

Section B — Make a sentence

Where are you right now?

I'm at the post office <u>mailing</u> a <u>letter</u>.

Where is she right now?

She's at the post office <u>buying</u> a <u>stamp</u>.

Learn: mailing, buying, choosing, checking, talking to

Section C — Make a question

Were you at the post office <u>talking to</u> the <u>mail carrier</u>?
Yes, I was. / No, I wasn't.

Was he at the post office <u>checking</u> a <u>zip code</u>?
Yes, he was. / No, he wasn't.

Section D — Learn a verb

check – checking – checked – checked 检查

I will **check** the zip code later.

She is **checking** the price of airmail now.

He **checked** when the mail carrier will be coming.

The teacher hasn't **checked** the homework yet.

Section E — Learn an idiom

To the letter

Meaning: To do something exactly as you're told to do.

"Her mom said she should follow the instructions *to the letter*."

Section F Write

Trace and fill in the words

1. Where are _____ right _____?

   I'm at _____ post office _____ a package.

2. _____ are _____ right now?

   They're _____ the _____ office mailing a _____.

3. Where _____ she _____ now?

   She's at the post _____ buying _____ _____.

4. _____ is he _____ _____?

   _____ at the _____ _____ buying a _____.

5. _____ she at the post office _____ the postcard?

   No, _____ wasn't.

6. Was _____ at the post office _____ the _____?

   _____, he _____.

7. _____ you at the _____ office _____ to the mail carrier?

   No, _____ _____.

8. Were _____ at _____ post _____ talking to the _____?

   Yes, _____ _____.

374

Section G Let's have fun

At the post office!

Across: →

1. She's talking to the _____.
2. He's talking to the _____.

Down: ↓

3. I'm at the post office buying a _____.
4. I'm at the post office checking a _____.
5. I'm at the post office mailing a _____.
6. I'm at the post office choosing a _____.
7. He's at the post office mailing a _____.
8. He's at the post office choosing a _____.

Lesson 82: Martial arts

武术

Which martial arts class are you thinking about taking?
I'm thinking about taking a tai chi class.
I'm not interested in learning judo.

Section A — Words

1. **karate**
   空手道
2. **taekwondo**
   跆拳道
3. **kung fu**
   功夫
4. **judo**
   柔道
5. **boxing**
   拳击
6. **kendo**
   剑道
7. **tai chi**
   太极拳
8. **sumo**
   相扑
9. **kickboxing**
   跆拳道
10. **fencing**
    西洋剑

Section B — Make a sentence

Which martial arts class are you thinking about taking? I'm thinking about taking a <u>kendo</u> class. I'm not interested in learning <u>taekwondo</u>.

Which martial arts class is she thinking about taking? She's thinking about taking a <u>judo</u> class. She's not interested in learning <u>kickboxing</u>.

Learn: think about, interest in

Section C — Make a question

Is he thinking about taking a <u>karate</u> class?
Yes, he is. / No, he isn't. He doesn't like <u>karate</u>.

Is she interested in taking a <u>boxing</u> class?
Yes, she is. / No, she isn't. She doesn't like <u>boxing</u>.

Section D — Learn a verb

kick – kicking – kicked – kicked 踢

Every week in kung fu class we **kick** the pads.

They were **kicking** each other in karate class.

Emily **kicked** the ball into the net.

He hadn't **kicked** a ball since he hurt his leg.

Section E — Learn an idiom

Kick the habit

Meaning: To stop doing a bad habit.

"We decided to start eating healthily and to *kick the habit* of eating junk food."

Section F — Write

Trace and fill in the words

1. Which _____ arts class is she thinking about _____?

_____ thinking about taking a _____ class. She's not _____ in learning _____.

2. _____ martial arts class are you _____ about taking?

_____ thinking about _____ a _____ class. We're not interested _____ _____ tai chi.

3. Which _____ arts class are you thinking about _____?

I'm _____ _____ taking a _____ class. I'm not _____ in _____ _____.

4. Is _____ thinking _____ taking a _____ class?

No, he _____. He _____ like fencing.

5. _____ she _____ in taking a kung fu class?

_____, _____ isn't. _____ doesn't like _____.

6. Is she _____ in _____ a _____ _____?

Yes, _____ _____.

7. Is he _____ in _____ a judo _____?

Yes, _____ _____.

378

Section G — Let's have fun

Martial arts!

Unscramble the words

- uodj
- atoekonwd
- cikbgoxikn
- nncfieg
- gukn uf
- tkraea
- ita ich
- xogibn
- okedn
- msuo

Write the sentence using the information above

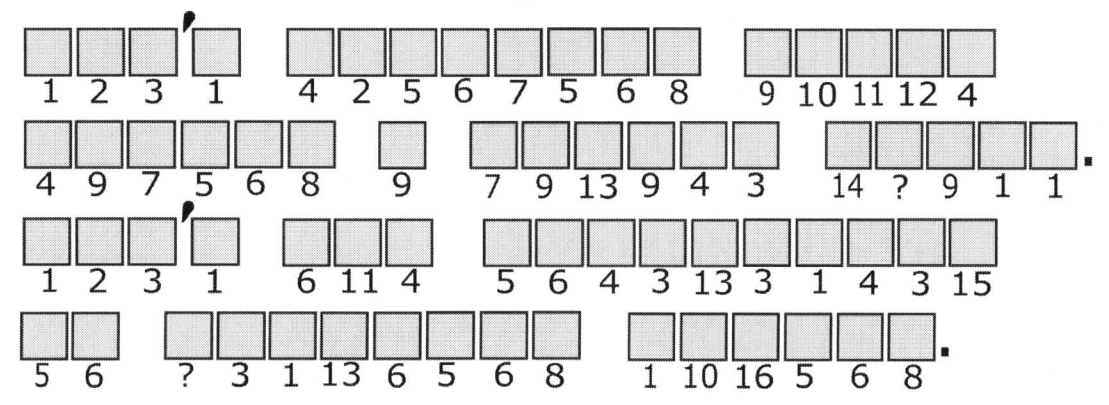

Lesson 83: Toiletries

梳妆用品

> What things do we need to get for the bathroom?
> We have everything we need except for floss and combs.

Section A   Words

1. a toothbrush
   牙刷
2. toothpaste
   牙膏
3. hand soap
   洗手乳
4. a razor
   刮胡刀
5. shaving cream
   刮胡膏
6. shampoo
   洗发精
7. floss
   润发乳
8. a hand towel
   擦手巾
9. deodorant
   体香剂
10. a comb
    梳子

Section B   Make a sentence

What things do we need to get for the bathroom?

We have everything except for <u>razors</u> and <u>deodorant</u>.

What things does he need to get for the bathroom?

He has everything except for <u>floss</u> and <u>a toothbrush</u>.

Learn: except for, enough, get

Section C — Make a question

Do we need to get any <u>hand towels</u> for the bathroom?
Yes, we do. / No, he has enough.

Does he need to get a <u>comb</u> for the bathroom?
Yes, she does. / No, I have enough.

Section D — Learn a verb

brush – brushing – brushed – brushed 刷

Brush your teeth before you go to bed.
Brushing your teeth is very important for health.
I **brushed** my hair, but it still looks messy.
She hasn't **brushed** her hair yet.

Section E — Learn an idiom

Comb through <u>something</u>

Meaning: To look through something very carefully.

"I *combed through* my homework to look for mistakes."

Section F — Write

Trace and fill in the words

1. What _____ do we need to get for the _____?

   We have _____ except for _____ and _____.

2. _____ things _____ she _____ to get for the bathroom?

   _____ has everything _____ for _____ and a _____.

3. What _____ do they _____ to _____ for the _____?

   _____ have _____ except _____ shampoo and a hand towel.

4. Do we _____ to get any _____ for the bathroom?

   No, _____ have enough _____.

5. Does _____ need to get a _____ for the bathroom?

   No, _____ has _____.

6. _____ we need to get any _____ for the _____?

   Yes, _____ _____.

7. _____ he need to get any floss _____ the _____?

   Yes, _____ _____.

Section G Let's have fun

Toiletries!

Write the 5 missing items on the shopping list

Shopping list

Answer the questions using the information above

1. What things do we need to get for the bathroom?

2. Do we need to get any floss for the bathroom?

3. Do we need to get any soap for the bathroom?

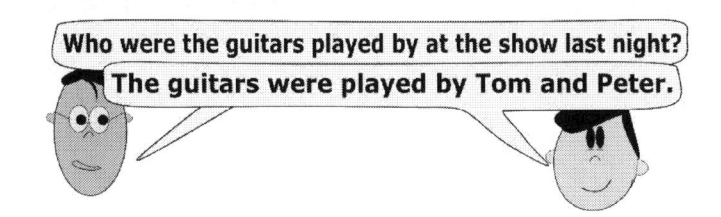

Lesson 84: Musical instruments

乐器

Who were the guitars played by at the show last night?
The guitars were played by Tom and Peter.

Section A — Words

1. **guitar** 吉他
2. **piano** 钢琴
3. **drums** 鼓
4. **violin** 小提琴
5. **cello** 大提琴
6. **trumpet** 小号
7. **trombone** 长号
8. **saxophone** 萨克斯風
9. **flute** 长笛
10. **accordion** 手风琴

Section B — Make a sentence

Who was the <u>violin</u> played by at the <u>concert</u> <u>last night</u>?

The violin was played by <u>me</u>.

Who will the <u>flute</u> be played by at the <u>party</u> <u>tonight</u>?

The flute will be played by <u>Tom</u>.

Learn: concert, party, show, festival

| Section C | Make a question |

Were the <u>drums</u> played by <u>Travis</u> <u>last night</u>?
Yes, they were. / No, they were played by <u>Lars</u>.

Will the <u>cello</u> be played by <u>Peter</u> <u>tomorrow night</u>?
Yes, it will be. / No, he will be playing the <u>guitar</u>.

| Section D | Learn a verb |

dance – dancing – danced – danced 跳舞

We like to **dance** slowly to this piano music.

They started **dancing** to his amazing guitar playing.

She **danced** until midnight.

They were laughing at me because I hadn't **danced** in years!

| Section E | Learn an idiom |

As tight as a drum

Meaning: When something is closed or sealed very tight.

"Before the storm came he closed the windows *as tight as a drum*."

| Section F | Write |

Trace and fill in the words

1. Who will the _____ be played by at the show _____?

   _____ guitar _____ be played by Matt.

2. Who _____ the piano be _____ by at the _____ tonight?

   The _____ will _____ played _____ Tim.

3. Who _____ the trumpet played _____ at the festival last _____?

   The _____ was _____ by me.

4. Who _____ the accordion _____ by at the _____ _____ month?

   The _____ was played _____ Melvin.

5. _____ the saxophone be played by Peter _____ night?

   Yes, _____ _____ be.

6. Will _____ _____ be played by Kim next _____?

   No, she _____ be _____ the trumpet.

7. Were _____ drums _____ by Scott last _____?

   No, _____ were _____ _____ Derek.

Section G — Let's have fun

Musical instruments!

concert — tonight
party — tomorrow night
festival — **last night**
show — two nights ago

Who was the guitar played by at the concert last night ?

concert — **tonight**
party — tomorrow night
festival — last night
show — two nights ago

_____?

concert — tonight
party — tomorrow night
festival — last night
show — **two nights ago**

_____?

concert — tonight
party — **tomorrow night**
festival — last night
show — two nights ago

_____?

Test 21   Lesson 81 - 84

Write the answer next to the letter "A"

A: ___ 1. ___ at the post office ___ a package.

a. She'll, mailing   b. She'd, mail   c. She's, mailing   d. She, mail

A: ___ 2. ___ you at the post office buying a ___?

a. Where, stamp   b. Will, letter   c. Were, postcard   d. When, package

A: ___ 3. She ___ when the mail carrier will be coming.

a. check   b. checked   c. checking   d. will checking

A: ___ 4. "I followed the teacher's words to the ___."

a. stamp   b. envelope   c. letter   d. package

A: ___ 5. She's not ___ in learning karate.

a. interest   b. interesting   c. interests   d. interested

A: ___ 6. ___ they thinking ___ taking a tai chi class?

a. Do, of   b. Were, on   c. Yes, about   d. Are, about

A: ___ 7. He was ___ hard in his taekwondo class.

a. kicking   b. kicks   c. kick   d. kicker

A: ___ 8. "He ___ the bad habit of going to sleep late."

a. kick   b. kicks   c. kicked   d. kicking

388

A: ___ **9.** We have everything ___ for razors and deodorant.

a. but	b. except	c. not	d. enough

A: ___ **10.** Does he need to get a toothbrush for the bathroom?

a. Yes, he does.	b. Yes, he needs.	c. Yes, he has.	d. Yes, he is.

A: ___ **11.** ___ your teeth before bed is very important.

a. Brush	b. Brushing	c. Brushed	d. Brushes

A: ___ **12.** "We ___ through the room looking for my lost ring."

a. brushed	b. flossed	c. combed	d. shaved

A: ___ **13.** Who ___ the cello be ___ by at the show tomorrow?

a. will, played	b. was, played	c. will, play	d. was, play

A: ___ **14.** ___ the guitar played by Eric last night? Yes, it ___.

a. Were, were	b. Is, is	c. Was, is	d. Was, was

A: ___ **15.** I haven't ___ since I was a child.

a. dance	b. dancing	c. dances	d. danced

A: ___ **16.** "No water will get in this tent, it's as ___ as a drum."

a. tight	b. loud	c. noisy	d. perfect

Answers on page 463

Lesson 85: Birds

鸟类

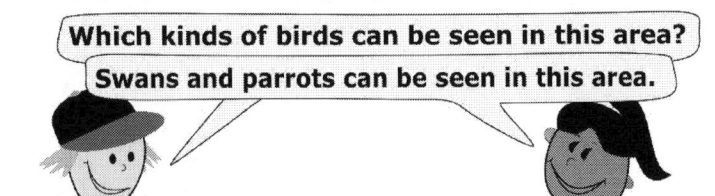

Which kinds of birds can be seen in this area?
Swans and parrots can be seen in this area.

Section A — Words

1. eagle
   老鹰
2. crow
   乌鸦
3. sparrow
   麻雀
4. seagull
   海鸥
5. pelican
   鹈鹕
6. ostrich
   鸵鸟
7. penguin
   企鹅
8. parrot
   鹦鹉
9. owl
   猫头鹰
10. swan
    天鹅

Section B — Make a sentence

Which kinds of birds can be seen in <u>this</u> area?

<u>Seagulls</u> and <u>pelicans</u> can be seen in this area.

Which kinds of birds can be seen in <u>that</u> area?

<u>Owls</u> and <u>eagles</u> can be seen in that area.

Learn: kind(s) of, area

Section C — Make a question

Can <u>ostriches</u> be seen in <u>this</u> area?
Yes, they can. / No, they can't be seen here.

Can <u>parrots</u> be seen in <u>that</u> area?
Yes, they can. / No, they can't be seen there.

Section D — Learn a verb

catch – catching – caught – caught 抓

I saw an eagle **catch** a rabbit.

The pelican was **catching** many fish at the beach.

The dog **caught** a stick in its mouth at the park.

The fishermen haven't **caught** any tuna in this area.

Section E — Learn an idiom

A night owl

Meaning: A person who stays awake late at night.

"She's *a night owl*, so she always does her work at midnight."

| Section F | Write |

Trace and fill in the words

1. Which _____ of birds can be seen in _____ area?

   _____ and _____ can be seen in that _____.

2. _____ kinds of _____ can be _____ in this area?

   _____ and _____ can be _____ in _____ area.

3. Which _____ of _____ can be seen in this _____?

   Swans and crows _____ be _____ in _____ area.

4. _____ _____ of birds can be seen in that _____?

   _____ and _____ can _____ seen in that area.

5. Can sparrows _____ _____ in that area?

   No, _____ can't be seen _____.

6. _____ penguins be seen _____ that _____?

   _____, _____ can.

7. Can _____ be _____ in this _____?

   Yes, _____ _____.

8. _____ _____ be _____ in _____ area?

   _____, they can't _____ _____ here.

Section G Let's have fun

Birds!
Find the missing birds!

1. **eagle**
- crow
- sparrow
- seagull
- penguin
- ostrich
- owl
- swan
- pelican
- parrot

2. _____
- swan
- ostrich
- owl
- eagle
- pelican
- seagull
- parrot
- penguin
- crow

3. _____
- sparrow
- ostrich
- owl
- penguin
- parrot
- eagle
- crow
- seagull
- pelican

4. _____
- seagull
- eagle
- ostrich
- sparrow
- owl
- parrot
- crow
- pelican
- swan

5. _____
- eagle
- sparrow
- swan
- penguin
- pelican
- seagull
- owl
- ostrich
- crow

6. _____
- swan
- sparrow
- parrot
- seagull
- penguin
- ostrich
- crow
- pelican
- eagle

7. _____
- parrot
- swan
- seagull
- owl
- eagle
- penguin
- crow
- sparrow
- pelican

8. _____
- eagle
- sparrow
- swan
- penguin
- parrot
- owl
- crow
- ostrich
- seagull

Lesson 86: At the bank

在银行

What do you have to do at the bank tomorrow?
I have to speak to the bank manager about my debit card.

Section A — Words

1. **bank teller**
   银行行员
2. **ATM**
   提款机
3. **vault**
   保险箱
4. **bank account**
   银行帐户
5. **currency exchange**
   货币兑换
6. **check**
   支票
7. **bankbook**
   存折
8. **credit card**
   信用卡
9. **debit card**
   现金卡
10. **bank manager**
    银行经理

Section B — Make a sentence

What do you have to do at the bank <u>today</u>?

I must speak with the bank manager about <u>my credit card</u>.

What do you have to do at the bank <u>this afternoon</u>?

I have to speak with the bank manager about <u>the ATM</u>.

Learn: have to, must

Section C | Make a question

Do you have to speak with the bank manager <u>later</u>?
Yes, I have to. / No, I don't have to.

Did you have to speak with the bank manager <u>before</u>?
Yes, I had to. / No, I didn't have to.

Section D | Learn a verb

open – opening – opened – opened 打开

I will **open** a new bank account next week.
The manager is **opening** the vault to get some money.
Mike **opened** the door for me at the bank yesterday.
The bank hasn't **opened** yet.

Section E | Learn an idiom

Bank on <u>someone</u> / <u>something</u>

Meaning: To rely on or count on something or someone.

"You can *bank on* her to get the job done."

| Section F | Write |

Trace and fill in the words

1. _____ do you _____ to do at the bank _____?

   I _____ speak with the bank manager about my _____.

2. What do _____ have to do at the _____ today?

   I must _____ with the bank _____ about _____ _____.

3. What _____ you have _____ do at the bank _____ morning?

   I _____ to speak with the _____ _____ about the _____.

4. _____ you have to _____ with the bank manager later?

   No, _____ don't _____ to.

5. _____ you _____ to speak _____ the bank manager before?

   Yes, I _____ _____.

6. Did _____ have _____ speak with the _____ _____ before?

   No, I _____ _____ _____.

Section G — Let's have fun

At the bank!

1. What do you have to do at the bank today?
I must speak with the bank manager about my bankbook.

2. What do you have to do at the bank later?
I must speak to the bank manager about the currency exchange.

3. Do you have to speak with the bank manager this afternoon?
No, I don't have to.

4. Do you have to speak with the bank manager tomorrow?
Yes, I do.

Read the sentences above. Circle True or False?

1. She must speak to the bank manager about her credit card. True False

2. She must speak to the bank manager about the currency exchange. True False

3. He has to speak to the bank manager this afternoon. True False

4. He has to speak to the bank manager tomorrow. True False

Connect the words

currency•   •account

bank•   •card

debit•   •exchange

bank•   •teller

Lesson 87: Household items

生活用品

> Why were you using the mop at seven o'clock?
> I was using the mop at seven o'clock because the chores in the dining room hadn't been done.

Section A — Words

1. **dish soap**
   洗碗精
2. **washing machine**
   洗衣机
3. **dryer**
   干衣机
4. **bleach**
   漂白剂
5. **rag**
   抹布
6. **flashlight**
   手电筒
7. **broom**
   扫帚
8. **mop**
   拖把
9. **dustpan**
   畚箕
10. **bucket**
    水桶

Section B — Make a sentence

Why were you using the <u>dustpan</u> at <u>four o'clock</u>?

I was using the dustpan at four o'clock because the chores in the <u>living room</u> hadn't been done.

Why were they using the <u>mop</u> at <u>a quarter past two</u>?

They were using the mop at a quarter past two because the chores in the <u>kitchen</u> hadn't been done.

| Section C | Make a question |

Had you been using the <u>dryer</u> at <u>half past five</u>?
Yes, I had been. / No, I hadn't been.

Hadn't he been using the <u>broom</u> at <u>a quarter to one</u>?
Yes, he had been. / No, he hadn't been.

| Section D | Learn a verb |

sweep – sweeping – swept – swept 扫

My uncle **sweeps** the floor every morning at ten o'clock.

I was **sweeping** up the dust in the living room.

We **swept** the kitchen floor.

I haven't **swept** the house since last Friday.

| Section E | Learn an idiom |

Mop the floor with <u>someone</u>

Meaning: To easily beat someone.

"When I played golf with him, he really *mopped the floor with* me."

Section F Write

Trace and fill in the words

1. Why _____ they _____ the _____ at a half past _____?

   _____ were using _____ bleach at a _____ past eight because the _____ in the _____ hadn't been _____.

2. _____ were _____ using the bucket at one _____?

   I _____ using the _____ at _____ o'clock because _____ chores in the _____ _____ been done.

3. Hadn't _____ been _____ the dryer at a _____ to seven?

   _____, she _____ been.

4. _____ they _____ using _____ flashlight _____ two _____?

   Yes, _____ had been.

5. Had _____ been _____ the _____ at half past _____?

   Yes, I _____ _____.

Section G | Let's have fun

Household items!

Make sentences with the words

I + dustpan + 10:00 + office
I was using the dustpan at ten o'clock because the chores in the office hadn't been done.

She + mop + 2:45 + living room

They + washing machine + 11:25 + laundry

Mary + bucket + 5:30 + garage

We + broom + 4:00 + bedroom

Peter + dish soap + 2:45 + kitchen

Susan and Matthew + rags + 7:00 + dining room

Lesson 88: The solar system

太阳系

> Which planet comes after Jupiter?
> Saturn comes after Jupiter.

Section A — Words

1. Mercury
   水星
2. Venus
   金星
3. Earth
   地球
4. Mars
   火星
5. Jupiter
   木星
6. Saturn
   土星
7. Uranus
   天王星
8. Neptune
   海王星
9. Pluto
   冥王星
10. the sun
    太阳

Section B — Make a sentence

Which planet comes before <u>Jupiter</u>?

Mars comes before Jupiter.

Which planet comes after <u>Saturn</u>?

Uranus comes after Saturn.

Learn: come(s) before, come(s) after, whether, or

| Section C | Make a question |

Do you know whether <u>Jupiter</u> comes after or before <u>Mars</u>?
Yes, I do. / No, I'm not sure.

Do you know whether <u>Venus</u> comes after or before <u>Earth</u>?
Yes, I do. / No, I'm not sure.

| Section D | Learn a verb |

come – coming – came – come 来

Would you like to **come** with me to look at the stars?
My friend is **coming** with us to the planetarium.
I **came** to this class to learn about the solar system.
Do you think aliens have ever **come** to Earth?

| Section E | Learn an idiom |

Rise with the sun

Meaning: To wake up and get out of bed when the sun comes up.

"He likes to get up early and *rise with the sun*."

| Section F | Write |

Trace and fill in the words

1. Which _____ comes _____ Neptune?

   _____ comes before _____.

2. _____ planet _____ before _____?

   Venus _____ _____ Earth.

3. Which _____ _____ after Jupiter?

   _____ comes _____ Jupiter.

4. _____ planet _____ _____ Mars?

   _____ _____ after _____.

5. Do you know _____ Saturn comes _____ or before _____?

   No, _____ not _____.

6. _____ you _____ whether Pluto comes after or _____ _____?

   Yes, _____ _____.

7. Does _____ know _____ Mercury _____ _____ or _____ Neptune?

   Yes, _____ _____.

Section G Let's have fun

The solar system!

Write the words in the solar system map

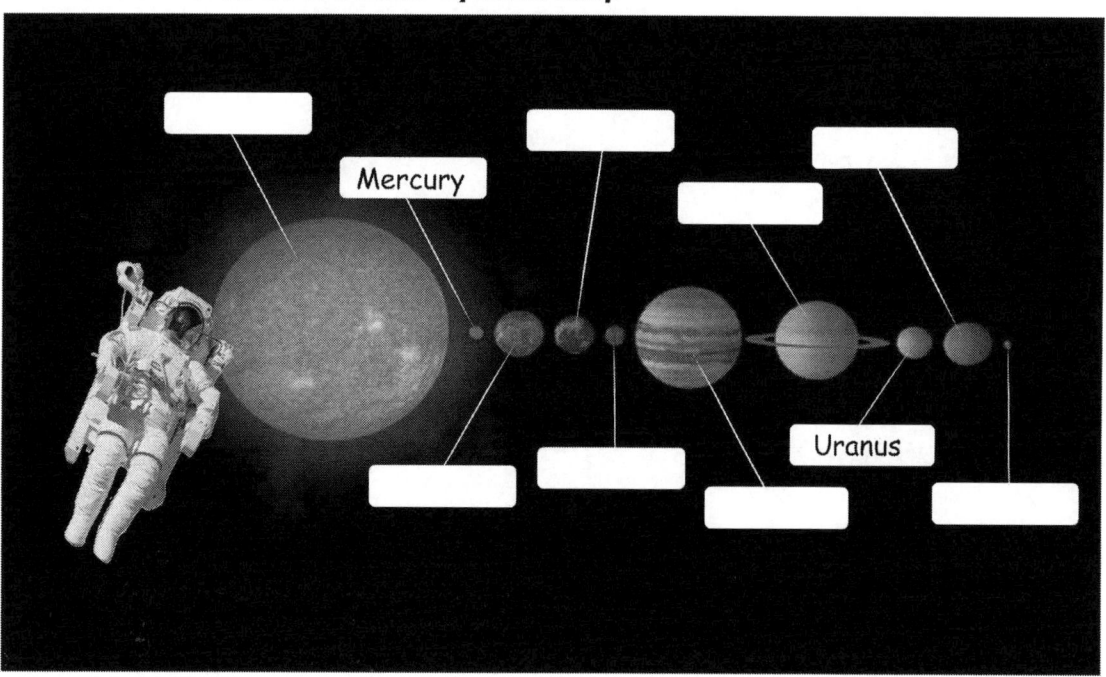

True or False?

1. Venus comes after Mercury.
   ☑ True   ○ False

2. Saturn comes before Mars.
   ○ True   ○ False

3. Mars comes before Earth.
   ○ True   ○ False

4. Pluto comes after Neptune.
   ○ True   ○ False

5. Earth comes after Venus.
   ○ True   ○ False

6. Jupiter comes before Mars.
   ○ True   ○ False

Answer the questions

Which planet comes before Uranus?
_____.

Which planet comes after Earth?
_____.

Test 22 — Lesson 85 - 88

Write the answer next to the letter "A"

A: ___ **1.** Sparrows and crows can be ___ in that area.

a. see   b. saw   c. seeing   d. seen

A: ___ **2.** ___ swans be seen in this area? No, they can't be seen ___ .

a. Do, there   b. Would, there   c. Were, then   d. Can, here

A: ___ **3.** The penguin ___ many fish yesterday afternoon.

a. catch   b. catches   c. caught   d. catching

A: ___ **4.** "His brother is a ___ owl, and he always stays up late."

a. late   b. night   c. dark   d. light

A: ___ **5.** She ___ to speak with the bank manager ___ the vault.

a. was, on   b. have, around   c. has, about   d. is, to

A: ___ **6.** ___ you have to speak with the bank manager ___?

a. Do, before   b. Did, before   c. Are, later   d. Were, later

A: ___ **7.** Yesterday, she ___ the vault to get some money out.

a. opens   b. open   c. opening   d. opened

A: ___ **8.** "She was ___ on me to finish the class project."

a. banking   b. vaulting   c. carding   d. booking

406

A: ___ **9.** I was ___ the broom because the chores ___ been done.

a. using, hadn't   b. use, had   c. uses, hadn't   d. using, were

A: ___ **10.** Had he been ___ the bleach at ___ past two?

a. using, over   b. use, quarter   c. dusting, ten   d. using, half

A: ___ **11.** He ___ the kitchen floor every evening for four years.

a. sweeps   b. swept   c. sweep   d. sweeping

A: ___ **12.** "I ___ the floor with him when we played games yesterday."

a. dried   b. swept   c. cleaned   d. mopped

A: ___ **13.** Which planet ___ Saturn?

a. go before   b. come after   c. comes before   d. go after

A: ___ **14.** Do you know ___ Venus ___ after or before Mars?

a. if, come   b. where, comes   c. whether, comes   d. how, comes

A: ___ **15.** Have they ever ___ to this place before?

a. come   b. came   c. comes   d. coming

A: ___ **16.** "She always ___ with the sun to start work early."

a. rises   b. moves   c. goes   d. eats

Answers on page 463

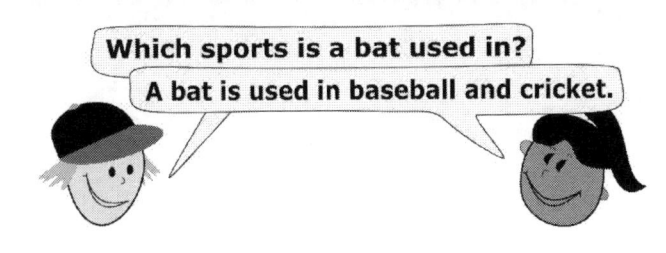

Lesson 89: Sporting equipment

运动器材

Which sports is a bat used in?
A bat is used in baseball and cricket.

Section A — Words

1. bat
   球棒
2. ball
   球
3. mitt
   棒球手套
4. net
   网子
5. ice skates
   溜冰鞋
6. helmet
   安全帽
7. racket
   球拍
8. knee pad
   护膝
9. board
   板
10. mouthguard
    护牙套

Section B — Make a sentence

Which sports is a **racket** used in?

A racket is used in **tennis** and **badminton**.

Which sports are **helmets** used in?

Helmets are used in **baseball** and **hockey**.

Learn: true, without

| Section C | Make a question |

Is it true that you can't play <u>hockey</u> without a <u>helmet</u>?
Yes, this is true. / No, that's not true.

Is it true that you can't play <u>baseball</u> without a <u>mitt</u>?
Yes, this is true. / No, that's not true.

| Section D | Learn a verb |

score – scoring – scored – scored 得分

She **scores** every time she plays basketball.
He hasn't been **scoring** many points since he hurt himself.
Simon **scored** his first goal last weekend.
Our team hasn't **scored** a goal for a month.

| Section E | Learn an idiom |

At bat

Meaning: To have your turn or chance to do something.

"Everyone else had tried, so then it was her *at bat*."

| Section F | Write |

Trace and fill in the words

1. Which _____ is a _____ used _____?

   A mouthguard is _____ in _____ and karate.

2. _____ sports _____ knee pads _____ in?

   _____ pads are used _____ _____ and _____.

3. _____ _____ are _____ used in?

   Nets _____ _____ in _____ and _____.

4. _____ sports is _____ _____ used in?

   _____ board _____ used in _____ and _____.

5. _____ it true _____ you can't play _____ without a helmet?

   No, _____ not _____.

6. Is _____ true that _____ can't _____ baseball _____ a _____?

   Yes, _____ is _____.

7. Is _____ _____ that you _____ play cricket without _____ _____?

   _____, _____ not _____.

Section G Let's have fun

Sporting equipment!

Unscramble the words. Connect the items and the sport

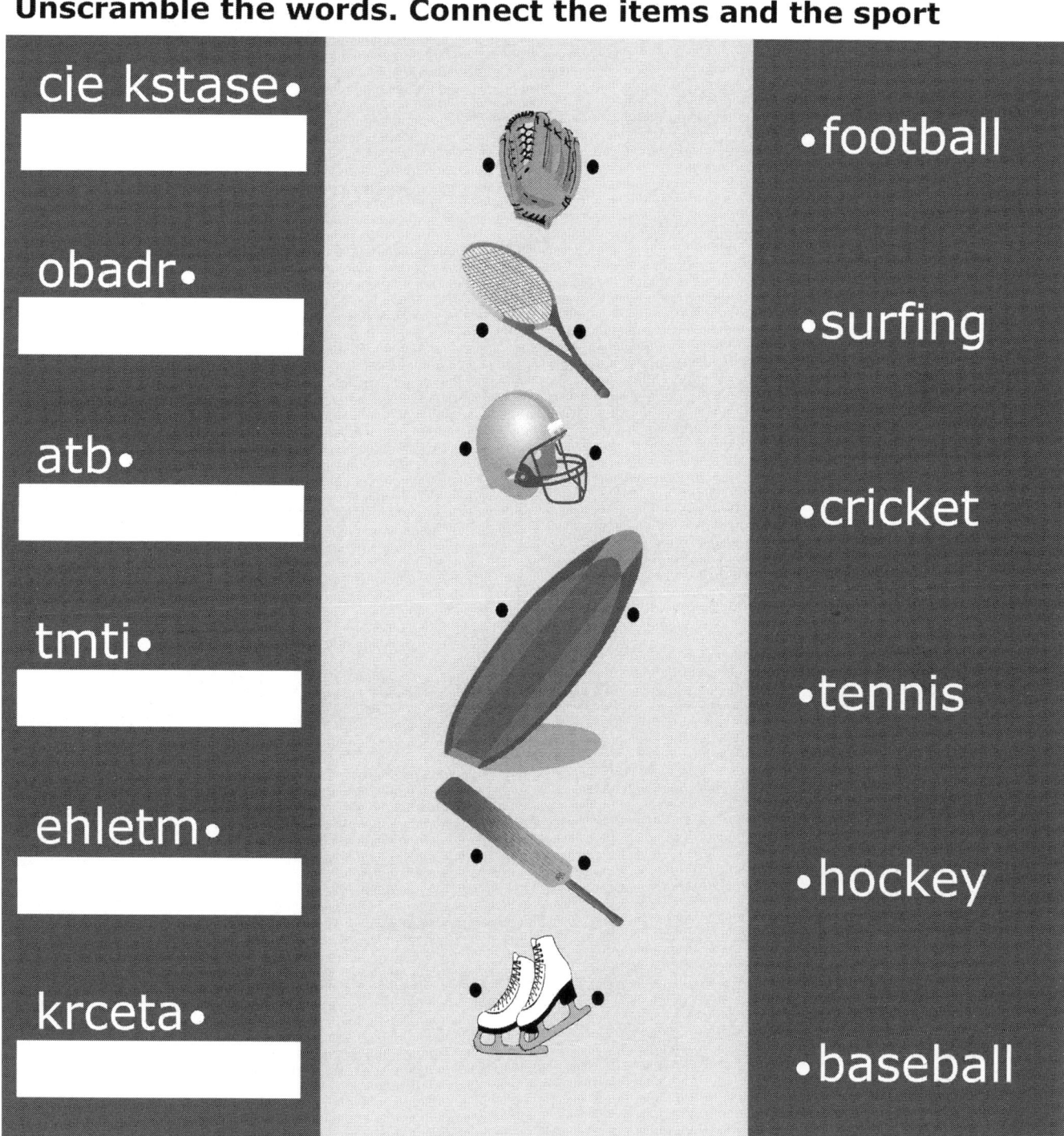

cie kstase•

obadr•

atb•

tmti•

ehletm•

krceta•

•football

•surfing

•cricket

•tennis

•hockey

•baseball

Lesson 90: Small animals

小动物

> Which animals have you never seen before in Canada? I have never seen a skunk, nor have I ever seen a hummingbird.

Section A — Words

1. **squirrel**
   松鼠
2. **frog**
   青蛙
3. **mouse**
   老鼠
4. **raccoon**
   浣熊
5. **skunk**
   臭鼬
6. **hummingbird**
   蜂鸟
7. **gecko**
   壁虎
8. **clownfish**
   小丑鱼
9. **bat**
   蝙蝠
10. **spider**
    蜘蛛

Section B — Make a sentence

Which animals have you never seen before in <u>China</u>? I have never seen a <u>skunk</u>, nor have I ever seen a <u>raccoon</u>.

Which animals have you never seen before in <u>Russia</u>? I have never seen a <u>gecko</u>, nor have I ever seen a <u>bat</u>.

Learn: nor, like, such as, of course

| Section C | Make a question |

Are mice seen in <u>cold</u> countries such as <u>Canada</u>?
Yes, of course. / No, of course not.

Are <u>skunks</u> seen in <u>hot</u> countries like <u>Thailand</u>?
Yes, of course. / No, of course not. / I don't know.

| Section D | Learn a verb |

discover – discovering – discovered – discovered 发现

Marine biologists **discover** new ocean life all the time.
They are still **discovering** many new species in the jungle.
We **discovered** a mouse living in our attic.
Scientists haven't **discovered** a cure for cancer.

| Section E | Learn an idiom |

Be as quiet as a mouse

Meaning: To be very quiet or shy.

"He *was as quiet as a mouse* whenever he got nervous."

| Section F | Write |

Trace and fill in the words

1. Which _____ have you _____ seen before in _____?

   I have never _____ a _____, nor have I _____ seen a _____.

2. _____ animals _____ he never _____ _____ in _____?

   He _____ never seen a hummingbird, _____ has _____ ever _____ a _____.

3. Are _____ seen in cold _____ such as Sweden?

   No, _____ course _____.

4. _____ geckos _____ in _____ countries _____ as Canada?

   _____, of _____ not.

5. Are _____ seen _____ hot _____ such _____ _____?

   Yes, _____ _____.

Section G Let's have fun

Small animals!

Draw the pictures! Write the words!

gecko

clownfish

spider   raccoon   skunk

Lesson 91: In the forest

在森林里

What are you hoping to find in this forest?
I'm hoping to find a swamp or maybe even a lake.

Section A — Words

1. tree
   树
2. plant
   植物
3. cave
   山洞
4. valley
   山谷
5. river
   河
6. lake
   湖
7. waterfall
   瀑布
8. swamp
   沼泽
9. nest
   鸟巢
10. log
    原木

Section B — Make a sentence

What are you hoping to find in <u>this</u> forest?

I'm hoping to find a <u>valley</u> or maybe even a <u>river</u>.

What is he hoping to find in <u>that</u> forest?

He's hoping to find a <u>cave</u> or maybe even a <u>waterfall</u>.

Learn: maybe, even, hope, hope so, doubt

| Section C | Make a question |

Do you think you'll find a <u>river</u> in the forest?
Yes, I hope so. / No, I doubt it.

Does she think she'll find a <u>river</u> in the forest?
Yes, she hopes so. / No, she doubts it.

| Section D | Learn a verb |

hope – hoping – hoped – hoped 希望

Peter **hopes** we can have a picnic in the forest this weekend.
I'm **hoping** they stop cutting the trees down in the forest.
I **hoped** she wouldn't get lost in the cave.
She had **hoped** it would rain on her plants, but it didn't.

| Section E | Learn an idiom |

Be swamped

Meaning: To be very busy.

"She had homework for every class, so she *was swamped*."

| Section F | Write |

Trace and fill in the words

1. What _____ you _____ to find in this _____?

_____ hoping to find a _____ or _____ even a

_____.

2. _____ is _____ hoping _____ find in _____

forest?

He's _____ to find a _____ or maybe _____ a

_____.

3. _____ are _____ hoping to _____ in _____

forest?

I'm _____ to _____ a nest or _____ even a log.

4. Do _____ think you'll _____ a swamp in the forest?

Yes, _____ hope _____.

5. _____ she think _____ find a _____ in the

_____?

No, she _____ it.

6. Does _____ think she'll _____ a lake in the forest?

Yes, _____ _____ _____.

Section G   Let's have fun

In the forest!

Circle the things in a forest

1.	racket	guitar	sumo	(cave)	floss
2.	lake	mitt	violin	bleach	razor
3.	bucket	river	cello	board	comb
4.	mop	ball	waterfall	judo	flute

Write the word

1. _____   2. _____

3. _____   4. _____

Write the answer using the information above

1. What is she hoping to find in this forest?
_____.

2. What is he hoping to find in that forest?
_____.

3. What is she hoping to find in this forest?
_____.

4. What is he hoping to find in that forest?
_____.

Lesson 92: Natural disasters

自然灾害

What should you be careful of in parts of Asia?
In parts of Asia, you should be careful of typhoons.

Section A | Words

1. **typhoon** 台风
2. **blizzard** 暴风雪
3. **earthquake** 地震
4. **wildfire** 野火
5. **tsunami** 海啸
6. **drought** 干旱
7. **tornado** 龙卷风
8. **flood** 淹水
9. **landslide** 山崩
10. **heat wave** 热浪

Section B | Make a sentence

What should you be careful of in parts of <u>Europe</u>?

In parts of Europe, you should be careful of <u>blizzards</u>.

What should you be careful of in parts of <u>Australia</u>?

You should be careful of <u>wildfires</u> in parts of Australia.

Learn: parts of, be careful of, Europe, Asia, North America, South America, Antarctica, Australia, Africa

Section C — Make a question

Do you have to be careful of <u>typhoons</u> in <u>Asia</u>?
Yes, you do. / No, you don't. / I'm not sure.

Do you have to be careful of <u>earthquakes</u> in <u>Africa</u>?
Yes, you do. / No, you don't. / I'm not sure.

Section D — Learn a verb

respond – responding – responded – responded 回应

The firefighters **respond** quickly to landslides.
The police are **responding** to calls in regards to the tsunami.
I **responded** to your email about the heat wave in Africa.
He hasn't **responded** to my message yet.

Section E — Learn an idiom

A disaster area

Meaning: A very messy or unclean place.

"His bedroom was extremely dirty. It was *a disaster area*."

| Section F | Write |

Trace and fill in the words

1. What _____ you be _____ of in parts of _____?

In parts of _____, you should be careful of _____.

2. _____ should you be careful of in _____ of Asia?

In parts of _____, you _____ be careful of _____.

3. What _____ you be _____ of in _____ of _____?

_____ parts of _____, you should _____ careful _____ _____.

4. _____ you _____ to be _____ of droughts in Asia?

I'm _____ sure.

5. Do _____ have to be careful of _____ in _____?

No, _____ _____.

6. _____ you have to _____ _____ of _____ in _____?

Yes, _____ _____.

7. Do _____ have to be careful of _____ in _____?

_____ _____ sure.

Section G   Let's have fun

Natural disasters!

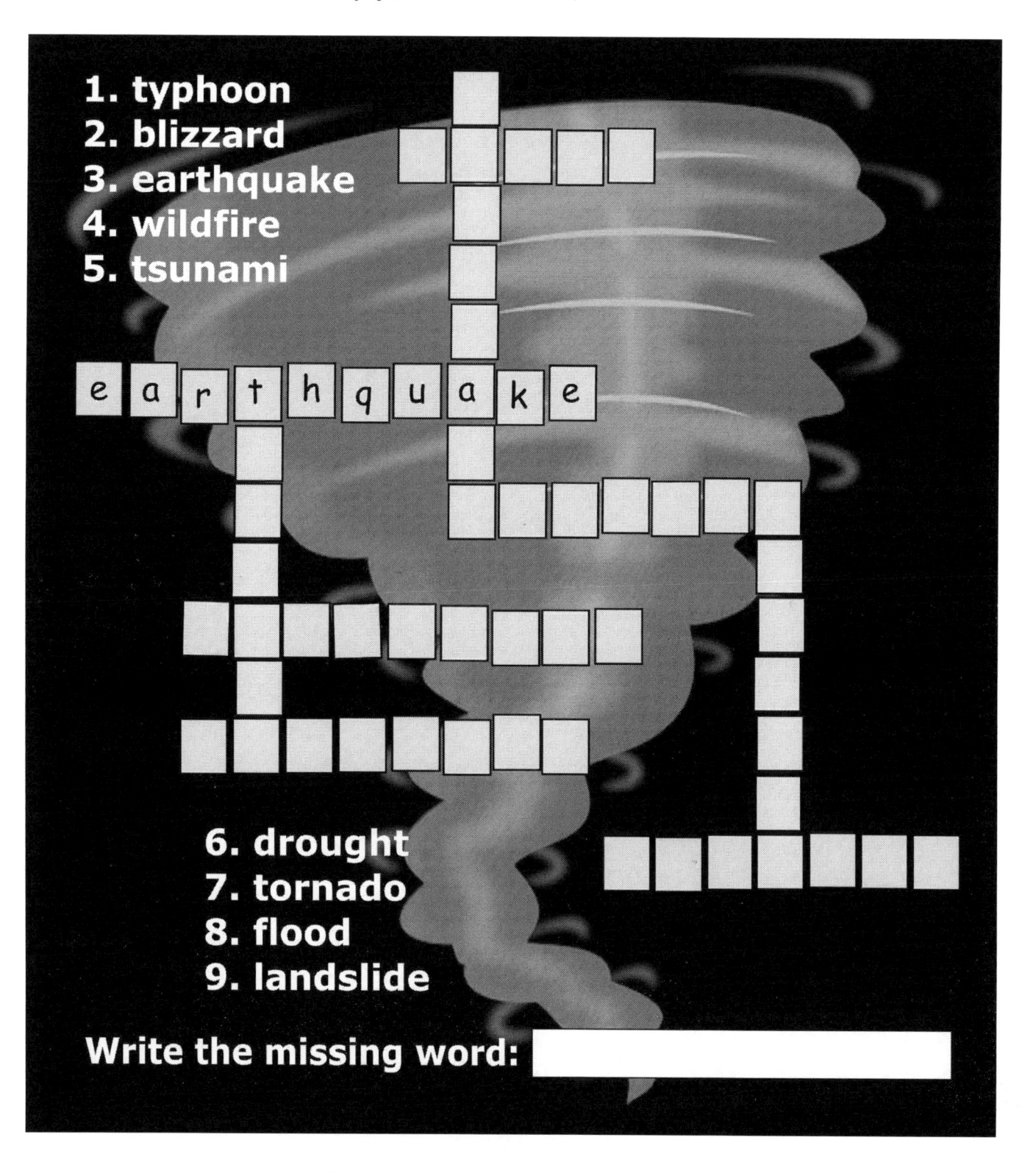

1. typhoon
2. blizzard
3. earthquake
4. wildfire
5. tsunami

e a r t h q u a k e

6. drought
7. tornado
8. flood
9. landslide

Write the missing word:

Test 23 Lesson 89 - 92

Write the answer next to the letter "A"

A: ___ **1.** Which ___ are helmets ___ in?

a. sport, using   b. sports, used   c. sports, use   d. sport, use

A: ___ **2.** Is it true that you can't play baseball ___ a mitt?

a. within   b. whenever   c. without   d. for

A: ___ **3.** She hasn't been ___ many goals this year.

a. score   b. scores   c. scored   d. scoring

A: ___ **4.** "No one else had done it, so it was his turn at ___."

a. bat   b. ball   c. net   d. racket

A: ___ **5.** She has ___ seen a frog, ___ has she ever seen a spider.

a. nor, never   b. ever, or   c. never, or   d. never, nor

A: ___ **6.** Are bats seen in cold ___ such as Norway? Yes, ___ course.

a. country, off   b. place, on   c. countries, of   d. cities, of

A: ___ **7.** He ___ a skunk walking behind his house.

a. discovered   b. discover   c. discovers   d. discovering

A: ___ **8.** "The new student was as quiet as a ___."

a. bird   b. mouse   c. spider   d. squirrel

A: ___ **9.** I'm ___ to find a valley or maybe ___ a river.

a. hope, ever   b. hopeful, there   c. holding, see   d. hoping, even

A: ___ **10.** Do you think ___ find a river in the forest? No, I ___ it.

a. you'll, doubt   b. you're, don't   c. you, done   d. you'll, can't

A: ___ **11.** They had ___ for better weather, but it started raining.

a. hope   b. hopes   c. hoped   d. hoping

A: ___ **12.** "During the busy holidays, he was ___ with work."

a. caved   b. swamped   c. nested   d. planted

A: ___ **13.** You should be ___ of floods in ___ of Europe.

a. careful, parts   b. caring, parts   c. care, part   d. cares, parts

A: ___ **14.** ___ you have to be careful of wildfires in Asia? I'm ___ sure.

a. Don't, so   b. Are, very   c. Do, not   d. Would, too

A: ___ **15.** She ___ very quickly to my email about natural disasters.

a. respond   b. responding   c. has respond   d. responded

A: ___ **16.** "My mom said my desk was a ___ area."

a. drought   b. disaster   c. blizzard   d. flood

Answers on page 463

Lesson 93: America

美洲

> Where in Central America would you like to travel to?
> If I had the chance, I'd travel to Belize.

Section A — Words

1. **Costa Rica**
   哥斯达黎加
2. **Belize**
   贝里斯
3. **Nicaragua**
   尼加拉瓜
4. **Canada**
   加拿大
5. **Mexico**
   墨西哥
6. **United States of America**
   美国
7. **Chile**
   智利
8. **Argentina**
   阿根廷
9. **Brazil**
   巴西
10. **Uruguay**
    乌拉圭

Section B — Make a sentence

Where in <u>North America</u> would you like to travel to?

If I had the chance, I'd travel to <u>Mexico</u>.

Where in <u>South America</u> would you like to travel to?

If I had the chance, I'd travel to <u>Chile</u>.

Learn: chance, Central America, North America, South America

Section C — Make a question

Have you been to any countries in <u>Central America</u>?
Yes, I've been to <u>Costa Rica</u>. / No, I haven't. / I can't remember.

Have you been to any countries in <u>South America</u>?
Yes, I've been to <u>Brazil</u>. / No, I haven't. / I can't remember.

Section D — Learn a verb

remember – remembering – remembered – remembered 记得

Remember to take your backpack to Argentina.
Remembering my childhood trip to Belize is difficult.
While hiking in Canada, I **remembered** to bring some water.
He hasn't **remembered** my birthday for two years.

Section E — Learn an idiom

Jog <u>one's</u> memory

Meaning: To remind someone about something they've forgotten.

"I'd forgotten about my trip to Belize until he *jogged* my *memory*."

Section F | **Write**

Trace and fill in the words

1. Where in North America _____ you like to _____ to?

   If I _____ the _____, I'd travel to _____.

2. _____ in South _____ would you like to travel to?

   _____ I had _____ chance, _____ travel to _____.

3. Where _____ _____ America _____ he like to travel _____?

   If he _____ the chance, _____ travel to Uruguay.

4. _____ you been to any _____ in South America?

   _____, I've _____ to _____.

5. Have _____ been to _____ countries _____ Central _____?

   No, _____ _____.

6. _____ you _____ to any _____ in North America?

   _____ _____ remember.

7. Have you _____ to any _____ in _____ America?

   _____, I've _____ to _____.

Section G Let's have fun

America!

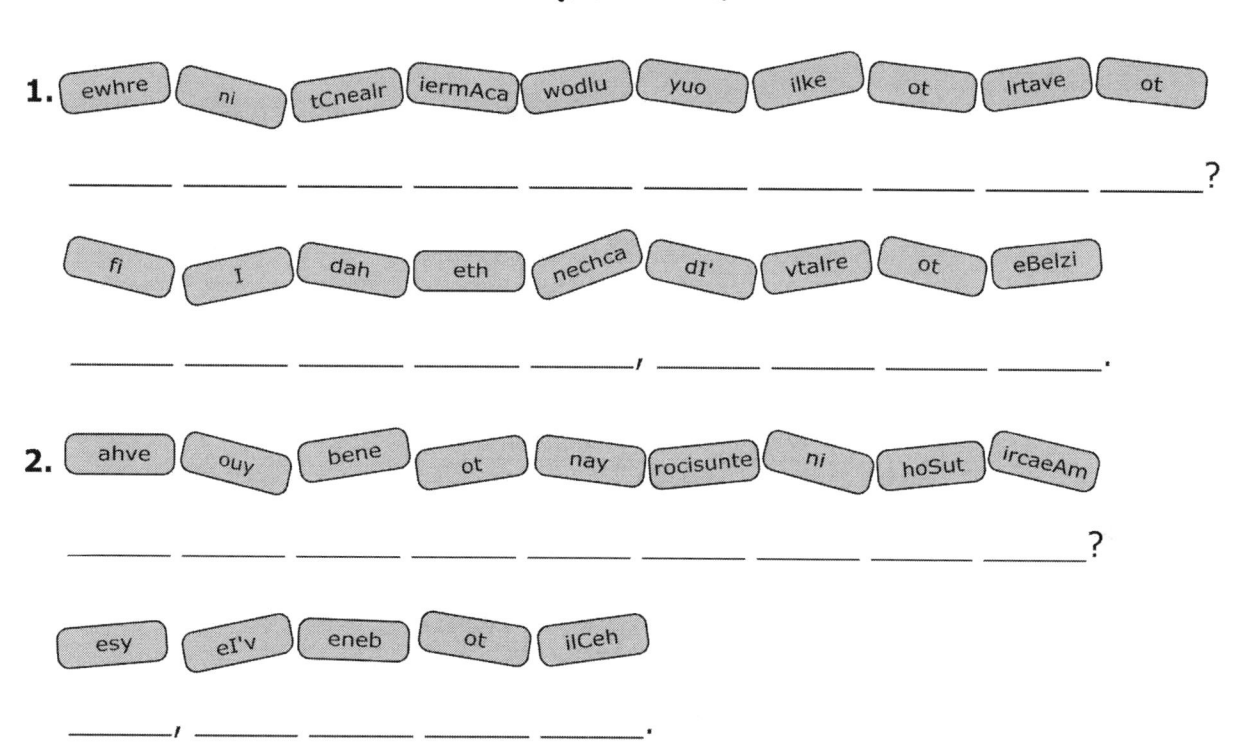

1. ewhre | ni | tCnealr | iermAca | wodlu | yuo | ilke | ot | lrtave | ot

_____ _____ _____ _____ _____ _____ _____ _____ _____ _____?

fi | I | dah | eth | nechca | dI' | vtalre | ot | eBelzi

_____ _____ _____ _____ _____ , _____ _____ _____ _____.

2. ahve | ouy | bene | ot | nay | rocisunte | ni | hoSut | ircaeAm

_____ _____ _____ _____ _____ _____ _____ _____ _____?

esy | eI'v | eneb | ot | ilCeh

_____ , _____ _____ _____ _____.

Complete the words & Connect the flag and continent

B_ _z_ _l •

_ _s_ a R_ c_ •

C_ n_ d_ •

• North America

• Central America

• South America

Where in North America would you like to travel to?
_____.

Where in Central America would you like to travel to?
_____.

Where in South America would you like to travel to?
_____.

Lesson 94: Beverages

饮料

> Which beverage don't you like to drink on a hot day?
> I don't like to drink coffee, and neither does Tom.

Section A — Words

1. **banana smoothies**
   香蕉冰沙
2. **cappuccinos**
   卡布奇诺
3. **beer**
   啤酒
4. **wine**
   酒
5. **green tea**
   绿茶
6. **soda water**
   苏打水
7. **sports drinks**
   运动饮料
8. **iced tea**
   冰茶
9. **soymilk**
   豆浆
10. **coconut water**
    椰子水

Section B — Make a sentence

Which beverage don't you like to drink on a <u>hot</u> day?

I don't like to drink <u>green tea</u>, and neither does <u>she</u>.

Which beverage doesn't he like to drink on a <u>cold</u> day?

He doesn't like to drink <u>soymilk</u>, and neither do <u>they</u>.

Learn: neither

Section C — Make a question

Don't you like to drink <u>beer</u> on a <u>hot</u> day?
Yes, I do. / No, I don't. / Only sometimes.

Doesn't he like to drink <u>cappuccino</u> on a <u>cold</u> day?
Yes, he does. / No, he doesn't. / Only sometimes.

Section D — Learn a verb

drink – drinking – drank – drunk 喝

I like to **drink** iced tea on a hot day.

Drinking coconut water is helpful during a heat wave.

He **drank** some sports drink after skateboarding.

She hadn't **drunk** much soymilk before living in Asia.

Section E — Learn an idiom

Drink up

Meaning: To drink your entire beverage.

"He gave me some green tea and told me to *drink up*."

Section F **Write**

Trace and fill in the words

1. Which _____ don't you like to _____ on a hot day?

   I don't like to drink _____, and neither does _____.

2. _____ beverage _____ she like to drink on a

   _____ day?

   _____ doesn't like to drink _____, and neither do they.

3. Which _____ _____ he _____ to _____ on a

   cold _____?

   He _____ like to drink _____, and _____ do they.

4. _____ he like to drink _____ on a cold _____?

   No, _____ _____.

5. _____ you _____ to drink sports drink on a hot day?

   _____ sometimes.

6. Don't you like to _____ _____ on a _____ day?

   Yes, _____ _____.

7. _____ she _____ to drink _____ on a cold day?

   _____, she _____.

Section G Let's have fun

Beverages!

Write the sentences

"I don't like to drink soda water." — "Me, neither."

He doesn't like to drink soda water, and neither does she.

"I don't like to drink green tea." — "We don't either."

_____

"I don't like to drink cappuccinos." — "Me, neither."

_____

"We don't like to drink soymilk." — "I don't either."

_____

And you...?

Which beverage don't you like to drink on a hot day?

_____

Lesson 95: At the beach

在海滩

> What did you notice at the beach today?
> I noticed there was a lot of coral at the beach.

Section A — Words

1. **lifeguards**
   救生员
2. **shells**
   贝壳
3. **sunglasses**
   墨镜
4. **waves**
   浪
5. **sandcastles**
   沙堡
6. **garbage**
   垃圾
7. **sunscreen**
   防晒乳
8. **coral**
   珊瑚
9. **seaweed**
   海藻
10. **sand**
    沙子

Section B — Make a sentence

What did you notice at the beach today?

I noticed there were many <u>lifeguards</u> at the beach.

What did you notice at the beach today?

I noticed there was a lot of <u>seaweed</u> at the beach.

Learn: many, a lot of

| Section C | Make a question |

Were there many <u>shells</u> at the beach?
Yes, there were. / No, there weren't.

Was there a lot of <u>coral</u> at the beach?
Yes, there was. / No, there wasn't.

| Section D | Learn a verb |

explain – explaining – explained – explained 说明

Can you **explain** to me how seaweed grows?

Dad was **explaining** to us where the garbage comes from.

The lifeguard **explained** how important coral is.

The teacher hasn't **explained** this to us yet.

| Section E | Learn an idiom |

Shell out

Meaning: To pay for something that's too expensive.

"I had *to shell out* too much money to fix my scooter."

| Section F | Write |

Trace and fill in the words

1. What did _____ notice at the _____ today?

I _____ there were many _____ at the beach.

2. _____ did _____ notice at the beach _____?

I noticed there _____ a lot of _____ at the beach.

3. What _____ you _____ at the _____ today?

_____ noticed _____ were many _____ at _____ beach.

4. _____ _____ you _____ at the beach _____?

I noticed _____ was a lot of _____ at the _____.

5. Was _____ a lot of _____ at the beach?

Yes, _____ was.

6. Were there _____ sunglasses _____ the beach?

Yes, _____ were.

7. _____ _____ many _____ at the _____?

No, _____ _____.

8. _____ _____ a lot of sand at _____ beach?

No, _____ _____.

Section G | Let's have fun

At the beach!

Find the words!

```
r h t q g x k f o k z j v j s s d i
x x l f w i m l b m u w a v e s d b
f s i s a n d c a s t l e s n h a k
c x f m v x w b z d h i c o z e e w
o x e w i t s u n s c r e e n l y f
r b g k s u n g l a s s e s d l g k
a f u z t p w v c n s a n d c s l a
l x a v y w s b v x s e a w e e d q
n w r s w x g m b z q a i d q g d j
i d d t i g w c p w g i d t i g s l
z s s b j o a g a r b a g e p i b k
l s k b r e t e p e x p o u b c u a
```

c_r_l   s_ _lls
gar_a_e   su_gl_ss_s
s_n_   se_w_ed
li_egua_ds   w_v_s
s_ns_ree_   s_nd_ast_es

Lesson 96: Africa

非洲

> Where in Africa would you like to travel?
> It is my dream to travel to Kenya one day.
> I heard Kenya is simply fascinating.

Section A — Words

1. **South Africa**
   南非
2. **Nigeria**
   奈及利亞
3. **Cameroon**
   喀麥隆
4. **Morocco**
   摩洛哥
5. **Egypt**
   埃及
6. **Senegal**
   塞內加爾
7. **Kenya**
   肯亞
8. **Ghana**
   迦納
9. **Mauritius**
   模里西斯
10. **Zimbabwe**
    辛巴威

Section B — Make a sentence

Where in Africa would you like to travel?

It is my dream to travel to <u>Egypt</u> one day.

I heard Egypt is simply <u>amazing</u>.

Where in Africa would you like to travel?

It is my dream to travel to <u>Morocco</u> one day.

I heard Morocco is simply <u>incredible</u>.

Learn: simply, one day, amazing, incredible, fascinating

| Section C | Make a question |

Do you think you will travel to <u>Cameroon</u> one day?
Yes, I think I will. / No, I don't think I will. /
I've never thought about it.

Do you think you will travel to <u>Senegal</u> one day?
Yes, I think I will. / No, I don't think I will. /
I've never thought about it.

| Section D | Learn a verb |

hear – hearing – heard – heard 听

I can't **hear** very well, can you speak up?
I've been **hearing** many good things about Kenya.
I **heard** that Mauritius has many great sites.
I haven't **heard** from him since he got back from Ghana.

| Section E | Learn an idiom |

Off the beaten path

Meaning: To travel to places where most people don't go to.

"His vacation in Ghana was really *off the beaten path*."

Section F — Write

Trace and fill in the words

1. _____ in Africa _____ you like to _____?

It is _____ dream to travel to _____ one day.

I _____ Nigeria is simply _____.

2. Where in _____ would you _____ _____ travel?

It is my _____ to _____ to Ghana one _____.

I heard _____ is _____ incredible.

3. _____ in _____ _____ you like to _____?

It is my _____ to _____ to _____ _____ day.

_____ _____ Mauritius is _____ _____.

4. _____ you think you will _____ to Senegal one day?

I've _____ thought _____ it.

5. Do _____ think you _____ travel to Egypt one day?

No, I _____ think _____ _____.

6. Do you _____ you will _____ to _____ one day?

Yes, _____ _____ I _____.

7. Do _____ think you will _____ to _____ one day?

Yes, _____ _____ _____ _____.

Section G — Let's have fun

Africa!

1 It is my dream to travel to Senegal one day.
I heard Senegal is simply incredible.

2 It is my dream to travel to Nigeria one day.
I heard Nigeria is simply amazing.

3 It is my dream to travel to Kenya one day.
I heard Kenya is simply fascinating.

Answer the questions using the information above

1A. Where in Africa would he like to travel?
_____

1B. What did he hear about Senegal?
_____

2A. Where in Africa would he like to travel?
_____

2B. What did he hear about Nigeria?
_____

3A. Where in Africa would she like to travel?
_____

3B. What did she hear about Kenya?
_____

Test 24 — Lesson 93 - 96

Write the answer next to the letter "A"

A: ___ 1. ___ in Mexico would you like to ___ to?

a. When, trip   b. Were, travel   c. Where, travel   d. Where, travels

A: ___ 2. Have ___ been to ___ countries in South America?

a. they, this   b. your, some   c. you, that   d. you, any

A: ___ 3. ___ to take your passport to Brazil.

a. Remembering   b. Remembers   c. Remembered   d. Remember

A: ___ 4. "My memories weren't clear until she ___ my memory."

a. ran   b. jogged   c. pulled   d. drew

A: ___ 5. He ___ like to drink beer, and neither do ___.

a. doesn't, I   b. don't, she   c. can't, we   d. does, them

A: ___ 6. ___ you like to drink coffee on a cold day? ___ sometimes.

a. Don't, Only   b. Do, On   c. Doesn't, Only   d. Does, If

A: ___ 7. He hadn't ___ iced tea since he was a child.

a. drinking   b. drunk   c. drinks   d. drink

A: ___ 8. "He gave me a sports drink and said to drink ___."

a. out   b. down   c. up   d. in

A: ___ **9.** I noticed there was ___ sand at the beach.

a. a lot of   b. many   c. lot of   d. much

A: ___ **10.** Were there ___ shells at the beach? Yes, there ___.

a. lot of, was   b. many, were   c. many, are   d. a lot of, is

A: ___ **11.** He ___ how to make a really big sandcastle yesterday.

a. explains   b. explain   c. explaining   d. explained

A: ___ **12.** "He had to shell ___ a lot of money for his trip to Africa."

a. over   b. on   c. out   d. to

A: ___ **13.** It is my ___ to travel ___ Morocco one day.

a. dreaming, to   b. dreams, in   c. dream, to   d. dreamt, through

A: ___ **14.** Do you think you ___ travel to Kenya one ___?

a. want, time   b. will, day   c. will, weeks   d. can, vacation

A: ___ **15.** It's too noisy, so he can't ___ very well.

a. hearing   b. hears   c. heard   d. hear

A: ___ **16.** "In Africa, she traveled to many places off the ___ path."

a. beaten   b. meeting   c. greeted   d. clearing

Answers on page 463

Lesson 97: Special days

特别的日子

What do you have planned this weekend?
I was invited to my aunt's birthday celebration.

Section A — Words

1. **birthday**
   生日
2. **Mother's Day**
   母亲节
3. **Father's Day**
   父亲节
4. **wedding day**
   婚礼
5. **wedding anniversary**
   结婚纪念日
6. **New Year's Day**
   元旦
7. **Valentine's Day**
   情人节
8. **graduation day**
   毕业日
9. **invitation**
   邀请函
10. **celebration**
    庆祝

Section B — Make a sentence

What do you have planned <u>this weekend</u>?

I was invited to my <u>friend's birthday</u> celebration.

What do you have planned <u>this Friday</u>?

I was invited to my <u>cousin's graduation</u> celebration.

Learn: invite, invitation, plan

Section C — Make a question

Have you received an invitation to Mary's <u>wedding day</u> celebration?

Yes, I have. / No, I haven't. / I'm not sure.

Have you received an invitation to Bob's <u>New Year's Day</u> celebration?

Yes, I have. / No, I haven't. / I'm not sure.

Section D — Learn a verb

invite – inviting – invited – invited 邀请

We'll **invite** the neighbors to join our celebration.

My boss is **inviting** everyone to celebrate his birthday.

I think I **invited** over fifty people to my Mother's Day party.

Did you notice that he hadn't **invited** anyone from work?

Section E — Learn an idiom

Throw a party

Meaning: To organize and have a party.

"It was his graduation day, so they *threw a party* for him."

| Section F | Write |

Trace and fill in the words

1. _____ do you have _____ this _____?

   I was _____ to my _____ _____ celebration.

2. What _____ you _____ planned _____ weekend?

   I _____ invited to my _____ _____ Day _____.

3. What _____ she _____ _____ this _____?

   _____ was _____ to her _____ _____ Day celebration.

4. _____ you _____ an invitation to Peter's _____ day celebration?

   No, _____ _____.

5. Have _____ _____ an _____ to Kim's _____ Day celebration?

   Yes, _____ _____.

6. _____ you _____ an _____ to Kevin's _____ Day _____?

   _____ not _____.

446

Section G — Let's have fun

Special days!

1. **Invitation**
Dear Helen,

I would like to invite you to my birthday celebration this weekend.

I hope you can make it!

From John

2. **Invitation**
Dear Matthew,

I would like to invite you to my wedding day celebration this weekend.

I hope you can make it!

From Jessica

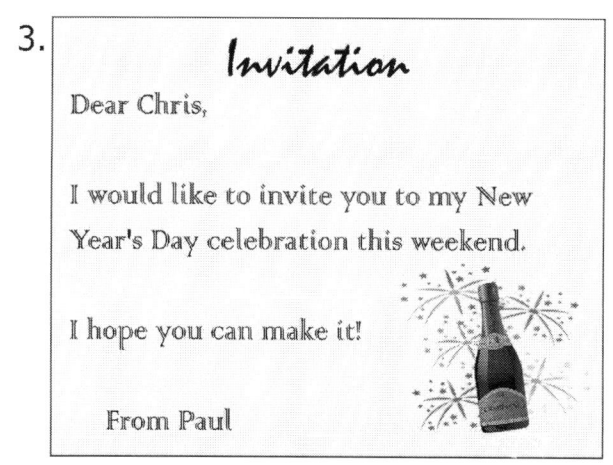

3. **Invitation**
Dear Chris,

I would like to invite you to my New Year's Day celebration this weekend.

I hope you can make it!

From Paul

4. **Invitation**
Dear Amanda,

I would like to invite you to my Valentine's Day celebration this weekend.

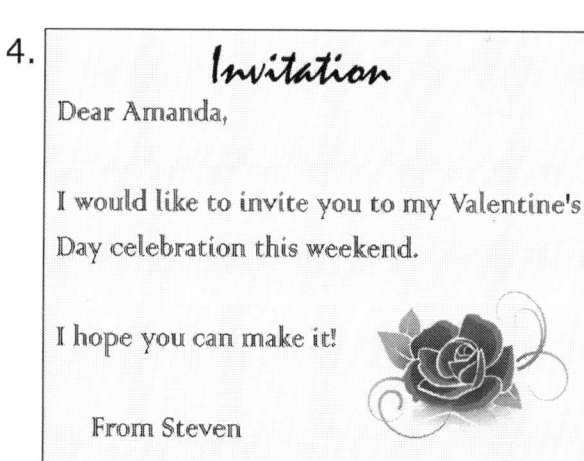

I hope you can make it!

From Steven

Answer the questions using the information above

1. What does Helen have planned this weekend?
_____.

2. What does Matthew have planned this weekend?
_____.

3. What does Chris have planned this weekend?
_____.

4. What does Amanda have planned this weekend?
_____.

Lesson 98: At the amusement park

在游乐园

> Which rides haven't you been on yet?
> I haven't been on the pirate ship yet and Peter hasn't either.

Section A — Words

1. **roller coaster**
   云霄飞车
2. **merry-go-round**
   旋转木马
3. **bumper cars**
   碰碰车
4. **pirate ship**
   海盗船
5. **Ferris wheel**
   摩天轮
6. **fireworks show**
   烟火表演
7. **parade**
   游行
8. **gift shop**
   礼品店
9. **haunted house**
   鬼屋
10. **food stand**
    小吃摊

Section B — Make a sentence

Which rides haven't you been on yet?

I haven't been on the <u>roller coaster</u> yet, and <u>Michael</u> hasn't either.

Where hasn't she been yet?

She hasn't been to the <u>gift shop</u> yet, and <u>I</u> haven't either.

Learn: either

Section C — Make a question

You haven't been on the <u>bumper cars</u> yet, have you?
Yes, I have. / No, I haven't. / I didn't know about them.

You didn't go to the <u>gift shop</u>, did you?
Yes, I did. / No, I didn't. / I didn't know about it.

Section D — Learn a verb

close – closing – closed – closed 关

What time does the amusement park **close**?
They are **closing** the haunted house for a week.
The cashier **closed** the gift shop and went home.
The food stand will have **closed** by seven o'clock.

Section E — Learn an idiom

Be a roller coaster

Meaning: Many sudden and big changes.

"We had many good and bad things happen on our trip. It really *was a roller coaster*."

Section F   Write

Trace and fill in the words

1. Where _____ he _____ yet?

   _____ hasn't been to the gift shop yet, and I haven't

   _____ .

2. _____ rides haven't _____ been on yet?

   I _____ been on the roller coaster yet, and Jan _____

   either.

3. Which _____ haven't you _____ on _____ ?

   I haven't _____ _____ the _____ yet, and Kurt

   hasn't _____ .

4. He _____ been on the _____ yet, has _____ ?

   _____ didn't _____ about them.

5. You _____ go to _____ haunted house, did _____ ?

   Yes, _____ _____ .

6. _____ haven't _____ on the pirate ship _____ ,

   _____ you?

   No, _____ _____ .

Section G | Let's have fun

At the amusement park!

haven't   been   either   yet

Underline the mistake and write the sentence correctly

1. Which rides haven't you <u>be</u> on yet?
_____

2. I hasn't been on the roller coaster yet, and Tom hasn't either.
_____

3. Where hasn't he been already?
_____

4. John hasn't been to the pirate ship, and Mary hasn't also.
_____

Complete the questions

1. You haven't been to the parade yet, _____?

2. She didn't go to the haunted house, _____?

3. He hasn't been to the gift shop yet, _____?

4. She didn't go to the roller coaster, _____?

Lesson 99: Dairy

乳制品

In which shop did you buy the milkshake?
I bought the milkshake from the shop that's around the corner.

Section A — Words

1. **milk**
   牛奶
2. **cheese**
   起司
3. **yogurt**
   优格
4. **ice cream**
   冰淇淋
5. **milkshake**
   奶昔
6. **whipped cream**
   鲜奶油
7. **butter**
   奶油
8. **chocolate milk**
   巧克力牛奶
9. **pudding**
   布丁
10. **fruit smoothie**
    水果冰沙

Section B — Make a sentence

In which shop did you buy the <u>butter</u>?

I bought the butter from the shop that's <u>around the corner</u>.

Which shop did you buy the <u>ice cream</u> in?

I bought the ice cream in the shop that's <u>on the corner</u>.

Learn: in which, around the corner, on the corner, from

Section C | Make a question

Did you buy the <u>cheese</u> from the shop that's <u>around the corner</u>?

Yes, that's right. / No, I didn't. / I have no idea.

Did you buy the <u>cheese</u> from the shop that's <u>on the corner</u>?

Yes, that's right. / No, I didn't. / I have no idea.

Section D | Learn a verb

create – creating – created – created 创造

You can **create** many different foods using milk.

We had a lot of fun **creating** new flavored fruit smoothies.

The chef **created** some delicious puddings for the party.

The students had **created** some amazing videos.

Section E | Learn an idiom

A big cheese

Meaning: An important or successful person.

"As the boss, he's *a big cheese* at that company."

Section F | Write

Trace and fill in the words

1. In _____ shop did _____ buy the _____?

   I _____ the milkshake _____ the shop _____ around the corner.

2. _____ shop _____ he buy the _____ in?

   _____ bought the pudding _____ the _____ that's on the _____.

3. _____ which _____ did you _____ the yogurt?

   I _____ the _____ from _____ shop _____ the corner.

4. _____ you buy the _____ from the _____ that's _____ the _____?

   No, _____ _____.

5. Did _____ buy _____ fruit smoothie _____ shop _____ on _____ corner?

   Yes, _____ right.

6. _____ you _____ the _____ from the _____ around the _____?

   I _____ no _____.

454

Section G Let's have fun

Dairy!

Circle the dairy words

1. cake   pizza   hot dog   (butter)   pie

2. soda   tea   beef   juice   ice cream

3. chicken   coffee   cheese   candy   juice

4. fish   yogurt   water   tea   bread

5. pudding   pork   apple   tomato   soda

6. pizza   cola   donut   juice   milkshake

7. milk   lettuce   orange   pie   mushroom

8. ham   whipped cream   soda   pie   cabbage

Write the word

1.
2.
3.
4.
5.
6.
7.
8.

Lesson 100: My job

我的工作

> What do you want to be when you're older?
> I think I'd like to be an engineer.
> I'm sure I'd be a good engineer.

Section A — Words

1. **engineer**
   工程师
2. **fashion designer**
   时装设计师
3. **receptionist**
   接待员
4. **architect**
   建筑师
5. **truck driver**
   卡车司机
6. **scientist**
   科学家
7. **musician**
   音乐家
8. **cashier**
   收银员
9. **janitor**
   守卫
10. **lawyer**
    律师

Section B — Make a sentence

What do you want to be when you're older?

I think I'd like to be a <u>lawyer</u>.

I'm sure I'd be a good lawyer.

What does she want to be when she's older?

I think she'd like to be a <u>fashion designer</u>.

I'm sure she'd be a great fashion designer.

Section C — Make a question

Do you think I'd be a good engineer?

Yes, I think you'd be a good engineer.

/ No, I don't think you'd be a good engineer.

/ How should I know?

Section D — Learn a verb

employ – employing – employed – employed 雇用

The company will **employ** a new engineer next month.

The boss is thinking about **employing** a truck driver.

The manager **employed** two receptionists for the new office.

I will have been **employed** by next year.

Section E — Learn an idiom

A bang up job

Meaning: To do very good work.

"The musician did *a bang up job* playing that song."

| Section F | Write |

Trace and fill in the words

1. What _____ you want to be _____ you're _____?

_____ think _____ like to _____ an architect.

I'm _____ I'd be a good _____.

2. What _____ she _____ to be when _____ older?

I _____ she'd _____ to be a _____.

_____ sure _____ be a _____ scientist.

3. _____ _____ _____ want to be when she's older?

I _____ _____ like to be a _____.

_____ _____ she'd _____ a _____ musician.

4. Do _____ think I'd _____ a good janitor?

Yes, I _____ you'd be a _____ _____.

5. _____ you _____ I'd be a _____ _____?

No, I _____ _____ _____ be a good receptionist.

6. _____ _____ think _____ be a good _____?

How _____ I _____?

7. _____ _____ _____ I'd be a good _____?

How _____ _____ _____?

458

Section G — Let's have fun

My job!

be / think / I / like / she'd / lawyer / a / to

1. _____.

he'd / be / sure / scientist / a / I'm / good

2. _____.

think / I / an / like / be / I'd / architect / to

3. _____.

cashier / good / you / I'd / think / be / Do / a

4. _____?

musician / a / think / be / I / you'd / Yes / great

5. _____ , _____.

What do you want to be when you're older?

_____

Test 25 — Lesson 97 - 100

Write the answer next to the letter "A"

A: ___ **1.** I was ___ my friend's New Year's Day celebration.

a. inviting to   b. invited in   c. invited to   d. invites in

A: ___ **2.** Have you received an invitation to his birthday celebration?

a. Yes, I have.   b. Yes, I do.   c. Yes, I will.   d. Yes, I am.

A: ___ **3.** They'll ___ their coworkers to join their graduation party.

a. invites   b. invite   c. invited   d. inviting

A: ___ **4.** "They want to ___ a party this weekend."

a. make   b. hide   c. set   d. throw

A: ___ **5.** I haven't ___ on the bumper cars yet, and he hasn't ___ .

a. been, either   b. tried, too   c. ride, also   d. sit, neither

A: ___ **6.** He hasn't been on the bumper cars ___ , ___ he?

a. still, have   b. today, will   c. now, can   d. yet, has.

A: ___ **7.** What time did the gift shop ___ ?

a. closes   b. close   c. closed   d. closing

A: ___ **8.** "Her time living in Asia really was a ___ ."

a. parade   b. bumper car   c. roller coaster   d. Ferris wheel

460

A: ___ **9.** I bought the yogurt in the shop that's ___ the ___.

a. in, corner   b. around, corner   c. through, corner   d. on, counter

A: ___ **10.** Did you buy the milk from the shop that's on the corner?

a. Yes, that's right.   b. Yes it is.   c. Yes, that's milk.   d. Yes, I do.

A: ___ **11.** She ___ a big ice cream dessert for the party.

a. creates   b. creating   c. created   d. create

A: ___ **12.** "After she got her new job, she was a big ___ in the office."

a. milkshake   b. pudding   c. dairy   d. cheese

A: ___ **13.** I think ___ like to be a lawyer. I'm sure ___ be a good lawyer.

a. I'm, I'd   b. I'd, I'm   c. I'd, I'd   d. I'd, really

A: ___ **14.** Do you think I'd ___ a good musician? How should I ___?

a. be, know   b. play, think   c. work, say   d. learn, do

A: ___ **15.** The company had ___ them for many years.

a. employing   b. employs   c. employ   d. employed

A: ___ **16.** "The engineer did a bang ___ job making the new bridge."

a. through   b. up   c. by   d. down

Answers on page 463

Answers Test 1 - 25

Test 1
1. a   2. c   3. a   4. d   5. d   6. c   7. c   8. b   9. d   10. b   11. b   12. a   13. a   14. a
15. c   16. d

Test 2
1. b   2. c   3. c   4. d   5. a   6. b   7. d   8. b   9. d   10. a   11. c   12. c   13. d   14. c
15. b   16. d

Test 3
1. d   2. b   3. d   4. c   5. b   6. a   7. c   8. a   9. d   10. c   11. c   12. d   13. a   14. c
15. c   16. d

Test 4
1. d   2. b   3. c   4. c   5. d   6. d   7. a   8. d   9. b   10. b   11. c   12. b   13. d   14. d
15. a   16. d

Test 5
1. a   2. a   3. c   4. b   5. d   6. d   7. b   8. a   9. c   10. d   11. c   12. b   13. d   14. c
15. a   16. c

Test 6
1. b   2. b   3. a   4. d   5. c   6. c   7. d   8. b   9. a   10. d   11. a   12. b   13. b   14. c
15. c   16. c

Test 7
1. c   2. c   3. b   4. a   5. b   6. a   7. c   8. d   9. d   10. c   11. a   12. c   13. b   14. b
15. d   16. d

Test 8
1. a   2. b   3. c   4. d   5. c   6. b   7. d   8. a   9. d   10. b   11. c   12. a   13. d   14. b
15. c   16. a

Test 9
1. b   2. c   3. c   4. a   5. d   6. d   7. a   8. b   9. d   10. a   11. c   12. b   13. b   14. a
15. c   16. d

Test 10
1. b   2. d   3. a   4. c   5. d   6. c   7. a   8. b   9. a   10. d   11. b   12. c   13. b   14. d
15. c   16. a

Test 11
1. d   2. d   3. b   4. b   5. a   6. a   7. c   8. d   9. c   10. c   11. a   12. b   13. d   14. a
15. b   16. c

Test 12
1. b   2. a   3. c   4. d   5. b   6. a   7. d   8. c   9. c   10. a   11. c   12. d   13. c   14. d
15. a   16. a

Test 13
1. b   2. d   3. a   4. b   5. c   6. b   7. d   8. d   9. a   10. c   11. c   12. b   13. a   14. b
15. d   16. d

Test 14
1. a   2. d   3. b   4. b   5. d   6. d   7. a   8. b   9. c   10. a   11. d   12. a   13. b   14. d   15. a   16. c

Test 15
1. d   2. b   3. a   4. d   5. a   6. b   7. c   8. d   9. b   10. d   11. a   12. c   13. d   14. b   15. c   16. b

Test 16
1. c   2. c   3. a   4. b   5. d   6. a   7. b   8. b   9. d   10. c   11. a   12. a   13. d   14. b   15. c   16. d

Test 17
1. a   2. b   3. b   4. c   5. d   6. a   7. c   8. a   9. c   10. d   11. b   12. b   13. c   14. b   15. a   16. c

Test 18
1. c   2. a   3. c   4. b   5. a   6. d   7. b   8. d   9. c   10. b   11. b   12. c   13. d   14. b   15. b   16. c

Test 19
1. a   2. c   3. d   4. d   5. a   6. a   7. b   8. a   9. c   10. c   11. d   12. c   13. a   14. d   15. b   16. a

Test 20
1. d   2. d   3. b   4. a   5. c   6. c   7. a   8. d   9. b   10. c   11. b   12. a   13. c   14. b   15. d   16. b

Test 21
1. c   2. c   3. b   4. c   5. d   6. d   7. a   8. c   9. b   10. a   11. b   12. c   13. a   14. d   15. d   16. a

Test 22
1. d   2. d   3. c   4. b   5. c   6. b   7. d   8. a   9. a   10. d   11. b   12. d   13. c   14. c   15. a   16. a

Test 23
1. b   2. c   3. d   4. a   5. d   6. c   7. a   8. b   9. a   10. c   11. d   12. b   13. a   14. c   15. d   16. b

Test 24
1. c   2. d   3. d   4. b   5. a   6. a   7. b   8. c   9. a   10. b   11. d   12. c   13. c   14. b   15. d   16. a

Test 25
1. c   2. a   3. b   4. d   5. a   6. d   7. b   8. c   9. b   10. a   11. c   12. d   13. c   14. a   15. d   16. b

Made in the USA
Middletown, DE
05 December 2018